AF761763

International Criminal Justice

George Andreopoulos • Rosemary Barberet
James P. Levine
Editors

International Criminal Justice

Critical Perspectives and New Challenges

Springer

Editors
George Andreopoulos
City University of New York
John Jay College of Criminal Justice
New York, NY
USA

James P. Levine
City University of New York
John Jay College of Criminal Justice
New York, NY
USA

Rosemary Barberet
City University of New York
John Jay College of Criminal Justice
New York, NY
USA

ISBN 978-1-4419-1101-8 e-ISBN 978-1-4419-1102-5
DOI 10.1007/978-1-4419-1102-5
Springer New York Dordrecht Heidelberg London

© Springer Science+Business Media, LLC 2011
All rights reserved. This work may not be translated or copied in whole or in part without the written permission of the publisher (Springer Science+Business Media, LLC, 233 Spring Street, New York, NY 10013, USA), except for brief excerpts in connection with reviews or scholarly analysis. Use in connection with any form of information storage and retrieval, electronic adaptation, computer software, or by similar or dissimilar methodology now known or hereafter developed is forbidden.
The use in this publication of trade names, trademarks, service marks, and similar terms, even if they are not identified as such, is not to be taken as an expression of opinion as to whether or not they are subject to proprietary rights.

Printed on acid-free paper

Springer is part of Springer Science+Business Media (www.springer.com)

Foreword

I am honored to have been asked to write the Foreword for this important book. As one of the plenary speakers at the John Jay College of Criminal Justice International Conference in San Juan, Puerto Rico, I spoke about the importance of research in international criminology and criminal justice, and the presence of global threats to human safety. What is unique about John Jay College of Criminal Justice and its international conferences is the effort to harness the thinking from a variety of disciplines to analyze crime and criminal justice issues. I am thus impressed that this has all materialized into this excellent edited collection, and that it represents so many disciplines: criminal justice, economics, philosophy, literature, sociology, and political science.

Here at Intervict, an international research center based at the University of Tilburg in the Netherlands, we also undertake an interdisciplinary approach and emphasize the importance of victims of crime and abuse of power in all the work that we do. The interdisciplinary approach of the research program ensures that research is undertaken about all aspects of victimization, which will ultimately contribute to preventing or reducing instances of criminal victimization across the world and to limiting the effects of such victimization on victims and their families including economic costs, pain, and suffering.

In our recent work, we have paid increasing attention to the victims of international crime. Throughout my career, both here and previously at the United Nations Office of Drugs and Crime, I have become convinced that criminologists can no longer confine their area of study to domestic crime, within the comfort of their national borders, when we know that the most heinous of crimes – genocide, war crimes, and crimes against humanity – are very likely to be undocumented, under-researched, and unpunished. Now, with the creation of the International Criminal Court in The Hague, the world is hopeful for a true enforcement mechanism for international criminal law serving the interests of individual and collective victims.

I am thus enthusiastic that this edited collection focuses on international crime. I am heartened by the number of papers in this volume that tackle issues of governance and human rights, and I am glad to see that terrorism is also a feature of a number of chapters. In reading this book, I have seen that the chapters mirror the objectives of the conference, which had the theme, "Justice and Policing in Diverse

Societies." The connection between the very technical and empirical nature of "criminal justice" studies and the larger philosophical and historical themes of "justice" cannot be broken, and we must continually strive as intellectuals to ensure that we do not lose the forest for the trees. Given that the mission of John Jay College of Criminal Justice is "educating for justice," I can truly say that that this collection fulfills its purpose of educating us all in these important matters.

Jan van Dijk

Introduction

One of the most remarkable developments in contemporary international affairs has been the pursuit of justice-related claims as a way of addressing a wide array of threats and challenges in the international system. Though interpretations as to the causes and impact of this development may vary, there is a growing consensus that accountability matters more than ever before in world politics, because it can constitute an effective instrument in the quest for a more just and secure world order.[1] Even a hard-nosed realist such as Henry Kissinger reluctantly acknowledged

> the general acceptance of the proposition that certain universal principles are deemed enforceable, either by the United Nations, or in extreme situations, by a group of states.... Moreover, such international conventions as those condemning genocide, torture or war crimes, are said to be enforceable by national judges.... These views...amount to a revolution in the way the international system has operated for more than three hundred years.
>
> (Kissinger, 2001, pp. 234–235)

There are several factors that have contributed to this expansion of the justice space. First, the evolution of human rights norms has legitimized international concern for human welfare. Despite its modest beginnings, the human rights movement has scored some notable successes, especially in the area of standard setting. Under the auspices of the United Nations, "an impressive normative architecture" (Falk, 2002, p. 23) pertaining to human rights has gained wider acceptance in the international community (though its implementation still leaves a lot to be desired).

This acceptance has been manifested in a variety of ways; one of its key facets is an increasingly dense transnational dialogue in which groups of government officials, as well as private individuals, exchange information and coordinate activities on the basis of shared understandings of human needs and aspirations, in order to address a whole set of critical issues affecting human well-being. As a result, greater attention is now given to good governance and codes of conduct at all levels

[1] Accountability is by definition a relational concept. At the most basic level, accountability refers to an agent's responsibility for some act or failure to act in ways that are consistent with certain accepted standards of behavior, as well as to someone or some institutional entity. In the context of our volume, these standards of behavior refer to shared understandings of appropriate conduct as prescribed by internationally recognized human rights and humanitarian norms; See Andreopoulos (2010).

than ever before. In addition, shifts in attitudes – and, at a slower rate, shifts in policy – are placing increasing emphasis on human rights and human needs in a model of *human security* that goes beyond traditional military and state-centric concepts of security.

Second, a series of modern-day conflicts have resulted in the increasingly visible victimization of innocents and civilians. According to one study, the number of civilian deaths as a percentage of all deaths in selected twentieth-century wars has risen steadily throughout the century: from 14% in World War I, to 67% in World War II, to 90% in the conflicts of the 1990s (Garfield and Neugut, 2000, p. 33). This trend is reflective of an increasing number of conflicts in which the parties involved have placed emphasis on methods of political control that have focused on population displacement, as opposed to popular support which was characteristic of the revolutionary warfare that developed during and after World War II.[2]

Third, and in response to the humanitarian tragedies in the former Yugoslavia and Rwanda, the United Nations established two ad hoc tribunals: one for the former Yugoslavia (ICTY) and one for Rwanda (ICTR). The political aspects of this particular process of tribunal formation stands out due to the particular approach followed in establishing the two tribunals. Instead of pursuing the treaty route, the international community opted for a Security Council resolution upon determination that the situation in both countries constituted a threat to international peace and security. Therefore, both the ICTY and ICTR are subsidiary organs of the principal political organ of the United Nations system, and their function is inextricably linked to the maintenance of international peace and security.

Fourth, and related to the previous point, the establishment of the ad hoc tribunals has been followed by the creation of the International Criminal Court (ICC), as well as other internationalized or "mixed tribunals." The Rome Conference led to the adoption of a Statute for the ICC in July 1998 and to the Statute's entering into force in July 2002 upon its ratification by 60 countries. In addition, and following rather protracted negotiations between the United Nations and the governments of Sierra Leone and Cambodia, special "mixed courts" were established for the prosecution of serious violations of international human rights and humanitarian law.

More specifically, the Special Court for Sierra Leone is mandated "to try those who bear the greatest responsibility for serious violations of international humanitarian law and Sierra Leonean law committed in the territory of Sierra Leone since 30 November 1996,"[3] and the Extraordinary Chambers in the Courts of Cambodia for the Prosecution of Crimes Committed during the period of Democratic Kampuchea is mandated "to try serious crimes committed during the Khmer Rouge regime 1975–1979."[4] While these courts differ in significant ways from the two ad hoc tribunals (ICTY and ICTR), they reflect the international community's converging

---

[2] For more on this, see Kaldor (2001), pp. 96–101.

[3] The Special Court for Sierra Leone, available at: http://www.sc-sl.org/.

[4] Extraordinary Chambers in the Courts of Cambodia, available at: http://www.eccc.gov.kh/english/about_eccc.aspx.

expectations on the need for the criminal accountability of perpetrators of gross violations of international human rights and international humanitarian law.

Fifth, domestic courts in several countries have initiated proceedings based on the principle of universal jurisdiction.[5] The most famous of these cases was the attempted extradition of former Chilean dictator Augusto Pinochet to Spain, on the basis of an international arrest warrant issued by Spain against him while he was in the United Kingdom seeking medical treatment. In the end of a lengthy process, the House of Lords overwhelmingly denied Pinochet's claim of state immunity and held that he was extraditable for the commission of torture. While medical considerations ultimately spared him the indignity of a criminal trial in Spain, the final decision by the House of Lords played a decisive role in expanding the universe of accountability and reinforced the potentially critical role of all domestic courts in the prosecution of perpetrators of human rights abuses. Equally important, the proceedings in the UK left a mark in Pinochet's home country, because they emboldened the "Chilean legal system to overcome their past embraces with impunity" (Falk, 2003, p. 119).

Last, but not least, the terrorist attacks of September 11, 2001, as well as subsequent attacks in other places (e.g., London, Madrid, Beslan, and Mumbai) have added a new dimension to the debate on the proper role of accountability mechanisms in the maintenance of international peace and security. Resolution 1373, adopted by the UN Security Council on the immediate aftermath of the September 11 attacks, highlighted the importance of international collaboration in enhancing the work of domestic mechanisms, as well as in strengthening a global response to this transnational threat.[6]

It is instructive to note here that although the international community has yet to agree on a comprehensive definition of the term *terrorism*, there is an emerging consensus that, whether in wartime or in peacetime, there can be no justification for the targeting of civilians and noncombatants. Irrespective of the merits of a particular cause, such targeting constitutes a violation of fundamental norms of international human rights and international humanitarian law.

In such a changing context, there has been a concerted effort to rethink some of the fundamental assumptions about threats and security, as well as about the existing institutions, mechanisms, and processes and their role in effectively addressing such threats. A report issued by a High-level Panel appointed by the UN Secretary-General, defined as threats as "any event or process that leads to large-scale death or lessening of life chances" (United Nations, 2004, p. 2).[7] The report went on to

---

[5] Universal jurisdiction is "criminal jurisdiction based solely on the nature of the crime, without regard to where the crime was committed, the nationality of the alleged or convicted perpetrator, the nationality of the victim, or any other connection to the state exercising such jurisdiction" ("The Princeton Principles," 2003, p. 21).

[6] UN Security Council Resolution 1373, S/RES/1373, September 28, 2001.

[7] The report also went on to add in the definition "and undermines States as the basic unit of the international system."

identify six clusters of threats; among these threats, the report included internal conflict such as civil war, genocide, and other large-scale atrocities and terrorism.

Our volume examines these two threats and the various justice-related claims that have been advanced as a way for addressing the challenges posed by them. The protection of human rights and humanitarian norms and combating terrorism intersect in multiple and complex ways. In some ways, and given the above-mentioned emerging consensus, they are clearly interrelated.[8] Moreover, human rights and particularly humanitarian law violations, as well as terrorist offenses, have been increasingly criminalized at the international level. In particular, the delinking of crimes against humanity from the war nexus requirement (Van Schaack, 1995, pp. 787–850), the growing reach of international humanitarian law applicable to noninternational conflicts (Meron, 1998, pp. 228–261), and the expanding corpus of international treaties dealing with terrorism,[9] are key indications of this process of international criminalization. Last, but not least, the evolving jurisprudence of the international tribunals has addressed the issue of the infliction of terror upon civilians in conflict situations. More specifically, in the Galic case, the ICTY identified the specific elements that constituted the crime of terror against the civilian population and held that the accused could be held responsible for it as a violation of the laws or customs of war.[10]

In other ways though, they have clearly worked at cross-purposes as several of our contributors indicate. Containing terrorism has often led to gross and systematic human rights and humanitarian law violations, and has placed the human rights deficit of both domestic and international initiatives on the international agenda as a pressing justice claim.

What has added a layer of complexity to all this is the discourse in which counter-terrorist initiatives have been framed. This discourse has not been consistent; rather it has alternated between the law enforcement framework and the law of war framework. Yet, as one analyst has pointed out these frameworks are based on very different moral premises. The law enforcement framework is based on a sharp moral distinction between policemen and outlaws, while the law of war framework is based on the moral equivalency of combatants, the acts of whom are judged lawful or unlawful on the basis of their battlefield conduct (de Torrente, 2002, p. 5).

In a similar vein, the UN Special Rapporteur on extrajudicial, summary or arbitrary executions, in a recent report on the practice of targeted killings, expressed concern over the re-characterization of many criminal acts "so as to justify addressing them within the framework of the law of armed conflict…. The result of this mix has been a highly problematic blurring and expansion of the boundaries of the

[8] The High-level Panel Report was rather emphatic on this issue: "Attacks that specifically target innocent civilians and non-combatants must be condemned clearly and unequivocally by all" (2004, p. 52).

[9] Currently the international community has adopted 16 counter-terrorism legal instruments; their texts are available at: http://www.un.org/sc/ctc/laws.html#t16.

[10] *Prosecutor v. Stanislav Galic*, Case No. IT-98-29-T, 5 December 2003, pars. 132–133.

applicable legal frameworks" (United Nations, 2010, May 28, p. 3). The guiding principle in the use of these competing frameworks seems to be the desire to achieve a predetermined outcome, as opposed to ensuring the proper application of the relevant legal framework.

Very early on, the contentious debate over framing had direct and decisive impact on the quest for accountability; in particular, one of the earliest post-9/11 controversies centered on the most appropriate forum to try the perpetrators of these attacks. The Bush administration's decision to establish military commissions to try suspected terrorists who were not U.S. citizens generated a major discussion on the merits of this option. Critics pointed out that federal district courts constitute the most appropriate forum, consistent with the due process provisions of the U.S. Constitution.

Others went further, suggesting an ad hoc international tribunal patterned—as to the legal basis for its formation and its process—after the ICTY and ICTR. By committing themselves to such a mechanism, states affected by the attacks[11] would be prepared to have their evidence subjected to international scrutiny, and the fate of the perpetrators decided by a tribunal that would have its proceedings likewise subjected to such scrutiny. In addition, such a forum would be easier for Islamic countries to extradite defendants to, as opposed to a court run by the U.S. military in which evidence would be presented in secret (Slaughter, 2001, November 17). Finally, an ad hoc tribunal on terrorism would have strengthened the emerging global ethos of accountability for the most serious of international crimes, a development with potentially far-reaching policy implications (e.g., enhanced legitimacy of proceedings and denial of safe haven to perpetrators of these crimes).

While the international option did not materialize, it was clearly indicative of the progress, albeit uneven, that international justice norms and corresponding claims have registered in the quest for accountability. To phrase it differently, it would be difficult to envisage a serious discussion that would include an international tribunal as a plausible forum for trying the perpetrators of 9/11, in the absence of the important precedents set by the establishment and operations of the ICTY, the ICTR, the establishment of the ICC, and the growing use of universal jurisdiction by a variety of domestic courts as the basis for asserting criminal jurisdiction over human rights violations.

The exploration of the inroads made by such norms, as well as the main challenges confronting the corresponding claims, constitute key concerns that shape the contributions to this volume. Whether the issue is addressing heinous crimes such as genocide, war crimes, and crimes against humanity; seeking to establish a common understanding of what constitutes humane conduct; confronting the inability or reluctance of governments to protect their own populations; or responding to the challenges posed by transnational terrorism, the international community has witnessed the proliferation of institutions and mechanisms, as well as the dynamic interplay between domestic and international processes, in the pursuit of justice-sensitive

[11] The reference here is to all states whose nationals died in the September 11 attacks.

outcomes. International and hybrid tribunals, UN-led and domestic counter-terrorist initiatives, and the use of force for human protection purposes have demarcated the space within which ethical, political, economic, and legal debates have unfolded in the quest for a more humane world order.

In the first chapter, Robert Schopp addresses one of the key issues relating to transnational normative development, and in particular the relevance of the law and practices of other countries in the interpretation by the U.S. Supreme Court of the evolving standards of decency (ESD) component of the analysis of the Constitution's Eighth Amendment. Schopp's interpretation rests partially on an understanding that the Eighth Amendment and, more generally, the Bill of Rights, place limits on the authority of the majority. In such a context, the rejection by other countries – which share with the United States certain fundamental principles concerning humane forms of punishment – of certain U.S. forms of punishment as inhumane does not, according to the author, carry constitutional weight. Instead, such rejection should trigger a "careful assessment of the relevant reasoning as a form of self-discipline" that will enhance responsible interpretations and applications of the principles to which U.S. citizens have committed themselves.

Addressing another issue area of transnational normative development, Toy-Fung Tung examines the "war against terrorism" in the context of the just war tradition. Tung critically analyzes the Bush administration rhetoric and its ability to appropriate just war–related claims within its securitization discourse to create a new script on the country's international legal obligations. This development led to a morally permissive approach that eroded every conceivable boundary that separated legitimate from illegitimate forms of conduct. Tung recognizes that the Bush administration legacy weighs heavily on his successor and it may not be easy to reverse the mistakes of the recent past. However, a fundamental commitment to human dignity should weather all storms, irrespective of the exceptionalist measures that may be called for by the situation under consideration.

One of the most troubling features of the "war on terror" is the cooptation of the human rights discourse for strategic political gains. As Paul Narkunas argues, this feature antedates the current "war" and constitutes part of a process that he calls *lawfare*. This is a process whereby war is less of an exception than the rule, due to a series of developments that include the proliferation of nonstate actors and the emergence of discontinuous patterns of violence, marked by periods of direct military engagement and followed by prolonged policing actions. In such a context, rules and norms place limits on what are considered legitimate and illegitimate networks of force and are instrumental in designations of the identities of legal parties. In this environment, policymakers, military lawyers, human rights advocates, and humanitarian workers are becoming more closely aligned and this alignment has clear policy implications for determinations on the limits of concepts of humanity. Ultimately, these decisions result in authoritative judgments as to which humans can be protected and which ones can be killed with impunity.

Martin Wallenstein's contribution shifts the focus to the "war on terror's" impact on civil liberties and in particular on First Amendment rights. His analysis is influenced by Packer's notion of the ongoing tension between crime control advocates and civil liberties advocates which, according to Wallenstein, informs the current debate. Wallenstein critically examines a series of troubling measures adopted as part of this ongoing "war" in light of two contending approaches as to the role of government: one that sees government as the guardian against all threats, and the other that sees an overzealous government as constituting the greatest threat to freedom. In this polarizing climate, the key challenge is finding the proper balance. This quest is imperative, especially in light of the prevailing dynamics that continue to favor a more benevolent reading of the government's role.

Maintaining the focus on civil liberties, Elena Pokalova's study explores the intricate relationships between civil liberties and terrorism. According to Pokalova, anti-terrorist measures in a liberal democracy have to meet the twin tests of effectiveness and legitimacy. She identifies two types of anti-terrorist responses: counter-terrorism and law enforcement and examines the role of civil liberties in the context of measures adopted under them. Pokalova argues that the analysis of the relevant empirical data demonstrates that an increase in civil liberties leads to a decrease in the probability of terrorist attacks. And while it is difficult to identify with any precision the effectiveness of anti-terrorist efforts in general, the fact that counter-terrorism has negative effects on democratic freedoms seems to indicate that law enforcement, as opposed to counter-terrorism, might constitute a more appropriate anti-terrorist approach.

The next two contributions situate the implementation of counter-terrorist strategies within the framework developed by the United Nations. Maria Victoria Perez-Rios notes that, despite an international legal framework developed and shared by many member states, key differences have emerged during the implementation phase. Perez-Rios' contribution is a comparative case study of counter-terrorist policies in the United States, Spain, and the United Kingdom after the terrorist attacks in these countries, with a focus on the prohibition of torture and due process rights. In this context, she examines the "war" approach in the United States, the criminal justice/rule of law approach in Spain, and the UK's mixed approach, which leans more toward the criminal justice/rule of law one. According to Perez-Rios, the absence of any further attacks in these three countries, which have pursued different counter-terrorist approaches, undermines the argument that one is more effective than the other. However, from a human rights perspective, the rule of law approach is preferable, because it is most respectful of international human rights norms and fosters interstate cooperation between the United States and its European allies.

Most of the counter-terrorist activities within the United Nations system have centered on the UN Security Council (UNSC). George Andreopoulos' study critically examines key aspects of the work of two UNSC committees, the Counter-Terrorism Committee (CTC) and the 1267 Sanctions Committee. By employing a combination of lenses from international relations theory, Andreopoulos argues that realism/neorealism best explains the behavior of these committees in the early phases of the global campaign against terrorism, while more normative-based lenses become relevant later on, as the UNSC seeks to address the challenges posed by the human rights deficit exhibited by the policies and practices of these two committees. He attributes the shift toward greater transparency and accountability to a variety of factors that include the work of the United Nations' human rights bodies, the advocacy of key human rights NGOs, and the use of regional judicial fora by individuals and entities affected by these policies. While a lot remains to be done, the situation is not as bleak as in the early phases of this global campaign.

Our volume concludes with the study of the Special Court for Sierra Leone (SCSL), the "mixed" tribunal dealing with the gross and systematic violations committed during the course of the civil war in that country. Richard Culp and Christopher Warburton address a key issue in the debate surrounding the establishment of accountability mechanisms, namely their location. As noted earlier, the international community has created a series of tribunals to deal with wartime atrocities; some of them have been located outside the country where the atrocities took place, while others were located within the subject country. Culp and Warburton critically discuss some of the major internationally sponsored projects directed toward peace-building in Sierra Leone and examine the various methods that have been used to evaluate justice-related activities. According to them, domestically situated courts not only contribute to accountability, but they help develop local institutions than can contribute to the prevention of such violations in the future.

The pursuit of justice is a key feature of any serious discussion on improving world order. Our contributors bring to bear the insights of a variety of disciplines and employ diverse methodological tools in their analysis and assessment of the challenges confronting various justice initiatives in the quest for a more humane order. We are cognizant of the formidable tasks that lie ahead and realize that advancing the justice agenda is always a work-in-progress. Our hope is that this volume makes a contribution to this important endeavor.

Contents

Contributors

George Andreopoulos
Department of Political Science, John Jay College of Criminal Justice and the Graduate Center, CUNY, New York, NY, USA
chrights@jjay.cuny.edu

Richard F. Culp
Department of Public Management, John Jay College of Criminal Justice and the Graduate Center, CUNY, New York, NY, USA
rculp@jjay.cuny.edu

J. Paul Narkunas
Department of English, John Jay College of Criminal Justice/CUNY, New York, NY, USA
jnarkunas@jjay.cuny.edu

M. Victoria Pérez-Rios
Department of Political Science, John Jay College of Criminal Justice, New York, NY, USA
mvictoriasp@hotmail.com

Elena Pokalova
Department of Political Science, Kent State University, Kent, OH, USA
elena.pokalova@gmail.com

Robert F. Schopp
Department of Philosophy, College of Law University of Nebraska-Lincoln, Lincoln, NE, USA
rschopp1@unl.edu

Toy-Fung Tung
Department of English, John Jay College of Criminal Justice CUNY, New York, NY, USA
ttung@jjay.cuny.edu

Martin Wallenstein
Department of Communications and Theater, John Jay College of Criminal Justice, New York, NY, USA
mwallenstein@jjay.cuny.edu

Christopher E.S. Warburton
Department of Economics, John Jay College of Criminal Justice and the Graduate Center, CUNY, New York, NY, USA
cwarburton@jjay.cuny.edu

It Counts, But Only When It Does Not Matter? Evolving Standards of Decency and the Law of Other Countries

Robert F. Schopp

Introduction

Recent decisions of the U.S. Supreme Court have excluded juvenile offenders and mentally retarded offenders from eligibility for capital punishment.[1] Each of these cases has included both majority and dissenting opinions addressing a set of arguments and counter-arguments regarding the proper application of Eighth Amendment analysis to this issue. In each case, the majority has interpreted the evolving standards of decency (ESD) component of the Eighth Amendment analysis as supporting the categorical preclusion of capital punishment for the specified categories of offenders. At the same time, in each case, dissenting opinions have objected to the majority's interpretation and application of the ESD analysis. In each case, the majority and dissenting opinions have differed regarding the relevance of several types of evidence used in the ESD analysis. These controversial sources of evidence include the laws and practices of countries other than the United States, the opinions of professional and religious organizations, and the views of the general population as represented by polls or surveys.[2]

The dispute regarding other countries resembles the broader contemporary debate regarding the relevance, if any, of the U.S. Supreme Court looking towards foreign law in its interpretation of the U.S. Constitution.[3] I do not purport to present a comprehensive review of that broader discussion here.

---

[1] *Roper v. Simmons*, 125 S.Ct. 1183 (2005); *Atkins v. Virginia*, 536 U.S. 304 (2002).

[2] See *infra* notes 5–27 and accompanying text.

[3] See, e.g., "Comment: The Debate Over Foreign Law in *Roper v. Simmons*," *Harv. L. Rev.* **119**, 103–67 (2005). Three authors provide separate comments on the use of foreign law in *Roper*, but each recognizes and discusses to some extent the more general questions regarding the use of foreign law in constitutional interpretation.

R.F. Schopp (✉)
Department of Philosophy, College of Law, University of Nebraska-Lincoln,
Lincoln, NE 68583, USA
e-mail: rschopp1@unl.edu

G. Andreopoulos et al. (eds.), *International Criminal Justice: Critical Perspectives and New Challenges*, DOI 10.1007/978-1-4419-1102-5_1,
© Springer Science+Business Media, LLC 2011

It is not obvious that the law and practice of other countries should carry the same type and degree of relevance for all aspects of constitutional analysis. One might plausibly advance a variety of arguments endorsing different approaches to particular aspects of constitutional interpretation for a variety of purposes and circumstances. One might make a plausible argument from commitment in law, for example, regarding the significance of treaties or conventions that the United States has ratified. Alternately, one might make an argument from practical considerations in circumstances in which recognizing the significance of the laws of other countries can reasonably be expected to elicit cooperation from those countries in advancing the purpose of the constitutional provisions at issue. Insofar as particular constitutional provisions embody particular principles as central to the U.S. Constitution, considerations of the laws of other countries that embody similar principles might enhance the ability of the courts to interpret and apply those provisions in a manner that most accurately reflects those principles. In this analysis, I address only the specific context of Eighth Amendment doctrine regarding ESD.

The Court's Eighth Amendment doctrine contains an extended series of cases that include the assessment of ESD as a component of more comprehensive analysis.[4] These opinions are not at all clear regarding the most defensible interpretation of the meaning and function of ESD or regarding the appropriate scope of evidence relevant to ESD. This chapter attempts to clarify our understanding of the legitimate form, functions, and range of ESD analysis. In pursuing this goal, I consider the relevance of various sources and categories of evidence with primary attention directed towards evidence regarding the laws and practices of other countries. I do not claim that the interpretation advanced here explains the approach taken by the Court. Rather, I advance an approach that coheres with a defensible interpretation of the function of ESD analysis.

The next section of this chapter, "ESD: The Dispute," explicates the ongoing dispute regarding the appropriate form of ESD analysis and the appropriate range of evidence relevant to that analysis. The following section then distinguishes three alternative interpretations of ESD. The fourth section specifically addresses the debate regarding the relevance of foreign law to ESD. The fifth section, "Integrating an Interpretation of ESD with the Laws and Practices of Other Countries," advances an argument regarding the most defensible interpretation of the significance of ESD in Eighth Amendment analysis, and thus, regarding the appropriate range of evidence relevant to this analysis. The final section concludes the analysis.

ESD: The Dispute

Recent Cases

Recent cases provide a variety of opinions that reflect the well-established structure of Eighth Amendment analysis in that they address historical interpretation of the amendment, ESD relevant to the amendment, the requirement of proportionality

---

[4] See *infra* notes 5–27 and accompanying text.

applied to punishment under the amendment, and the requirement that punishment not be merely the gratuitous infliction of pain, but rather that it serve some legitimate purpose of punishment.[5] For the purposes of this discussion, I focus primary attention on the portions of these opinions that address ESD. All of the opinions accept United States legislation and jury decisions as relevant evidence of ESD – although they disagree regarding the significance of various patterns of legislation or sentencing.[6] The majority opinions in recent cases have applied ESD analysis and have concluded that developing patterns of legislation in the United States have demonstrated that contemporary standards of decency preclude capital punishment of offenders who have committed their capital offenses before reaching the age of 18 or who qualify as mentally retarded.[7] The opinions recognize that the degree of convergence among United States jurisdictions is less than has been found in prior cases that relied on ESD analysis. Each opinion relies partially on the rate of recent change in the law of the United States jurisdictions and on the unidirectional pattern of change.[8] The dissenting opinions reject the majority claims of consensus among United States jurisdictions, contending that preclusion of punishment as cruel and unusual under the Eighth Amendment requires a much more decisive consensus than that claimed by the majority in either case.[9] Neither the majorities nor the dissenting opinions provide clear reasoning to support their contentions that the developments cited should, or should not, qualify as consensus for this purpose. Neither provides clear analysis that persuasively justifies any particular threshold of "consensus."

In addition to disagreeing regarding the degree of convergence needed to establish a consensus among United States jurisdictions, the opinions differ regarding the relevance of various sources of evidence. The controversial sources of evidence include public opinion polls; the opinions of professional, learned, or religious organizations; and foreign law and practices. Some opinions explicitly assert that those sources are relevant to the Court's assessment of ESD, although these opinions appear to relegate these sources to secondary status as compared to state legislation and jury decisions.[10] Other opinions reject these sources, including the laws and practices of other countries as irrelevant to Eighth Amendment analysis.[11]

[5] *Roper*, 125 S.Ct. 1190–98; *Atkins*, 536 U.S. 311–21.

[6] Compare *Roper*, 125 S.Ct. 1192–94 with 1217–21 (Scalia, J., dissenting); *Atkins*, 536 U.S. 313–16 with 321–23 (Rehnquist, J., dissenting), 339–48 (Scalia, J. dissenting).

[7] *Roper*, 125 S.Ct. 1190–98; *Atkins*, 536 U.S. 311–21.

[8] *Roper*, 125 S.Ct. 1192–94; *Atkins*, 536 U.S. 313–16.

[9] *Roper*, 125 S.Ct. 1218 (Scalia, J., dissenting); *Atkins*, 536 U.S. 321–22 (Rehnquist, J., dissenting), 342–44 (Scalia, J., dissenting).

[10] *Roper*, 125 S.Ct. 1198–1200 (majority), 1215–16 (O'Connor, J., dissenting); *Atkins*, 534 U.S. 316n21. (All discussing the law and practices of other countries as relevant.)

[11] *Roper*, 125 S.Ct. 1225–29 (Scalia, J., dissenting); *Atkins*, 536 U.S. 324–26 (Rehnquist, J., dissenting), 347–48 (Scalia, J., dissenting).

Neither the accepting nor the rejecting opinions provide clear reasoning to justify their claims that the sources at issue are, or are not, relevant to ESD analysis. I focus here on that question: What reasoning supports claims of relevance, or irrelevance, and what does that reasoning reveal regarding the most defensible interpretation of what constitutes ESD that merit constitutional recognition?

Relevance and Reliability

Although the opinions discussed above debate the relevance of the proposed sources of evidence of ESD, some passages in some opinions seem to address reliability, rather than relevance. Some opinions characterize legislation as "the clearest and most reliable objective evidence of contemporary values."[12] Similarly, some passages in Justice William Rehnquist's dissenting opinion in *Atkins* appear to endorse legislation as the most reliable source of evidence regarding ESD, rejecting the majority reference to polls because the Court lacks sufficient basis to evaluate the validity and reliability of those sources.[13]

Justice Antonin Scalia's dissenting opinion in *Roper* endorses Justice Rehnquist's concerns regarding the validity and reliability of studies and polls.[14] In these opinions, Justices Sandra Day O'Connor, Rehnquist, and Scalia apparently rely on legislation and jury decisions rather than on nonlegal sources, at least partially because they believe that the legal sources differ from the nonlegal sources in that the former, but not the latter, provide reliable evidence of ESD.

Proffered evidence lacks relevance if it lacks logical connection to the matter at issue.[15] Evidence that is relevant because it is logically related to the matter might lack reliability in that it might mislead the jury because it does not provide a trustworthy or consistent indicator.[16] If the matters at issue were the practices or beliefs of American juries, for example, measures of legal standards or popular opinion in other countries with different histories, traditions, and standards would be irrelevant, regardless of the quality of the measures in terms of reliability. Post-trial interviews with American jurors would be relevant, but they might not be reliable if they were poorly executed or applied to a nonrepresentative sample.

The most relevant and reliable sources of evidence regarding ESD might vary with the applicable conception of ESD. The Court's opinions are not entirely clear

[12] *Roper*, 125 S.Ct. 1207 (O'Connor, J., dissenting) quoting *Penry v. Lynaugh*, 492 U.S. 302, 331 (1989); *Atkins*, 536 U.S. 312.

[13] *Atkins*, 536 U.S. 322–37 (Rehnquist, J., dissenting).

[14] Roper, 125 S.Ct. 1222–23 (Scalia, J., dissenting).

[15] *Fed. R. Evid.* 401; *Black's Law Dictionary*, 8th ed., Eagan, MN: Thomson-West, 1316 (2004).

[16] *Fed. R. Evid.* 403; *The New Shorter Oxford English Dictionary*, New York: Oxford University Press, 2536 (1993) (hereinafter NSOED).

regarding the conception of ESD that applies to the Eighth Amendment. According to one interpretation, ESD refers to the "current moral sentiments of the American people."[17] Assume first that informal moral and political views widely endorsed by the citizens of the United States constitute the most defensible interpretation of ESD for the purpose of the Eighth Amendment analysis. Various sources of evidence would then be relevant if they were logically related to these widely held informal views. These sources would be reliable to the extent that they provided accurate and consistent indicators of those views.

According to this interpretation, polls, surveys, and the positions of various organizations in the United States would provide relevant evidence of the informal opinions that contribute to ESD. Insofar as these informal social attitudes constitute the ESD relevant to the Eighth Amendment analysis, Justice Rehnquist was correct in raising concern regarding the phrasing and sampling of a series of polls and surveys.[18] Polls, surveys, empirical studies, and opinions of relevant organizations should receive critical scrutiny designed to identify the strengths and weaknesses of these sources as accurate indicators of widely held social attitudes.

The degree of reliability of various sources would depend upon the methods through which they were identified, applied, and interpreted. The degree to which these sources provide accurate information might vary substantially, calling for critical review by the courts of such considerations as design, sampling, statistical analysis, and interpretation. Thus, the reliability of various sources might vary substantially.

It is not at all obvious, however, that these nonlegal sources provide less reliable measures of the views widely held among American citizens than do legislation and jury decisions. What evidence supports the premise that statutes and case decisions are reliable sources of evidence regarding widely held views among American citizens about the decency of various practices of punishment? Juries are small samples specifically selected to exclude those citizens who hold certain views regarding capital punishment.[19] As representative samples of the general population, they are further skewed by the use of peremptory challenges, challenges for cause, and various additional concerns that lead individuals or categories of individuals to be excused from service on capital juries. Furthermore, they are explicitly instructed regarding the relevant law in the jurisdiction in which they serve, and they take an oath to apply that law as instructed to the circumstances of the case.[20] Thus, insofar as they conform to their oath and instructions, they apply law, regardless of the degree to which that law converges with, or diverges from, their personal beliefs regarding the decency of that law and of the legal punishment at issue.

[17]*Atkins*, 536 U.S. at 348 (Scalia, J., dissenting).

[18]*Atkins*, 536 U.S. 322–37 (Rehnquist, J. dissenting).

[19]*Morgan v. Illinois*, 504 U.S. 719 (1992); *Wainwright v. Witt*, 469 U.S. 412 (1985).

[20]See, e.g., Kevin F. O'Malley, et al. (Eds.), *IA Federal Jury Practice and Instructions*, 6th ed., Eagan, MN: Westlaw, 4 (2006). "It is your duty to accept and to follow the law as I give it to you, even though you may disagree with the law."

Similarly, statutes are passed by legislatures, rather than by referendum of the general population. As such, they are subject to influence by a wide range of sources beyond the moral and political views of the legislators' constituents. Some evidence suggests that some countries outside of the United States have rejected capital punishment through legislation although the majority of the citizens endorsed the practice of capital punishment.[21]

Thus, statutes and jury determinations resemble polls, surveys, and opinions of organizations in that they provide some evidence of informal views widely held among citizens, but the accuracy of that evidence might vary significantly across time, circumstances, and specific instances. For these reasons, it remains unclear that statutes and jury decisions provide more reliable evidence of these informal views than would polls, surveys, and opinions of organizations. In short, it seems at least plausible to suggest that a combination of these nonlegal sources, statutes, and jury decisions might provide a more accurate representation of widely held informal views than would either the legal or nonlegal sources taken in isolation from the alternative category.

There is no obvious reason to consider judicial decisions in bench trials or at the appellate level relevant to ESD interpreted as informal social attitudes. Judges are a small nonrepresentative sample of the population who at least purport to decide on the basis of law, rather than on their own views or the views that they take to be popularly accepted.[22] Thus, insofar as ESD address widely held informal social views, it is not clear why judicial interpretation of the Constitution in the appellate process or application of law in bench trials should carry any weight regarding the ESD analysis.

It also remains unclear whether widely held informal views constitute the relevant conception of ESD. Notice an apparent ambiguity in the claim that legal sources provide objective evidence upon which the Court can rely. Objective evidence is "based on externally reliable phenomena."[23] The Court can rely with confidence on objective evidence because it provides observable, quantifiable evidence, relatively free of distortion by feelings, opinions, or bias.[24] If informal moral and political beliefs widely held among the citizens constitute ESD, then the relative weight of statutes, jury decisions, polls, surveys, or opinions by organizations depends upon the degree to which these sources reliably represent those informal moral beliefs. The justification for relying on some combination of these sources would require some good reasons to believe that this combination provided a more accurate representation of these informal beliefs than that provided by any available alternative.

---

[21] Paul G. Cassell, "In Defense of the Death Penalty," In: *Debating the Death Penalty* (Hugo Bedau & Paul G. Cassell, Eds.). New York: Oxford University Press, 199–200 (2004).

[22] See, e.g., *Furman v. Georgia*, 408 U.S. 238, 375 (Burger, J., dissenting), 405–14 (Blackmun, J., dissenting), 431–33 (Powell, J., dissenting), 465–70 (Rehnquist, J., dissenting) (1972).

[23] *Black's Law Dictionary*, *supra* note 15, at 1103.

[24] *Id.*; II NSOED, *supra* note 16, at 1963, 2536.

In short, if the ESD analysis refers to the widely held informal attitudes and opinions of the population, legislation provides only indirect inferential evidence of those standards. Thus, legislation provides reliable evidence of ESD only insofar as there is reason to believe that this legislation reflects the widely held views of citizens without substantial distortion through the influence of alternative sources such as interest groups, lobbyists, or the personal and nonrepresentative views of legislators.

The Court's reliance on statutes in American jurisdictions as the primary source of evidence regarding ESD suggests an alternative interpretation of ESD as the standards of decency to which the citizens of the United States have collectively committed themselves by embodying those standards in law through the democratic process.[25]

If this is the applicable interpretation of ESD, statutes fulfill a fundamentally different function. According to this interpretation of ESD, statues are not relevant because they provide evidence of widely held informal beliefs. Rather, statutes that have passed through the democratic process constitute the standards of decency that carry weight for the purpose of Eighth Amendment doctrine. By electing and retaining the legislators who pass these statutes, the citizens adopt the law passed by these legislators as the standards that define the legitimate exercise of coercive force by the state.[26] The claim here is not that the legislators always pass the statutes that the citizenry would adopt if those statutes were subject to popular vote. Rather, according to this interpretation of ESD, it is the responsibility of the citizenry to exercise the democratic process in a manner that replaces those legislators and that legislation if the citizenry chooses not to be so bound.

Insofar as citizens in a democracy elect legislators and refrain from removing those legislators from office or resorting to alternative procedures such as referenda to reject the laws passed by those legislators, they accept those laws as the standards that bind them. Interpreted in this manner, statutes do not merely provide evidence of ESD. Rather, the statutes that have passed through the legislative process and have been applied by the judiciary constitute the standards that bind a democratic society.[27]

In short, the manner in which legislation informs the most defensible interpretation of ESD depends partially upon the applicable conception of ESD. If ESD are understood as the standards to which the citizens currently bind themselves in law through the democratic process, then laws that the citizens enact through the democratic process constitute the ESD. Alternately, if the ESD are those standards represented by widely held informal social views, the laws enacted through the democratic process provide only one source of evidence regarding ESD.

Thus, identifying the most relevant and reliable sources of evidence regarding ESD requires that one address the following question: What constitutes ESD such

---

[25] Robert F. Schopp, "Reconciling 'Irreconcilable' Capital Punishment Doctrine as Comparative and Noncomparative Justice," *Flor. L. Rev.* **53**, 475, 508–17 (2001).

[26] *Id.* at 513–17.

[27] *Id.*

that this conception of ESD justifies recognition of ESD as a source of constitutional legitimacy regarding the interpretation and application of the Eighth Amendment?

Alternative Interpretations of ESD

Standards of Acceptance

The language in various opinions suggests at least three distinct answers to this question above. The first two alternatives discussed in the preceding section interpret ESD as standards defined by two distinct forms of acceptance by the population. Some language in some opinions is consistent with an interpretation of ESD as informal social attitudes widely held among the relevant population.[28] As discussed above, legislation, jury decisions, polls, studies, and opinions of various religious or professional organizations might provide some evidence relevant to these informal attitudes. Some opinions reject the nonlegal sources as not reliable, but they provide no reason to believe that legal sources provide more valid or reliable evidence of informal social attitudes than those nonlegal sources.[29]

Although some opinions apparently reject nonlegal sources as unreliable, other opinions apparently reject them as irrelevant.[30] The opinions that discuss ESD for the purpose of the Eighth Amendment analysis as "societal standards" or "standards of our citizenry" suggest the previously discussed interpretation of ESD as those standards to which the citizens have collectively committed themselves by embodying those standards in law.[31]

According to this interpretation, only legal sources are relevant. These alternative interpretations of ESD as widely held informal social views or as societal standards embodied in law represent standards of acceptance in that they rest upon the claim that general acceptance in informal opinion or in legal institutions defines the applicable ESD.

Justificatory Standards

Justificatory interpretations of ESD generate standards that differ from standards of acceptance in that they purport to rest upon reasoning that justifies the application

[28] *Roper*, 125 S.Ct. at 1183, 1222–23 (Scalia, J., dissenting); *Atkins*, 536 U.S. at 304, 316n21; *Gregg v. Georgia*, 428 U.S. 153, 175–76 (1976) (plurality opinion).

[29] See *supra* note 17–21 and accompanying text.

[30] See *supra* note 11.

[31] Schopp, *supra* note 25 at 508–09.

of these standards by appeal to justificatory principles, rather than merely upon general acceptance. Justificatory analysis can take conventional or critical forms.

Conventional standards of justice blur the boundary between justificatory standards and standards of acceptance in that they identify the principles, criteria, or practices that are generally believed to be just within a particular legal system or moral culture. Thus, conventional justificatory standards are standards of acceptance insofar as they reflect a pattern of general acceptance within a particular culture. They are also justificatory, however, in that they reflect the generally accepted view that such principles and practices are just, rather than some alternative view, such as general acceptance as effective, efficient, or popular.

Critical justificatory standards, in contrast, are those that reflect persuasive justificatory reasoning that appeals to principles of justice that are defensible in turn by rigorous critical reasoning.[32]

A particular law or practice might satisfy both critical and conventional requirements of justice in that it is supported by rigorous justificatory reasoning and widely accepted as just among the target population. The critical and conventional standards remain distinct, however, in that meeting the criteria for either type of standard does not entail meeting the criteria for the alternative type. The interpretations of ESD as widely accepted informal social views or as those to which the citizenry have committed themselves in law represent conventional standards of justice insofar as they rest upon the general acceptance of a specific form or application of punishment as just in informal opinion or in the standards embodied in law respectively.

Neither of these two variations of acceptance rests upon critical evaluation of justificatory arguments, although such arguments may have influenced the acceptance by some actors in either context. For the purpose of this chapter, I will include conventional justificatory standards within the category of standards of acceptance. I will address critical justificatory standards as a third category of standards that is distinct from the two identified standards of acceptance. Some language in some early cases suggests this third interpretation of ESD as a critical standard requiring critical review of the justifications for the standards at issue.

A Civilized Society

Some passages in a series of early opinions suggest that the Court gradually moved from a standard of acceptance to one that also included a critical interpretation in that the later opinions in this series frame the ESD analysis as one that addresses the enlightened standards of a civilized or maturing society. Prior to *Furman v. Georgia*

---

[32] Joel Feinberg, *Harmless Wrongdoing*, New York: Oxford University Press, 124 (1988). (Distinguishing critical and conventional morality.)

in 1972,[33] a few cases raised questions regarding the scope and interpretation of the Eighth Amendment that arguably carry some relevance to the ESD analysis.

In 1878, the Court upheld a sentence of death by public shooting for the crime of murder.[34] The Court upheld this method of execution as consistent with the Eighth Amendment by referencing the law of the territory of Utah, the rules and articles of war, and military laws, as well as the corresponding laws of other countries as reported by authors in these fields.[35] This opinion appears to accept the proposition that a mode of punishment is not cruel and unusual under the Eighth Amendment if it is currently accepted under relevant rules of law, including those of other countries. Thus, this opinion appears to apply a standard of acceptance in law, and insofar as the Court inferred acceptance as justified from acceptance in law, this opinion appears to apply a standard of conventional justification.

In 1890, the Court rejected a challenge to New York's use of the electric chair as a method of execution.[36] This challenge was brought under a state constitutional provision that closely mirrored the Eighth Amendment of the U.S. Constitution.[37] The Court cited a lower court's findings that the legislature had selected the electric chair as a humane method of execution and that electrocution produces instantaneous and painless death.[38] The Court characterized cruel and unusual punishments as those that "involve torture or a lingering death... something inhumane and barbarous...more than the mere extinguishment of life."[39]

These two opinions share a common focus on the decisions of lawmakers. They differ, however, in that the earlier *Wilkenson* opinion appears to rely only upon a general pattern of acceptance by those who adopted various laws, but the *Kemmler* opinion addresses the purpose of the lawmakers to promote instantaneous and painless death. The latter opinion articulates a standard involving the absence of torture or lingering death that appears to carry weight independent of acceptance by lawmakers. Although not entirely clear, it apparently vested weight in the decisions of lawmakers at least partially because they acted to promote instantaneous and painless death as well as to avoid inhumane or barbarous methods of punishment.

Taken together, these opinions consider acceptance by lawmakers, but they also suggest that the legislative purpose to select a method that is humane, rather than barbarous, is relevant to the assessment of a punishment as within the limits set by the Eighth Amendment. It is not clear whether the legislative purpose to promote instantaneous and painless death is important only as evidence that the chosen method is effective in preventing torture and lingering death or whether the Court treats this legislative purpose as important in itself for establishing legitimacy under the Eighth Amendment. According to either of these interpretations, however, the

---

[33] *Furman*, 408 U.S. at 238.

[34] *Wilkerson v. Utah*, 99 U.S. 130 (1878).

[35] *Id.* at 132–36.

[36] *In re Kemmler*, 136 U.S. 436 (1890).

[37] *Id.* at 446.

[38] *Id.* at 443–44.

[39] *Id.* at 447.

Court appears to move beyond mere acceptance. The opinion appears to consider either the legislative purpose to adopt a humane method, the effect of that purpose in achieving a humane method, or both the legislative purpose and the effect of that purpose in avoiding unjustifiable application of torture or lingering death as relevant to the Eighth Amendment analysis.

Although the *Kemmler* opinion indicates that inhumane or barbarous punishments are those that extend beyond the taking of life, two later opinions struck down punishments that did not involve the taking of life. In *Weems*, the Court struck down a sentence of 20 years at hard and painful labor as greatly disproportionate to the offense.[40] Thus, it interpreted the Eighth Amendment as prohibiting punishments that are excessive in proportion to the offense. Further, the opinion indicated that the meaning of the amendment might change "as public opinion becomes enlightened by a humane justice."[41]

This language arguably suggests that the interpretation and application of the Amendment might reflect changes in the principles of humane justice that are recognized by public opinion. Taken on its face, this language suggests that the constitutionality of particular punishments might change over time as public opinion comes to recognize and embrace more humane standards of punishment. Interpreted in this manner, revisions in standards of constitutional punishments require both that a standard reflects a more humane justice and that it is recognized as such in public opinion. That is, the amendment requires both the critical judgment that a method is justifiable because it is humane and the acceptance of that critical judgment in conventional standards of justice.

In *Trop v. Dulles*, the Court rejected denationalization as punishment for desertion during war, but the opinion explicitly rejects excessiveness as the-justification for that conclusion.[42] The opinion emphasizes the requirement that punishment conform to civilized standards. The opinion interprets the Eighth Amendment as drawing meaning from "the evolving standards of decency that mark the progress of a maturing society."[43] It also refers to the unanimity among "civilized nations" that statelessness should not be imposed as criminal punishment.[44] This reference to the opinions of civilized nations in conjunction with the reference to the evolving standards of a maturing society arguably reflects the premise that the laws and practices of civilized nations fulfill some function in identifying the evolving standards of humane justice in a maturing society.

Thus, the *Kemmler*, *Weems*, and *Trop* sequence of opinions can reasonably be understood to reflect the premise that the standards of acceptable punishment under the Eighth Amendment can evolve in the critical sense that they can become more enlightened by humane justice and that acceptance by public opin-

---

[40] *Weems v. United States*, 217 U.S. 349, 371–82 (1910).

[41] *Id.* at 378.

[42] *Trop v. Dulles*, 356 U.S. 86, 99 (1958).

[43] *Id.* at 101.

[44] *Id.* at 102.

ion and by the standards of other civilized countries can fulfill some unspecified function in identifying these standards. Interpreted in this manner, ESD evolve in the critical sense that they become more consistent with critically defensible standards of justice. Acceptance by civilized countries serves an evidentiary function in that acceptance by these countries provides some affirmation that these practices of punishment are consistent with those critically defensible standards of justice. These opinions do not provide, however, any clear criteria or factors that would qualify specified practices of punishment or principles of justice as enlightened or humane, nor do they provide criteria or factors that qualify societies as civilized or mature.

Insofar as the practices of civilized, mature, evolved, or enlightened societies are relevant because they provide evidence of critically justifiable practices of punishment, application of this interpretation requires some criteria or guidelines that reliably identify such societies. A society might be considered to be "civilized" in an anthropological sense or in a justificatory sense.

A society might be considered civilized in the anthropological sense to the degree that it is developed at the state level, rather than at the tribal level, with complex social stratification, literacy, and established social institutions.[45] The standard of civilization in this sense for the Eighth Amendment analysis would be conventional in that civilized practices are those that such societies endorse and practice. Insofar as standards and practices are civilized in this sense, it is not clear why such acceptance would carry Eighth Amendment doctrinal significance or justificatory force. Societies that qualify as civilized in this sense might vary substantially in the underlying principles of political morality they endorse in their constitutions, laws, institutions, and traditions. They might also vary substantially in the degree to which their practices successfully embody those principles. Thus, some societies that are civilized in this anthropological sense might embody principles that converge closely with those embodied in the Eighth Amendment specifically and in the Constitution more generally.

Other societies that are civilized in this sense might adopt principles of punishment and more general principles of political morality that diverge markedly from those embodied in the U.S. Constitution. Similarly, societies that qualify as civilized in this anthropological sense might engage in practices of punishment that vary markedly in the degree to which they converge with critically defensible justifications of punishment. Societies could qualify as civilized in this sense although they routinely inflict torturous punishments involving lingering death through the application of developed institutions of torture under the supervision of a civil authority.

Furthermore, some societies might share common principles in their constitutions, but they might address specific questions of punishment in a manner that fails to accurately represent the more general principles embodied in their broader system of legal institutions. Thus, their acceptance or rejection of a particular type or

[45]Robert H. Winthrop, *Dictionary of Concepts in Cultural Anthropology*, Westport, CT: Greenwood Press, 33–36 (1991); I NSOED, *supra* note 16, at 409.

application of punishment might, or might not, conform to the more general principles they endorse.

This anthropological interpretation is arguably inconsistent with the opinions that refer specifically to other nations that share our values, traditions, or heritage.[46] Many countries that arise from traditions that differ from those that provide the heritage of the United States and endorse principles and practices that differ from those endorsed in the Constitution, laws, and heritage of the United States can clearly qualify as civilized in this anthropological sense. Thus, relying on the practices of all anthropologically civilized societies in the interpretation of the ESD doctrine might require that the Court develop some process of analysis to address conflicting principles and practices of punishment among "civilized" societies.

Alternately, in referring to societies as "civilized," the opinions might be read to direct attention to those societies that are advanced or enlightened in matters of justice, spiritual knowledge, or political morality.[47] Arguably, this justificatory interpretation of "civilized" is more consistent with the function of the Eighth Amendment in precluding cruel and unusual punishments. The drafters could have phrased the amendment to prohibit punishments that were not widely accepted among nations. By describing the prohibited punishments as cruel, rather than merely as not widely accepted among nations, the Eighth Amendment apparently addresses those methods of punishment that a country should not apply, rather than those methods that are merely different from those that are generally accepted. This interpretation appears more consistent with the passages in the opinions that refer to societies that are "mature," "evolving," or "enlightened" in that they apply a more "humane justice."

These opinions appear to refer to societies that practice punishment in a morally justified or defensible manner.[48] This interpretation is consistent with the apparent implication that the practices of these societies provide evidence regarding the practices of punishment that the Court should accept as within the range of justified punishments or reject as cruel and unusual because they fall outside that range of justified punishment. That is, recognizing societal practices that are civilized in this justificatory sense explains why those practices carry prescriptive significance.

This interpretation of the ESD raises a different concern. Understood in this manner, attempts to identify ESD by appeal to the standards of punishment that are widely accepted is a non sequitur because the question at issue is one of justification, rather than one of acceptance. Alternately, if the Court appeals only to the practices of societies that apply punishment that is civilized in the justificatory sense, this approach appears vacuous. Identifying societies that apply punishment in a manner that qualifies as civilized in this sense requires justificatory analysis of the relevant practices in order to identify societies that qualify as civilized by virtue of the principles and practices of punishment they adopt and apply.

---

[46] *Roper*, 125 S.Ct. 1183, 1198–1200 (2005).

[47] I NSOED, *supra* note 16, at 409, 824.

[48] See *supra* notes 36–43 and accompanying text.

In order to perform this analysis, one needs some previously identified standards of justifiable punishment. If the Court has such standards, it can apply them directly to the punishment in question without the detour through the evaluation of other societies. Rather, the Court can apply the justificatory analysis directly to the form of punishment or the application of that punishment that is at issue. If it is not justified, then we should refrain from applying it, regardless of whether it is practiced by societies that are civilized in other ways. If it is justified, then those other civilized societies that reject it as uncivilized are mistaken.

Alternately, if the Court lacks such justificatory standards for punishment, then it lacks standards that will enable it to accurately identify other countries that are civilized in their principles and practices of criminal punishment. Finally, if such a justificatory analysis extends beyond the constitutional role of the Court as an institution that interprets and applies law, then it does so whether the Court applies that analysis directly to certain forms of punishment or indirectly to identify other countries as "civilized" in this sense.

Three Interpretations of ESD and the Law and Practices of Other Countries

As previously discussed, the Supreme Court's opinions addressing the Eighth Amendment include several that either endorse the evidence regarding the laws and practices of other countries as relevant, or reject it as irrelevant, but they do not provide clear reasoning to justify either position.[49] The significance, if any, that the Court should grant to this evidence might vary according to which of the previously identified interpretations of ESD is most defensible.

If ESD are understood as addressing acceptance by widely held informal social attitudes, determining the relevance of foreign sources requires that one address three questions.

First, when interpreting the Constitution, what range of social attitudes are relevant? Should the Court vest significance only in widely held attitudes among the citizens of the United States, or should the Court also consider the attitudes of citizens of other countries? If the Court should consider only the informal social attitudes held by the citizens of the United States, then the laws and practices of other countries are irrelevant to the ESD in the absence of some reason to believe that these laws provide reliable indicators of informal social attitudes that are widely held in the United States.

Second, if the Court should consider the attitudes of citizens of other countries, should the Court consider the attitudes of the citizens of *all* countries or only of some select subset of countries, such as those that share common heritage or political principles with the United States?

---

[49] See *supra* notes 10–11.

Third, insofar as the court should consider the informal social attitudes prevalent in at least some other countries, do the legal developments in other countries cited by these sources reflect widespread beliefs of the citizens of these countries?

Some sources suggest, for example, that the governments of Canada and England abandoned capital punishment when the majority of the citizens of those countries still supported it.[50] If those sources are accurate, the laws of those countries might not provide reliable evidence of ESD among the citizens of those countries. Thus, insofar as ESD should address the informal social attitudes widely held by the citizens of other countries, the Court should review a more comprehensive body of evidence, including law, surveys, polls, and other sources.

If the most defensible interpretation of the ESD addresses those standards of acceptance to which the citizenry have bound themselves by embodying them in law, the law and practices of other countries appear to be irrelevant. International treaties, conventions, or other forms of international law to which the citizenry of the United States have committed themselves through ratification or some alternative method of formal commitment would provide relevant evidence of ESD. Absent some form of explicit commitment, however, it is not clear what reasoning would justify granting substantive weight to the laws and practices of other countries as relevant to ESD interpreted in this manner. This interpretation of ESD as standards to which the citizens have bound themselves in law precludes the granting of any binding force to foreign law and practices to which the citizens have not bound themselves. It also precludes consideration of polls, surveys, or other evidence of informal social attitudes in this country or in other countries because the citizens have not bound themselves to those informal attitudes, even if they are widely endorsed as informal social beliefs.

Some opinions refer to the standards of a civilized society, but as previously discussed, this approach is ambiguous in that a society might be considered civilized in the anthropological sense or in the justificatory sense. If ESD refer to the standards of civilized societies in the anthropological sense, one could reasonably argue that the standards of all societies that meet the minimum level of institutionalization to qualify as civilized in this sense should be considered relevant. There is no obvious reason why this interpretation would grant any more weight to the laws and practices of countries in the Western liberal tradition than it would grant to those of countries with roots in markedly different political, religious, or moral traditions. Countries that adopt and apply practices of criminal punishment as well as broad principles of political morality that differ from those represented by the Constitution and political institutions of the United States would qualify as civilized in this sense. It is not clear that any coherent interpretation of the justification and limits of criminal punishment could apply to this broad range of societies.

More fundamentally, if one adopts the anthropological interpretation, it is not clear why these laws or practices would carry any justificatory significance for the purpose of constitutional interpretation or for the purpose of identifying those

[50] See *supra* note 21 and accompanying text.

punishments that are, or are not, cruel. Absent some persuasive reasoning to support the proposition that particular laws and practices are justified, why would the mere fact that other countries employ these laws or practices support the conclusion that they are not cruel?

Correspondingly, absent some persuasive reasoning to support the proposition that particular practices were cruel, why would the mere fact that other countries do not employ these laws or practices support the conclusion that they are appropriately categorized as cruel and unusual for the purpose of the Eighth Amendment?

Finally, if reference to other civilized countries in this sense establishes only that such practices are, or are not, widely accepted, with no inference that acceptance reflects justice, or that lack of acceptance reflects cruelty or injustice, why would wide acceptance, or lack of acceptance, carry any prescriptive force? Absent an inference that general acceptance provides a reliable indicator of justification according to the principles or political morality represented by the Constitution, there is no obvious reason why courts should vest any significance in general acceptance among nations when interpreting an amendment to the Constitution written to protect individual liberty by placing limits on the power of government to infringe on specified liberties.[51]

Arguably, the opinions that refer to "enlightened," "humane," or "maturing" societies or practices suggest that only the laws and practices of some subset of anthropologically civilized societies are relevant.[52] These opinions provide no clear interpretations of these terms, however, nor do they provide any clear justification for granting constitutional significance to the laws and practices of those societies. Furthermore, insofar as one attempts to advance interpretations of these terms that provide persuasive reasons to grant justificatory force to some identifiable subset of countries, laws, or practices, this process appears to meld the anthropological interpretation into the justificatory one.

If the applicable interpretation of "civilized," "enlightened," or "maturing" is justificatory, it remains unclear why the mere fact that other countries accept or reject such practices should carry any weight. That is, this interpretation raises the concern discussed previously: If the appropriate standard of civilization is a justificatory one, must the courts evaluate the justificatory force of the reasons why these countries accept or reject capital punishment or its application in particular circumstance? If so, why should the Court not simply evaluate the various justificatory arguments, without regard to whether other countries have endorsed or rejected them?

Thus, this justificatory interpretation of "civilized" appears to encounter the following dilemma. If the inquiry regarding ESD addresses the justification of certain practices, then why would the mere fact that various countries accept or reject those practices carry any significance? Alternately, if the mere fact of acceptance or rejection is relevant to the ESD analysis, then why should the Court grant any justificatory or constitutional significance to ESD?

---

[51] Ronald D. Rotunda & John E. Nowak, *Treatise on Constitutional Law*, 4th ed., St. Paul, MN: Thomsen-West, §14.2 (2007).

[52] See *supra* notes 33–48 and accompanying text.

Integrating an Interpretation of ESD with the Laws and Practices of Other Countries

Foreign Law and Confirmation of Consensus

Some opinions assert that foreign law can confirm the Court's conclusion that the Constitution prohibits application of capital punishment to specified populations, although it cannot control the outcome of that constitutional interpretation.[53] At first glance, this is puzzling. If foreign law can only confirm a conclusion supported by national consensus within the United States, it seems that foreign law counts only when it does not matter.

If there is a national consensus and foreign law confirms that national consensus, then the consensus establishes ESD. If there is a national consensus, but foreign law does not confirm that national consensus, then the national consensus establishes ESD. The lack of consensus among other nations cannot negate the national consensus because if the Court accepted the lack of consensus among other nations as fulfilling that function, then foreign law would control the outcome of the ESD analysis, and the Court explicitly states that the foreign law cannot control.[54] Thus, foreign law is redundant in that it merely augments a national consensus that would suffice for the purpose of the Eighth Amendment analysis. If there is no national consensus, and no consensus among other nations, then the lack of consensus provides no basis to establish ESD. Finally, if there is no national consensus and foreign law can confirm our consensus but it cannot control, then foreign law cannot confirm a national consensus that does not exist, regardless of the extent of convergence among other nations.

It might seem reasonable to suggest that foreign law matters in cases in which the pattern among United States jurisdictions approaches but does not attain a consensus. In such a near consensus situation, foreign law might tip the balance towards consensus.

Given the relatively low number of states accepted as forming a consensus in *Simmons* and in *Atkins*, one might reasonably suspect that this describes the influence that foreign law had on the majority opinions applied in those cases.[55] Although one might reasonably ponder whether foreign law had this effect in these opinions, accepting such a function for foreign law directly contradicts the majority opinions contention that foreign law can confirm our consensus but cannot control. That is, insofar as foreign law provides the influence that leads the Court to conclude that a consensus exists with a relatively limited number of United States jurisdictions that would not be sufficient to establish a consensus in the absence of the foreign law, then the claim that foreign law cannot control is apparently false.

---

[53] *Roper*, 125 S.Ct. at 1183, 1198–1200; *Atkins*, 536 U.S. at 304, 316n21.

[54] *Id.*

[55] *Roper*, 125 S.Ct. at 1217–21 (Scalia, J., dissenting); *Atkins*, 536 U.S. at 341–48 (Scalia, J., dissenting).

It seems then, that according to this interpretation, foreign law carries confirmatory significance only when it is superfluous because it merely confirms an independent national consensus that would be sufficient to establish ESD for the Eighth Amendment analysis in the absence of that foreign law. It cannot establish a consensus in the absence of a national consensus because it can only confirm a national consensus if that national consensus exists. Thus, foreign law counts only when it does not matter.

ESD and the More Comprehensive Eighth Amendment Analysis

The Court does not apply ESD analysis in isolation. Consider the relationships among ESD analysis and the other components of the Court's Eighth Amendment analysis. Several opinions make explicit that this analysis is not limited to history and ESD. These opinions explicitly assert that a consensus among the states is not dispositive and that the justices must exercise "[their] own independent judgment, whether the death penalty is a disproportionate punishment for juveniles."[56]

Taken on its face, this language is puzzling. From one perspective, it seems trivial; of course the justices must exercise their own judgment, as they must in any case. Some opinions object to this claim that the justices must bring their own judgment to bear because these opinions interpret this claim to mean that the justices apply their personal moral beliefs or intuitions, rather than their professional judgment regarding the most defensible interpretation of the Constitution.[57]

Some early opinions contain language that invites this interpretation. The plurality opinion in *Coker*, for example, includes reference to the "abiding conviction" of the justices.[58] The reasoning in that opinion interprets the general pattern of legislation and jury sentencing as confirming the judgment of the justices that death is a disproportionate punishment for the crime of the rape of an adult woman. One plausible reading of the opinion would interpret it as addressing legislation and jury sentencing as sources of information that the justices consider in making their personal moral judgments regarding proportionality.[59]

More recent opinions reflect an alternative interpretation. These opinions review the evidence of ESD. They then apply their own judgment to confirm the conclusion supported by the ESD analysis by applying two further steps in the Court's well-established Eighth Amendment analysis. First, they examine the penal

---

[56]*Roper*, 125 S.Ct. at 1192; *compare*, *Atkins*, 536 U.S. at 312.

[57]*Roper*, 125 S.Ct. 1221–22 (Scalia, J., dissenting); *Atkins*, 536 U.S. at 348–49 (Scalia, J., dissenting).

[58]*Coker v. Georgia*, 433 U.S. 584, 598 (1977).

[59]*Id.* at 597–60.

purposes served by the punishment at issue in order to determine whether applying that punishment to this offender or this class of offenders serves some previously recognized legitimate purpose and, thus, does not involve the gratuitous infliction of pain.[60] Second, these opinions examine the proportionality of the punishment according to the established standards involving severity of the offense and the moral responsibility of the offender.[61]

This pattern of analysis applies the traditional sequence of inquiries grounded in the 1976 cases. In *Gregg v. Georgia*, the plurality began the analysis by reaffirming that the Eighth Amendment did not preclude capital punishment at the time it was adopted.[62] The plurality then made clear that the amendment also requires that punishment conform to the ESD analysis and that it must not be excessive.[63] The opinion interprets this requirement regarding excessiveness as precluding punishment that involves the unnecessary and wanton infliction of pain, or that is grossly disproportionate to the offense.[64] The opinion identifies retribution, deterrence, and incapacitation as legitimate social purposes of punishment, rendering punishment that serves these purposes not the wanton infliction of pain.[65]

This opinion reveals a pattern of Eighth Amendment analysis that places substantial weight on ESD but retains the consideration of the legitimate purposes of punishment and of proportionality as a method for confirming the legitimacy of common practice. Insofar as the Court applies this pattern of analysis, punishments that are commonly accepted among the states could violate the Eighth Amendment if they were administered in circumstances in which they served no legitimate purpose or if they were clearly disproportionate to the offenses or to the personal responsibility or blameworthiness of the offenders.

I do not claim that the opinions of the Court reveal a consistent and clearly established pattern of analysis that fully integrates the ESD, legitimate purposes, and proportionality components. Various opinions might reasonably be interpreted as reflecting different interpretations of these components and of the relationships among them. Some opinions appear to address the legitimate purposes of punishment and the proportionality of the punishment as elements of the comprehensive Eighth Amendment analysis that are distinct from the ESD analysis and from one another.[66]

Other opinions appear to evaluate the legitimacy of various purposes and the proportionality of certain punishments for certain offenses or offenders by comparing those punishments to those applied to similar offenses and offenders in

---

[60] *Roper*, 125 S.Ct. at 1194–98; *Atkins*, 536 U.S. at 317–21.

[61] *Id.*

[62] *Gregg*, 428 U.S. at 153, 176–77 (plurality opinion).

[63] *Id.* at 179–87.

[64] *Id.* at 153, 169–73.

[65] *Id.* at 182–83 n28.

[66] *Roper*, 125 S.Ct. at 1183, 1192–98; *Gregg*, 428 U.S. at 153, 169–87 (plurality opinion).

other states.[67] These latter opinions arguably blend the legitimate purpose and proportionality elements into the ESD analysis. I claim only that the Court applies the ESD analysis as part of a more comprehensive Eighth Amendment analysis, rather than as a necessary and sufficient criterion that establishes or precludes constitutionality independent of other considerations.[68]

As initially articulated by the Court, the inquiry regarding legitimate purposes of punishment recognizes retribution, deterrence, and incapacitation as legitimate purposes, although incapacitation has been less clearly accepted in later opinions. This initial formulation apparently required only that punishment serve some legitimate purpose and prohibited only punishments that involved the gratuitous infliction of suffering because they served no legitimate purpose.[69] Some later opinions appear to emphasize the retributive principle in that they address punishment in proportion to the severity of the offense or to the moral or personal responsibility or blameworthiness of the offender.[70]

Although some of these opinions seem to require punishment in proportion to moral responsibility, the Eighth Amendment sets limits on constitutional punishment, rather than requiring specified punishments. Thus, these opinions might reasonably be interpreted as requiring negative retribution in that they limit punishment by precluding punishment that is disproportionate to the offender's personal responsibility for the offense.

Retributive principles that prescribe punishment in proportion to culpability arguably are embodied in institutions of criminal law that prescribe more severe punishment for more severe harm and more culpable mental states.[71] The insanity defense, duress, and related mitigating factors in sentencing arguably reflect at least a negative retributive structure in that these provisions limit criminal punishment to offenders who are culpable for their crimes, and they recognize circumstances that limit the offenders' culpability for their crimes as factors that provide good reasons to punish those offenders less severely than offenders who are fully culpable.[72]

I do not claim here that contemporary criminal law in the United States is purely retributive in purpose and justification. I claim only that the requirements of culpability, the relative severity of criminal offense definitions, and sentencing factors that aggravate or mitigate severity of punishment are reasonably interpreted as embodying retribution as one important principle embodied in current formulations of criminal law.

---

[67] *Atkins*, 536 U.S. at 304, 311–12; *Enmund v. Florida*, 458 U.S. 782, 788–93 (1982); *Coker*, 433 U.S. at 584, 592–97 (plurality opinion).

[68] Some opinions contend that the Court should limit the analysis to history or to history and ESD. *Roper*, 125 S.Ct. at 1217–18 (Scalia, J., dissenting); *Atkins*, 536 U.S. at 339–40 (Scalia, J., dissenting).

[69] *Gregg*, 428 U.S. at 182–87 (plurality opinion).

[70] *Penry v. Lynaugh*, 492 U.S. 302, 319–28 (1989); *Spaziano v. Florida*, 468 U.S. 447, 461–62 (1984).

[71] See, e.g., Model Penal Code, §§210.1–210.4; 211.1 (Proposed Official Draft, 1962). (Grading homicide and assault offenses as more serious if they cause more severe harm or are performed with a more culpable mental state.)

[72] *Id.* at §§ 4.01 (insanity), 2.09 (duress), 210.6(4) (sentencing mitigation).

Retribution as a legitimate penal purpose and the requirement of proportionality converge insofar as proportionality is understood as addressing punishment in proportion to the offender's culpability for the crime. Although the general requirement that the punishment be proportionate to the crime, or at least that it be no greater than proportionate, might seem intuitive to many people, it can be very difficult to articulate and justify standards of proportionality beyond ordinal proportionality.[73]

In the Eighth Amendment context, the Court relies heavily on comparison to punishments applied in the United States to related categories of offenders and offenses as defined by the severity of the harm done and the degree of offender culpability.[74] This approach arguably reflects an interpretation of proportionality that converges with retribution and with ESD as those standards to which the citizenry have committed themselves by embodying them in law. That is, the citizens collectively define the structure and limits of punishment that they are willing to apply to themselves by embodying them in the criminal laws addressing culpability requirements, excuses, and sentencing. Courts then apply those standards to specific offenders and offenses, and they use them to interpret the underlying principles and limits. Thus, citizens are bound by the standards of criminal responsibility, culpability, and proportionality to which they collectively have committed themselves through the democratic process.[75]

This commitment binds at two levels of abstraction. First, at a relatively concrete level, the specific statutes passed in the legislative process define the criminal offenses, culpability requirements, and sentencing standards that apply to the citizens who select the legislators. Trial courts apply those statutes to specific offenders and offenses. Second, at a relatively abstract level, appellate courts use those statutes and the resulting sentences as guidelines to define applicable principles of punishment and the boundaries of proportionate criminal sentences when performing the Eighth Amendment analysis.

According to this interpretation, citizens of the United States would not be bound by the standards that other countries have adopted or by standards that are endorsed only by informal social views either in the United States or more broadly.[76] I do not claim that the Court's opinions explicitly endorse this interpretation. I claim only that this interpretation is consistent with the general pattern of the Court's Eighth Amendment opinions and with a democratic process of self-rule through law.

---

[73] Joel Feinberg, *Doing and Deserving: Essays in the Theory of Responsibility*, Princeton: Princeton University Press, 116–18 (1970).

[74] *Roper*, 125 S.Ct. at 1183, 1194–98; *Coker*, 433 U.S. at 584, 592–97 (plurality opinion).

[75] See *supra* notes 25–27 and accompanying text.

[76] Schopp, *supra* note 25 at 508–17.

Interpreting the Law and Practices of Other Countries and ESD

Although various justices and commentators advocate various approaches to constitutional interpretation, it is not controversial that the Court must interpret and apply the Constitution. According to the interpretation of the Court's Eighth Amendment opinions presented here, the Court arguably derives the retributive principle to which the citizens of the United States have bound themselves from the history and current practices of criminal punishment in the United States. These opinions arguably derive generally applicable standards of retributive proportionality from ESD represented by the standards of offense severity, culpability, and sentencing that the citizens have adopted through the democratic process. The Court then tests the application of a particular sentence to a specified category of offenses or offenders against these standards, and it rejects the sentence as inconsistent with the Eighth Amendment if it is disproportionate to the severity of the offense or to the culpability of a recognizable class of offenders.[77] The citizens collectively define the bases for these standards through the legislative process that defines offenses and sentences, as well as through jury sentencing decisions. The citizens can modify the standards applied under the Eighth Amendment to some degree through the legislative process by modifying the criminal sentencing statutes and practices from which the Court partially derives the ESD regarding the severity of punishment that falls within the limits of the Eighth Amendment for a particular category of offenses or offenders.

According to this interpretation, there is no obvious role for foreign law in the interpretation of the Eighth Amendment because it does not represent the laws to which the citizens of the United States have bound themselves through the legislative process or through jury sentencing decisions. Other nations might or might not converge with United States law in identifying retribution as an important principle that partially defines the limits of criminal sentencing as applied to particular categories of offenses and offenders. Among those that do adopt this general principle, they may or may not adopt similar standards of proportionality for similar offenses.

Finally, insofar as the constitutional significance of the retributive principle rests on the decisions of the citizens to collectively bind themselves by enacting those principles into law and by applying them in jury sentencing decisions, standards of proportionality in other societies do not carry this binding force on those who have not had the opportunity to participate in the decision to adopt those standards.

Insofar as other societies adopt principles of criminal sentencing in common with those reflected in the Constitution and the criminal law of the United States, however, the relevant laws and practices of those societies might serve a legitimate triggering function in constitutional interpretation. Recall the opinions that discuss foreign law as a source that can confirm our consensus but cannot control in the absence of a

---

[77] See *supra* note 74.

consensus in the United States. As previously discussed, this interpretation appears to provide no substantive function for foreign law because it apparently counts only when it does not matter.[78]

Foreign law might serve a legitimate triggering function, however, if sentencing standards and practices in the United States differ substantially from corresponding standards and practices in other countries that have adopted similar principles. Such differences among countries that purport to adopt similar principles might signal a potential discrepancy between the interpretation and application of common principles as applied to particular offenders or offenses in the law of the United States and alternative interpretations and applications of those principles in other countries that have adopted them. According to this interpretation, such a discrepancy does not provide legally binding authority regarding the appropriate interpretation and application of these principles because the laws of other countries are not among those to which the citizens of the United States have chosen to bind themselves. Neither does such a discrepancy provide persuasive evidence that standards applied in the United States are in error because we have no clear criteria of retributive proportionality and no reason to infer from the mere discrepancy that the practices of those other countries provide a more defensible standard than those of the United States.

Insofar as practices in the United States markedly depart from those of other countries that purport to pursue common principles, however, that discrepancy can serve as notice that should trigger critical review and reflection. That is, insofar as the Court applies the analyses of proportionality and legitimate penal purposes as a method of review designed to determine whether specific sentencing standards or practices cohere with the more general principles of punishment to which the citizens have bound themselves, clear evidence that other countries that adopt similar principles of political morality, including similar principles of criminal responsibility and punishment, reject certain punishments as unjustifiable provides the Court with reason to ask whether these punishments violate the principles that the United States shares with these other countries. Such a discrepancy provides good reason to think that at least one of these interpretations and applications of the common principles might be misguided.

This triggering function serves as a cautionary device that should alert the Court to the possibility that the manner in which some United States jurisdictions currently interpret and apply the principles held in common with these countries to particular categories of offenses or offenders might not represent defensible interpretations of those principles. Hence, it provides good reason to pause and critically review the applicable principles and the relevant reasoning in light of the broader institutions of criminal punishment to which the citizens of the United States have bound themselves.

This critical review might provide the Court with good reason to revise or to confirm the current interpretation and practices. According to this interpretation, the practices of other countries do not carry constitutionally binding force. That is, the

[78] See *supra* notes 53–55 and accompanying text.

mere fact that many, or even all, other countries reject specific practices does not render those practices inconsistent with the Eighth Amendment. Furthermore, the standards and practices of other countries are not in themselves persuasive because a Court that applied this interpretation would not accept the mere fact that these countries adopted these standards and practices as providing good reason for the United States to conform to these standards and practices as a matter of constitutional doctrine. Rather, convergence in rejecting specified practices of punishment among other countries that embrace similar principles to those embraced under the U.S. Constitution should serve to trigger rigorous review of the reasoning that purports to justify those practices as consistent with those principles and rigorous review of the alternative reasoning that purports to repudiate those practices as inconsistent with those principles.

This process would apply critical analysis of the relevant reasoning to determine whether these practices were, or were not, consistent with the relevant principles represented by the Constitution and by the laws defining the criminal offenses and punishments to which the citizens have bound themselves. This process would constitute an exercise of self-discipline designed to protect the integrity of the Constitution and of the rule of law in a democratic society by requiring that the specific standards and practices of punishment converge with the broader underlying principles of punishment that the citizens have embodied in law.

Recognition of an apparent discrepancy between the practices of punishment in the United States and those broadly applied by countries that purport to embrace and apply principles similar to those embedded in the Constitution and laws provides the Court with good reason to critically question and reflect upon the reasoning that supports those practices. That critical reflection might support the conclusion that some of our standards and practices are inconsistent with the principles that we have endorsed and attempted to apply through the democratic process. If that reflection supports that conclusion, it provides good reason to revise those standards and practices.

That comparison to other countries would not, however, support revision merely because the practices of other countries differed from those in the United States. Rather, that divergence of practices would support modification of practices in the United States only if the reflection triggered by recognition of those differences provided persuasive reasoning to support the conclusion that some practices in the United States violated the principles to which the citizens of the United States have bound themselves as constitutional principles. If critical reflection on the reasoning supporting the current practices in the United States supports the conclusion that those practices converge with those principles, that reflection would reaffirm the legitimacy of those practices, despite their divergence from the practices of other countries. In short, the interpretation suggested here recognizes the practices of other countries that at least purport to endorse relevant principles in common with those embedded in United States law as relevant to the practice of self-discipline in the interpretation and application of those principles through rigorous analysis of the reasoning and principles embodied in the Eighth Amendment doctrine.

This approach to self-discipline pursues the integration of constitutional principles to which the citizens have committed themselves with the forms and limits of punishments they have endorsed through the legislative process and through the sentencing process. The integration of constitutional principles with the more specific legislation and sentencing decisions pursues coherence of principles with judgments regarding rules and specific applications of those rules similar to the coherence approach of reflective equilibrium.[79]

As applied to moral and political theory, reflective equilibrium pursues the integration of considered moral judgments with more abstract principles that explain and justify those judgments. Discrepancy between considered judgments and apparently defensible principles requires critical assessment of the reasoning that supports each in pursuit of a coherent set of principles and judgments that can be supported by consistent reasoning. That critical analysis might provide persuasive reasoning that justifies revision of the considered judgments regarding the justification of particular practices or of specific applications of those practices. Alternately, such analysis might provide persuasive reasoning that requires modification of the relevant principles. The process of pursuing coherence of particular practices or of specific applications of those practices with more abstract principles serves as a form of discipline in which the requirement of coherence of principle and judgments promotes the application of critical reasoning at both levels of abstraction.[80]

The Eighth Amendment prohibits cruel and unusual punishments, but it provides no clear criteria for the application of that prohibition.[81] As previously discussed, the Court has adopted the ESD doctrine as a component of its more comprehensive Eighth Amendment analysis.[82] A standard is "[a] criterion for measuring acceptability, quality, or accuracy."[83] Decency refers to "[p]ropriety of behavior or demeanor... avoidance of impropriety, obscenity, or immorality."[84] Thus, a standard of decency is a criterion or measure of proper behavior that precludes improper or immoral behavior. In the context of criminal punishment, a standard of decency provides a criterion or measure of the practices of criminal punishment that precludes practices that violate the applicable principles of retributive justice. Evolution refers to "[t]he process of developing in detail what is implicit in an idea or principle."[85] Thus, evolving standards of decency for the purpose of criminal punishment would develop more precisely the measures of punishment that conform to the applicable principles of retributive justice and preclude those forms or applications of punishment that violate those principles.

---

[79] John Rawls, *A Theory of Justice*, Cambridge, MA: Belknap Press, 19–21, 48–51 (1971); *The Cambridge Dictionary of Philosophy*, 2nd ed., (Robert Audi, General Ed.), New York: Cambridge University Press, 782 (1999).

[80] *Rawls, id.* at 48–51.

[81] U.S. Const. amend. VIII.

[82] See *supra* notes 56–68 and accompanying text.

[83] *Black's Law Dictionary*, *supra* note 15, at 1441.

[84] I NSOED, *supra* note 16, at 606.

[85] *Id.* at 868.

Interpreted in this manner, ESD neither purport to provide a critical justification of punishment nor are they merely a survey of those methods and applications that are conventionally accepted. Rather, analysis of ESD seeks to integrate conventional and critical analysis by accepting the principles of punishment that the citizens of the United States have adopted by embodying them in law and testing specific practices of punishment to determine whether they are consistent with those principles.

The Court's approach discussed in the prior section begins the ESD analysis by reviewing the laws and practices of the United States jurisdictions, but it then tests those practices by assessing their consistency with the identified legitimate purposes of retribution and deterrence. Insofar as retribution and deterrence represent the generally accepted legitimate purposes of the institutions of criminal punishment embodied in the criminal law of the United States, they represent the decisions of the citizens, through their legislators, to adopt practices that apply punishment in proportion to culpability for the wrong done and that are expected to discourage such crimes.[86] The Court's approach that tests ESD by asking whether the punishment in question is consistent with these legitimate purposes arguably adopts a process that resembles reflective equilibrium in that it seeks coherence of the practices of punishment accepted by ESD with the principles of retribution and prevention that the citizens have adopted by embodying them in law.

I do not claim that the Court explicitly adopts reflective equilibrium as a constitutional doctrine. I claim only that the Court identifies generally accepted modes and applications of punishment through the ESD analysis and tests those standards by asking whether they comport with the retributive and consequentialist principles of punishment generally embodied in the institutions of criminal punishment. This pattern of analysis seeks coherence of practices and principles similar to that represented by reflective equilibrium.

Insofar as this pattern of Eighth Amendment analysis can reasonably be understood as an attempt to pursue coherence of principles and practices, evidence that other countries that adopt similar principles do, or do not, accept similar practices can serve a triggering function. That is, evidence that other countries with similar principles of punishment and of political morality generally reject particular practices of punishment as contrary to those principles provides good reason to engage in careful analysis of the relevant reasoning in order to determine whether those practices are consistent with the principles that those countries and the United States endorse in common.

According to this approach, however, the critical question is not whether the practices of the United States converge with, or depart from, the practices of these other countries. Insofar as the rigorous application of critical reasoning is an exercise in self-discipline, simply accepting the practices of other countries as persuasive would undermine that pursuit of self-discipline. Rather, the pursuit of Eighth Amendment analysis as a form of self-discipline requires that the courts ask whether the practice

[86] *Black's Law Dictionary*, *supra* note 15, at 1343 (retribution), 481 (deterrence).

of punishment at issue reflects rigorous application of the principles of punishment to which the citizens of the United States have committed.

This approach is more consistent with the function of ESD as a component in democratic self-government through the rule of law than are the alternative approaches of including foreign countries along with the states in the count of the jurisdictions that comprise the basis for the ESD or of disregarding the law and practices of countries other than the United States.

The U.S. Constitution provides the basic principles of government and the institutional structure through which the citizens of the United States govern themselves through the rule of law. The Bill of Rights protects individual liberties by placing limits on government power.[87] These provisions partially define the principles to which the citizens bind themselves by setting limits on the government's authority to infringe on liberty through the use of coercive force. Rigorous interpretation and application of principles requires critical assessment of all relevant information and reasoning. Consideration of the standards and practices of the states and of other countries that purport to apply similar principles can provide one method through which the citizens collectively discipline themselves in the interpretation and application of law. Thus, consideration of the reasoning presented by these nonbinding sources provides one element in a more comprehensive exercise of self-discipline in the democratic process of self-rule through law.[88]

The alternative approach of including the law and practices of other countries along with the states in the count of jurisdictions in tabulating a consensus for the ESD analysis undermines the democratic process of self-rule through law. The citizens of the United States have no opportunity to vote regarding the laws that govern criminal punishment in other countries. Similarly, the Eighth Amendment carries no prescriptive force regarding the laws and practices of criminal punishment in countries other than the United States.

Insofar as the laws and practices of other countries were accepted by the Court as sufficient to establish a binding consensus that was not established by the laws and practices of the states, foreign law would control the ESD analysis in a manner that effectively recognized the authority of other countries to amend the Eighth Amendment of the U.S. Constitution. That is, recognizing the laws and practices of other countries as sufficient to establish a consensus when combined with a pattern of laws and practices among some states in the United States that would not have

[87] See *supra* note 51 and accompanying text.

[88] Similarly, amicus briefs from professional or religious organizations presenting the opinions that we should or should not apply specified punishments to specified categories of offenders, offenses, or circumstances would carry no weight. Amicus briefs from such organizations that provided information and reasoning relevant to the Court's analysis of the most defensible interpretation or application of the retributive principle or of the preventive functions of punishment would be relevant. Insofar as such briefs provide the Court with accurate information and reasoning relevant to the interpretation and application of the legitimate penal functions of punishment in general, or as applied to particular categories of offenses or offenders, they can assist the Court in interpreting and applying the constitutional principles to the questions at issue.

been sufficient to establish a consensus in the absence of the foreign law recognizes the authority of other countries to revise the effective interpretation and application of the Eighth Amendment, although those other countries and their citizens are not bound by that amendment. This approach undermines democratic self-rule because the citizens of the United States are bound by laws regarding which they cannot vote and because the foreign countries take on a power to revise the effective interpretation of a Constitution to which they are not bound.

The alternative approach of entirely disregarding the laws and practices of other countries that purport to adhere to similar principles undermines the process of self-discipline through rigorous interpretation and application of the principles to which the citizens bind themselves. This process requires careful critical review of the available reasoning that supports specific interpretations of the principles represented by the Eighth Amendment and by the criminal law that has been enacted and applied in the various states. Recognizing that other countries that endorse similar principles draw different conclusions about the legitimacy of capital punishment, about other forms of punishment, or about particular applications of those punishments should facilitate the rigorous pursuit of self-discipline by encouraging justices and legislators to engage in the critical analysis of the reasoning that justifies the conclusion that specific types of punishment in general, or as applied to particular categories of offenses or offenders, are consistent with those principles.

By requiring of ourselves that we critically review the available reasoning that supports the conclusion that such punishment is, or is not, consistent with the most defensible interpretation and application of the principles embedded in the Constitution and in the relevant legal institutions, we promote the disciplined exercise of democratic self-rule through law. This process of self-discipline in the interpretation and application of constitutional principles mirrors the process of reflective equilibrium in that it applies rigorous reasoning to the integration of those principles with specific judgments regarding the legitimacy of particular forms or applications of punishment.[89] In short, recognizing the legitimate function of the law and practices of other countries as a triggering device for self-discipline is more consistent with democratic self-rule through law than is either of the two identified alternatives.

This interpretation of the most defensible approach to considering the significance of the laws and practices of other countries applies to the interpretation of ESD as the standards to which the citizens have bound themselves by embodying them in law. That interpretation is more consistent with democratic self-rule through law than either of the previously identified interpretations of ESD. The interpretation of ESD as widely held informal social views undermines the exercise of democratic self-rule through law because it promotes sentencing based on standards to which neither the citizens generally nor those engaged in the sentencing and appellate process have bound themselves. Sentencing judges or jurors could apply those informal views in sentencing a particular offender without adopting a

---

[89] See *supra* text accompanying notes 79–80 discussing reflective equilibrium.

rule that would also be applicable to themselves. Similarly, appellate court justices could apply interpretations of ESD that were not grounded in democratically enacted laws to which they were subject.[90]

I do not suggest here that informal social views have no effect on the decision making of jurors, sentencing judges, or appellate justices. Neither do I deny that the decisions made by these individuals and juries can influence the perception of informal views that would apply to them if they were to become defendants. Unlike standards embodied in law, however, these interpretations of informal views do not establish specific legal standards to which they are bound.

Similarly, the interpretation of ESD as the most defensible critical justificatory standard shifts the focus from the standards that the citizens have adopted as rules of law through the democratic process to those that are most consistent with the most defensible justifications of punishment. This approach might be the most effective method for identifying the standards to which citizens *should* bind themselves. Insofar as appellate justices apply the ESD component of the Eighth Amendment analysis by seeking the most defensible critical justification of punishment, they arguably shift from the interpretation and application of law to the pursuit of moral justification. Insofar as they pursue rigorous interpretation and application of the moral principles of justified punishment embedded in the Constitution and laws the citizens have adopted, they pursue conventional moral justification that converges with the interpretation of ESD as the standards to which the citizens have committed themselves. This pursuit of conventional moral justification falls within the responsibilities of the justices. If the justices interpret the ESD as the most critically defensible moral justification, however, they depart from the limitation to those standards the citizens have embodied in law. This approach undermines democratic self-rule through law because it allows justices to interpret and apply principles and practices of punishment to which the citizens have not bound themselves and which may not be consistent with those embedded in law. Furthermore, because justices are ordinarily educated and experienced in legal analysis, this approach raises serious questions regarding the qualifications of justices to interpret and apply ESD.

Finally, this interpretation of ESD is consistent with the opinions that contend that ESD is not determinative in that the justices must bring their own judgments to bear. As discussed previously, recent opinions that articulate this approach call for the justices to exercise their own judgment by applying the legitimate purposes of punishment and the proportionality principle.[91] Insofar as ESD are understood as representing the principles that the citizens have embodied in law, it is possible that a large majority of states might pass specific statutes applying punishment that conflicts with the principles of criminal punishment embodied by the more comprehensive body of criminal law.

Suppose, for example, that a terrorist organization triggered a series of bombings resulting in mass murders by placing explosives in the lunch boxes of small children and sending them into schools. Suppose further, that these events were so horrific

---

[90] Schopp, *supra* note 25, at 516.

[91] See *supra* notes 60–65 and accompanying text.

that many states passed statutes defining an offense of mass murder and stipulating that all those who participated in such offenses would be subject to mandatory capital punishment, regardless of their culpability regarding the conduct they performed that contributed to the offenses. Thus, some young children who were manipulated in a manner that facilitated such murders would be sentenced to death, despite their lack of awareness of the purpose or effects of the conduct they performed.

If the ESD analysis is interpreted as restricted to a survey of the practices of punishment accepted by the laws of the states, such punishment would meet the ESD component of the Eighth Amendment analysis. If the ESD analysis is understood as requiring rigorous reasoning regarding the integration of practices of punishment with the principles embodied in the broader body of criminal law, in contrast, the Court could reasonably conclude that the passage and application of such statutes would violate the principles of responsibility and culpability that permeate the standards of criminal punishment to which the citizens have bound themselves by establishing them in law.

Conclusion

One might advance plausible arguments for the inclusion or exclusion of the law and practices of other countries in the most defensible approach to the interpretation of various provisions of the United States Constitution. The interpretation advanced here addresses only the ESD component of the Eighth Amendment doctrine. This analysis reflects the premise that identifying the most defensible role, if any, for the law and practice of other countries requires a more comprehensive assessment of the purpose of the specific constitutional provision at issue and of the legitimate functions various sources might fulfill in appropriately interpreting and applying that provision. The interpretation and application of a complex system of law requires the integration of rules and principles in a manner that is consistent with the principles of political morality underlying the particular legal institutions at issue.

The interpretation advanced here rests partially upon an understanding of the Eighth Amendment specifically, and of the Bill of Rights generally, as placing limits on the authority of the majority. The Court's approach to Eighth Amendment cases disciplines the majority by asking whether the general acceptance of specific forms or applications of punishment in ESD is consistent with the retributive and deterrent purposes of punishment contained in the broader institutions of criminal law that the citizens have adopted.

In this context, recognizing that other countries that adopt similar principles reject certain categories or applications of punishment as unjustified should trigger careful analysis of the coherence of these punishments with the principles to which the citizens have bound themselves by enacting them into law. According to this interpretation, the mere fact that other countries accept or reject a particular form of punishment does not carry constitutional weight. Rather, a general pattern of rejection by countries that generally adopt similar principles to those embodied in the law of the United States serves to trigger careful assessment of the relevant reasoning as a form of self-discipline that can enhance the ability of the courts to responsibly interpret and apply the principles to which the citizens of the United States have committed themselves.

Just War Claims: Historical Theory, Abu Ghraib, and Transgressive Rhetoric

Toy-Fung Tung

Old Theories, New Global Reality

A misguided understanding of the new global reality traced a trajectory from September 11, 2001, to the March 2003 invasion of Iraq, and finally to Abu Ghraib. Wars take place within contexts of global power, and they are rationalized within certain historical norms of thought. After September 11, the United States possessed the moral advantage, but as the Iraqi invasion took shape, the legitimacy of the United States' responses became questionable. The Iraqi invasion triggered renewed interest in "just war" claims, but contemporary commentators did not always fully understand the historical and humanistic origins of just war theories.[1] Just war paradigms evolved through centuries of conventional warfare marked by the gradual emergence of modern nation-states. One can question whether traditional just war theory obtains in the contemporary world, defined as it is by new technologies of warfare and communication, changing economic conditions, and transnational geopolitical realities (Murnion 2006). Still, the rhetoric of just war played a paramount role in shaping the war on terror, the Iraqi invasion, and the Abu Ghraib fiasco.

The "war against terrorism" has been called a "war everywhere" (Brooks 2004, pp. 681–682) and a war without any foreseeable end. This chapter argues that an almost inevitable path leads from the unrestricted "war against terrorism"

[1] Walzer's (2006a) well-known work, *Just and Unjust Wars*, is based on historical examples, but he does not openly confront historical just war theory. Walzer's issues, however, all have precedents in just war theory. For example, in discussing "double effect" in detail (pp. 152–159), he never mentions Aquinas, the originator of this theory (Aquinas 2002, pp. 263–264), although he elsewhere mentions Vitoria. While Walzer does not situate his own work within the context of historical just war theory, many other scholars did (Bellamy 2006b; Fiala 2008; Guthrie & Quinlan 2007; Patterson 2007; Stover 2004; Wester 2004), not to mention the multitude of treatments in the popular media. The important point here is the prevalence of the rhetoric focused on "just war."

T.-F. Tung (✉)
Department of English, John Jay College of Criminal Justice, CUNY, New York, NY, USA
e-mail: ttung@jjay.cuny.edu

G. Andreopoulos et al. (eds.), *International Criminal Justice: Critical Perspectives and New Challenges*, DOI 10.1007/978-1-4419-1102-5_2,
© Springer Science+Business Media, LLC 2011

to Abu Ghraib. That course was set by the Bush administration's use of rhetoric, not only to defend its going to war (*jus ad bellum*),[2] but afterwards, unilaterally, to "rewrite" international law and the United States' own military regulations, in order to override restrictions on war conduct. Many limits were erased that regulated the status and conduct of noncombatants and occupying forces; regular soldiers and the military police (MPs); MPs and military intelligence (MIs); MIs and civilian interrogators from Other Governmental Agencies (OGAs) or private contractors. As will be argued, the new global reality and the unbounded nature of the war on terror laid the foundations for the Bush administration's erosion and violation of every boundary of conduct: geopolitical, legal, moral, and finally, even plainly human.

This breakdown was facilitated through official pronouncements – speeches, national strategies, memos, and CPA orders – and unofficial rhetorical complicities, with the aim of undercutting written law in the name of a supposedly higher law. Because so much discussion after September 11 swirled around the idea of a pre-emptive "just war," we must examine and question the contemporary distortion of the just war tradition. The vast array of today's views about just war cannot be fully accounted for here, nor can justice be done to the nuanced tradition as a whole.[3] But the historical outlines of just war theory will be examined, and a proper precedent will be proposed for the Iraqi invasion.

Finally, the Bush administration's rhetoric will be analyzed for how it appropriated the moral force of just war claims within its "securitization" discourse to create a culture that fostered transgressions of the permissible limits of war conduct, first in the general war on terror, as evidenced in the Yemeni strike, and afterwards, in "Operation Iraqi Freedom" and Abu Ghraib.

---

[2]I have followed contemporary usage by generally writing "*jus*" for the Latin "*ius*" except in a couple of instances, such as "*ius gentium*" and "*ius cosmopoliticum*." The word "*ius*" is laden with significances and is hotly debated in the historical literature concerning "rights," so the reader should be aware that "*jus*" is the same word as "*ius*."

[3]Good contemporary editions and translations exist for all the theorists discussed in this chapter. See: Thomas Aquinas, *St Thomas Aquinas: Political Writings*, trans. and ed. R.W. Dyson (Cambridge: Cambridge University Press, 2002); Alberico Gentili, *De iure belli libri tres* (On the Law of War), trans. J.C. Rolfe, vol. 2 (1588, rev. 1598; Oxford: Clarendon Press, 1933); Francisco de Vitoria, *Francisco de Vitoria: Political Writings*, trans. and ed. Anthony Pagden and Jeremy Lawrance (Cambridge: Cambridge University Press, 2001); Hugo Grotius, *De iure belli ac pacis libri tres* (On the Law of War and Peace), trans. Francis W. Kelsey, vol. 2 (1625; Washington, DC: Carnegie Institution of Washington, 1925). While this writer does not agree with all the conclusions, an excellent background work for understanding the context of early modern just war theorists is Richard Tuck (2001), and a balanced historical treatment is found in Bellamy (2006b). Additional contemporary viewpoints grounded in analyses of historical events include: Fiala (2008), Orend (2006), Walzer (2006a); as well as essay collections by Hensel (2008), Lee (2006), and Shue and Rodin (2007).

Waging a Global War on Terrorism?

September 11 marked a turning point in global and national consciousness of the United States' role in the world.[4] President George W. Bush's response in the aftermath of the Pentagon and World Trade Center attacks was to declare a "war against terrorism" and a "monumental struggle of good versus evil," in which nothing less was at stake than "freedom and democracy" for the entire world (2001, September 11; 2001, September 12).[5]

By not equating these "acts of terror" with international criminal activity, but instead elevating them to the status of a "war,"[6] President Bush set the United States as a nation against a small band of enemies located possibly anywhere. Participants in today's conflicts are not only traditional nation-states, such as the United States, but also a host of other nonstate actors (NSAs), including "rogue" states as well as roaming terrorist groups such as al-Qaeda. If the assaults of NSAs are legitimized as acts of "war," rather than viewed as criminal acts, what are the rules of engagement?

In describing the global framework of the war on terrorism, the president labeled the enemy, in his 2002 State of the Union address, as a new "axis of evil" (2002, January 29). The original "axis" referred to Japan, Germany, and Italy in World War II, but Osama bin Laden and al-Qaeda are not state-sponsored foes. As late as 2007, Bush leveled the same accusation against Iraqi insurgents: "Today, the violent Islamic extremists who fight us in Iraq are as certain of their cause as the Nazis, or the Imperial Japanese, or the Soviet communists were of theirs" (2007, August 22).[7]

---

[4]A sampling of book-length analyses dealing with new global realities includes: Bobbitt (2008), Khanna (2008), and Zakaria (2008). Robert Kagan's 2002 article, circulated widely by e-mail, caused a stir. For an analysis of Kagan's effect, see Steven Erlanger, The world: America the invulnerable? The world looks again, *New York Times*, July 21, 2002. For a view and comments from the perspective of cultural anthropology, see Knauft's article (2007).

[5]On September 12, 2001, Bush declared: "This enemy attacked not just our people but all freedom-loving people everywhere in the world."

[6]Though not a formal declaration of war, a joint resolution was passed nearly unanimously by Congress (with one dissenting vote in the House), three days after 9/11, which authorized the president "to use all necessary and appropriate force…in order to prevent any future acts of international terrorism against the United States." Jane Perlez, After the attacks; The overview; U.S. demands Arab countries 'choose sides,' *New York Times*, September 15, 2001. In October 2002, another resolution was passed by Congress authorizing the president to wage war against Iraq: Authorization for Use of Military Force Against Iraq Resolution of 2002, Pub. L. No. 107–243, 116 Stat. 1498.

[7]See also Rudy Giuliani's remark about "radical Islamic fascism" (Is it war? 2007, December 23). A *Washington Post* editorial shortly after September 11 called the enemies of the United States "contemporary counterparts of the Nazis" (Neier 2001, October 9).

The leap from the September 11 terrorists to the Iraqi invasion was made by linking Iraq with so-called "weapons of mass destruction" (WMDs), and then suggesting that Saddam Hussein was likely to give WMDs to al-Qaeda. The Bush administration, therefore, claimed not to be fighting a war against Iraq per se, but (1) firstly, a pre-emptive,[8] defensive war to remove WMDs *from* Iraq; and (2) secondly, a war of humanitarian intervention, to provide support *for* the rights of the Iraqis to be part of an "international order…integrated into a world consistent with the values and interests we share with our partners," as the 2003 Counterterrorism Strategy stated (U.S. State Department 2003, February 14). From the earliest origins of just war theory, defensive war was the most justifiable war.[9] When no WMDs were found in Iraq, however, the administration began highlighting the "humanitarian" aim of turning Iraq into a "beacon" of hope for the Arab world.[10] This second aim is more problematic in terms of traditional just war theory.[11]

Spreading democracy is an old idea advanced by conservatives such as Samuel Huntington and Francis Fukuyama. Huntington had argued in 1996 that the world was arrayed along "fault line conflicts" (2003, pp. 207–208) determined by a "clash of civilizations" and that this kind of war was "particularly prevalent among Muslims" (p. 268), who tended to identify themselves in opposition to Western values. Fukuyama's 1992 idea of the "end of history" is part of the old story of Western hegemony as an inexorable march of progress towards ever-increasing acceptance of liberal democracy as the guarantor of human progress (2006, pp. 47–51, 342–354).[12]

---

[8] The general question of pre-emptive war is beyond the scope of this paper, but a good article from a contemporary military and ethical perspective is Rodin, in Shue & Rodin (2007), pp. 143–170.

[9] According to Augustine: "[I]t is the injustice of the opposing side that lays on the wise man the duty of waging wars; and this injustice is assuredly to be deplored by a human being, since it is the injustice of human beings" (Augustine 1972, p. 862). Also, the maxim of repelling force with force derived from Roman law and was passed down to the Middle Ages through Gratian's *Decretum*.

[10] According to many commentators, humanitarian intervention was the "default" reason for going to war (Farer 2008b, p. 363). "The initial justification for the U.S. invasion, the search for nonexistent weapons of mass destruction, was made palatable to the public by a conjoining of the 9/11 attacks and Saddam Hussein's political record. But soon the leap was made from removing him, to remaking the political map of the Middle East by transforming Iraq into a beacon of democracy and reforms" (Lazreg 2008, p. 260). Burke poses the question of "*who* gets to wage just war? Does every sufferer of harm and injustice, or merely those who have the power and the means, and who can turn their justifications into truth? … In short, the weak do not get to wage just war" (2004, p. 348).

[11] Walzer defines humanitarian intervention as "justified when it is a response (with reasonable expectations of success) to acts that 'shock the moral conscience of mankind'" (2006a, p. 107). This contemporary idea of humanitarian intervention is not found in early modern thinkers or the Thomists. For more on the contemporary debate, see Walzer, "The politics of rescue" (1994), in Walzer (2004a, pp. 67–81). For other viewpoints, see: Fiala (2007, pp. 28–47); Martin, along with other articles, in Part III of Lee (2006, pp. 75–88; 89–134); and Bellamy (2006b, pp. 199–228). See also the 2008 debate between Farer (2008a) and Elshtain (2008), covering three articles in *Human Rights Quarterly* 30, 356–403, 758–766, 767–771.

[12] Despite the Bush Administration's allusions to Fukuyama's 1992 opinions, in 2008 Fukuyama supported Obama for president and wrote that the cost of the regime change in Iraq "was hugely disproportionate," especially since it undermined the United States' moral authority by setting the "most recent precedent for a big power intervening to change a regime it didn't like, without the sanction of the U.N. Security Council" (2008, August 15).

These theories assume an international order of nation-states and are inapposite to the war on terror, even though they speak to Bush's 2001 call to defend "freedom and democracy." While the Bush administration adamantly denied any "clash of civilizations,"[13] in September 2001, Bush remarked: "This crusade, this war on terrorism, is going to take awhile (Salisbury 2001, September 30)."[14] In the 2003 Counterterrorism Strategy, he reiterated Fukuyama's vision by insisting that "what we are ultimately fighting for [are] our fundamental democratic values and way of life" and "the kind of world we want to live in" (U.S. State Department 2003, February 14). The re-emergence of these old ideas in the wake of September 11 contributed to redirecting the war against terror towards the nation-state of Iraq, which provided the unbounded war on terror with a delimited battleground.

Though persistently colored by Huntington's and Fukuyama's language, the new global reality is not shaped by the singular influence of the United States, but by a complex web of interrelationships made possible by changes in technology, communications, and economics, as well as new multinational alliances, such as the European Union. In such a world, NSAs, such as nongovernmental organizations (NGOs) and terrorist groups, can play increasingly significant roles.[15] Philip Bobbitt (2008) explains the new global reality by the transition from nation-states to market-states.[16] The legitimizing function of the "Nation State" is to better our "material well being," while "the Market State earns its legitimacy by providing the

---

[13] Bush disavowed any "clash of civilizations," because he thought that only one civilization exists today, that of the United States. The "twentieth century ended with a single surviving model of human progress," and while "America cannot impose this vision [it] can support and reward governments that make the right choices," through its "overwhelming power" (Lindberg 2002, June 4). In the 2003 National Counterterrorism Strategy, the administration denied making war against "a religion," while also quoting bin Laden to the effect that al Qaeda's obtaining WMDs was a "religious duty" (U.S. State Department 2003, February 14). The Bush administration's rhetoric had it both ways. While declaring the United States the winner in the "clash of civilizations," Bush spoke more openly after 2003 of "violent Islamic extremists [who are] as certain of their cause as the Nazis, or the Imperial Japanese, or the Soviet communists." American democracy was no longer just a civilizing force, but an imperative sanctioned by God, since "the desire for liberty [is] written into the human heart by our Creator" (2007, August 22). For a study, based on survey data, of religious factors raised by the Bush administration's rhetoric as an element in the Iraqi invasion, see Smidt 2005, pp. 243–261.

[14] In commenting on the deaths of three supporters in Pakistan, bin Laden responded: "these brothers are among the first martyrs in Islam's battle in this era against the new Christian-Jewish crusade led by the big crusader Bush under the flag of the Cross" (Salisbury 2001, September 30). The endpoint of this rhetoric came in 2008, when the Bush administration banned the word "jihadist" as "unintentionally portraying terrorists, who lack moral and religious legitimacy, as brave fighters, legitimate soldiers" (Lee 2008, April 24).

[15] "War can lead directly to political reconstruction.... But there is another form of direct action, which involves what we might call 'politics short of force,' noncoercive politics, the work of nongovernmental organizations, like Human Rights Watch or Amnesty International, which also aim, in their own way, at regime change" (Walzer 2006a, p. xvii; Walzer 2006b; Andreopouloss, 2006b; Falk 2006, pp. 120–121).

[16] Khanna agrees with Bobbitt. "Power has migrated from monopoly to marketplace.... In the geopolitical marketplace, legitimacy is based on effectiveness – and must be *proven* in comparison with other superpowers" (2008, p. xvi).

opportunity to its citizens to advance their own well being" (Scoblete 2004, September 8). The nation-state assumes moral responsibility for the common weal; while the market-state is an enabler of opportunity. This transition is crucial to contemporary war strategy, because, as Bobbitt (2008) argues in his latest book, *Terror and Consent*, wars mirror the constitutional order of the combatants. Al-Qaeda's "new form of terrorism…reflects the emerging constitutional order of the market-state" (p. 78). While al-Qaeda is not a state of any kind, in today's global economy it functions both as a "virtual market state" and as an "imagined" or "virtual caliphate" (pp. 64–65, 70–73, 93, 182). As a result of Bin Laden's immense personal wealth and influence, al-Qaeda can avail itself of the global resources of war making, in the same way as any geographically constituted market-state.[17] Huntington's idea of a "clash of civilizations" might seem appropriate because of the religious affiliations of the two sides of the war on terror, Judeo-Christian and Islamic.[18] But Huntington's clashes are envisioned as occurring between geographically proximate factions. The war against the terrorists is happening irrespective of geographical boundaries. We do not even know where Bin Laden's headquarters are.

Nothing shows more clearly that today's "clashes" are not between civilizations. After all, civilizations are only "intellectual construct[s]…to establish the *boundaries* of a field of study" – much as we speak of "gardens." These "can be described, analyzed and interpreted" but can never "clash" (Matlock 1999, p. 439; my italics). Even speaking metaphorically, we cannot conceive of the "war against terrorism" as a "clash" of cultures or civilizations, because al-Qaeda and other terrorist groups succeed by operating outside of all geopolitical, religious, and legal boundaries. They have no international standing to wage war – that is, no state, no citizens, and no national leadership positions. Yet Osama bin Laden agrees with President Bush that he is at war with the United States, and he has formulated his own policy statements, claiming the authority of a religious fatwa, without any ostensible religious authority. In fighting the terrorists by their rules, as combatants in a market-state "war" without boundaries – rather than as international criminals subject to state-sponsored

---

[17]"Market state terrorism will be just as global, networked, decentralized, and devolved and rely just as much on outsourcing and incentivizing as the market state. It does not depend on state sponsorship; indeed, it would appear that al-Qaeda had more influence over the government in whose jurisdiction it worked than did that government over it." Also, because "[m]arket state terrorism 'neither relies on the support of sovereign states nor is constrained by the limits on violence that state sponsors have observed themselves or place on their proxies'…it is horrifyingly more violent." Bobbitt (2008, p. 45), quoting Steve Simon and Daniel Benjamin.

[18]President Bush's rhetoric casts al-Qaeda's aims in terms of religious rather than political motives, as in his September 20, 2001, address to a Joint Session of Congress: "The terrorists practice a fringe form of Islamic extremism…. The terrorists' directive commands them to kill Christians and Jews, to kill all Americans, and make no distinctions among military and civilians, including women and children." Of course, bin Laden replied in kind by dubbing Bush a "crusader" (Salisbury 2001, September 30). Both sides imputed religious values to political goals (Byrm 2008, p. 102).

diplomatic or policing actions – the United States risks betraying its own values as a nation-state.[19]

If the United States and American democracy are indeed under attack, then we must take care that in fighting terrorists, we do not lose the war against terror and become a state of terror ourselves, due to "the acts of [our] own misguided defenders" (Bobbitt 2008, p. 391). Ironically, by legitimizing the "war against terrorism," while declaring the enemy's agents "unlawful combatants," the Bush administration embarked on a course that eventually transformed Iraq into an unruly market-state[20] and violated the boundaries of war conduct. In wars between states, enemy soldiers and civilians are both shielded from illegitimate violence. But from the outset, the war against terrorism was construed as a "war" directed against combatants acting in their personal capacities and not as soldier-agents of a state. This mentality prevailed during the Iraqi invasion, and afterwards, at Abu Ghraib, thanks to the persistent identification of Iraq with al-Qaeda. Starting shortly after September 11, the Bush administration mounted a media campaign, first linking al-Qaeda and Iraq, and then, Iraq and WMD – without presenting a shred of evidence (Bellamy 2006b, pp. 176–177; Kramer et al. 2005, pp. 57–60). This rhetoric succeeded. By the start of the invasion, "70% of Americans surveyed believed that Iraq was directly involved in the planning of the September 11 attacks" (Kramer et al., p. 57). Bush also played on the public's fears that al-Qaeda would get WMDs from Iraq (Bush 2002, September 12).[21] Identifying Iraq with the terrorists worked to undermine protections guaranteed to members of a warring state. In short, the war on terror and the Iraqi invasion were intentionally construed as two sides of the same market-state war.

The new targets in a market-state war are not visible state-held military installations, strategic bridges, or land and sea positions, but vast networks of money,

[19] The United States responded as a "global state" – another word for Bobbitt's "market-state" – by undertaking war actions instead of "by revamping international law enforcement through greatly augmented resources and cooperative procedures [which would have] vindicated the viability of the statist framework of world order and its ability to meet the challenge mounted by a nonstate network within the framework of international law" (Falk 2006, p. 125). Other commentators have analyzed the Iraqi invasion from the perspective of international criminology. See Agozino (2004), Hamm (2007), and Kramer et al. (2005). Choosing the war paradigm rather than the policing model "has been a strategy of the Bush Administration…. The prospect of an imminent threat posed by terrorists and terrorism is utilized by security states to expand the scope and purview of executive power and to engage in a certain state of lawlessness to counter the supercriminality that terrorism is made out to be" (Denike 2008, p. 110).

[20] Because occupation forces failed to establish a "monopoly of legitimate violence" and "largely abdicated this responsibility," Iraq's nation-state identity was compromised, and opportunities were opened for Iraqi insurgents to destroy infrastructure and interrupt basic services – for which the United States was blamed (Danner 2004, pp. 56–58; Kramer et al. 2005, pp. 68–69).

[21] In an October speech in Cincinnati, Bush said: "Iraq's weapons of mass destruction are controlled by a murderous tyrant…. We have experienced the horror of September 11…. Our enemies would be no less willing – in fact they would be eager – to use a biological, or chemical, or nuclear weapon…. [W]e have every reason to assume the worst, and we have an urgent duty to prevent the worst from occurring" (2002, October 7).

communication, and information, and the people who direct them. In one message, Bin Laden justifies making war against noncombatant American civilians, including women and children, even though this is considered by other interpreters to be forbidden by Islamic law (*Sharī'a*).[22] All Americans are legitimate war targets, he says, because "the American people are the ones who fund the attacks against us [acting] through their elected candidates" (Bin Laden's letter, 2002, November 24). President Bush, for his part, targeted Bin Laden and his associates (2001, September 20). This intense personalizing of the terror wars – outside of the traditional boundaries separating soldier and civilian – clearly reveals the new face of Bobbitt's market-state war.

A further complication is that this new war is being prominently waged in the communications marketplace. Because of instant global interconnectivity (via Internet, cell phones, newswires, etc.), noncombatants are drawn more intimately into the field of virtual combat. Three prominent examples of this are the Internet video clips of the gruesome beheadings attributed to Abu Musab al-Zarqawi; the worldwide dissemination of the Abu Ghraib photographs; and the constant replay on television of the World Trade Center bombings.[23]

Targeting civilians is part of a growing global tendency. In the new conflicts involving both state and nonstate actors, George J. Andreopoulos has noted that both sides engage in "the deliberate targeting of civilians, who often constitute *the principal aim* rather than the unintended consequence of otherwise legitimate military operations" (2006a, p. 141; my italics). The Iraqi invasion may have started off as a nation-state war, but Abu Ghraib was the result of focusing on individuals rather than states, and there, civilians – their identities merging with al-Qaeda's – did become "the principal aim" of military operations.

The conflicts initiated by September 11 and the rhetoric of both the United States and al-Qaeda, may seem to fit Huntington's paradigm of "Muslim and Asian societies" against the West (2003, p. 183). But the power distribution is no longer along Huntington's lines. In a January 2008 article in the *New York Times* and in a book that followed, Parag Khanna notes: "The web of globalization now has three spiders," which are America, the European Union, and China (2008, January 27, p. 64). Thus, Western hegemony is divided between America and the European Union, while the Islamic countries are part of the "key second-world countries" – swing states that will decide the balance of power in the twenty-first century (pp. xxiv–xxv, pp. 37–39).

Significantly, since 1996 (when Bin Laden first declared war on America for stationing troops in Saudi Arabia), al-Qaeda has taken pains to be more conciliatory "towards European publics it believes can be peeled away from association with the U.S."

---

[22] *Sharī'a* is Islamic law, drawn from Revelation and Wisdom (Qur'ān and *Sunna/Hadīth* or Traditions), as well as other authorities (such as *ijma* or consensus and analogy). But the Islamic legal tradition is far from unified. The Prophet prohibited killing women and children, but others, like Shāfi'ī said they could be slain, along with other categories, such as the infirm, old, and hermits (Peters 2005, pp. 33–35).

[23] The U.S. Department of State, in its annual report of 1999, classified "money and the Internet," along with "human rights," as the "three universal languages of mankind" (Pagden 2003, p. 193).

(Bobbitt, 2008, p. 79). Khanna notes that while Max Weber and Karl Marx disparaged the East as lacking the elements for "organizational" success, Oswald Spengler correctly understood that "mankind both lives and thinks in unique cultural systems, with Western ideals neither transferable nor relevant" everywhere (2008, January 27, p. 62). In the future, we may be bypassed rather than opposed. The new global economy and geopolitics, not cultural dissonance, underlie the conflicts of the twenty-first century.[24] Winning on those grounds means winning the "hearts and minds" of the Muslim world, and that is why Sir Michael Howard insists we should not be thinking of our engagement as a "war" at all (2002).

Just War Theory in Historical Perspective

The plethora of opinions about what constitutes "just war" played an important part in the "war of ideas" that the Bush administration pinpointed early on as a virtual battlefield in its strategy papers.[25] But most contemporary discussions have distorted the just war tradition by invoking the moral legitimacy of medieval theologians such as Augustine and Thomas Aquinas, without sufficiently distinguishing the framework of their discussion from the legalism and expediency advanced by early modern proponents.

In a 2004 article,[26] Michael Walzer, a leading contemporary just war theorist, proposed to amplify the traditional discussion by adding a just peace (*jus post bellum*) to the two traditional categories of just conditions for war (*jus ad bellum*) and just conduct in war (*jus in bello*), which he says were "first worked out by Catholic philosophers and jurists in the Middle Ages" (2004, p. xiii). History is compressed here as Walzer seems to posit a direct arc from Augustine in the late fourth or early fifth century to Aquinas in the fourteenth century. By "jurists in the Middle Ages," he presumably means the canon lawyers. But he omits the early modern Thomists, as well as any mention of the secular early modern jurists, who should be our focus. And, as Brian Orend (2006) has shown, Immanuel Kant already laid the groundwork for the peacemaking aspect of war (*jus post bellum*), with his idea of the transnational or "cosmopolitan man" as the foundation of human identity. Without detracting from the value of Walzer's work, a historical look at the just war tradition reveals two distinct contexts of discussion, one moralistic, grounded in theological values and the other, legalistic, concerned mainly with political legitimacy (excepting Kant).

---

[24] "The unifying element among the groups to which al-Qaeda outsources its operations is not a mystical, retrograde form of Islam but a shared hatred of the U.S" (Bobbitt 2008, p. 83).

[25] In Part III of the September 20, 2002 National Security Strategy, the Bush administration announced a "war of ideas to win the battle against international terrorism," including "kindl[ing] the hopes and aspirations of freedom of those in societies ruled by the sponsors of global terrorism" (U.S. State Department 2002). See also the 2003 National Counterterrorism Strategy (U.S. State Department 2003, February 14).

[26] Walzer, 2004a, p. xiii. Walzer's 2004 article, entitled "To war or not to war" was subsequently published as the Introduction to *Arguing About War*.

The Bush administration was a true heir to the political-legalistic framework, but wanted always to be perceived as waging a moral "war," whether this was aimed at al-Qaeda or Saddam Hussein's Iraq. It was aided in this duplicity by the legitimate discussions of Walzer and others who too easily conflated the moral and political traditions, allowing for the moral patina of one to rub off on the expediency of the other.[27] The Bush administration's pervasive rhetoric of morality enveloped a callous legalism and created a context for certain troubling events, particularly at Abu Ghraib. How the rhetoric of moral outrage helped shape the Iraqi invasion is evident from the news headlines touting the successful bombing raids as an exercise in "Shock and Awe."[28] The rhetorical value of just war discourse was integral to what went wrong at Abu Ghraib.

Just war theories from Augustine through Grotius fall into three main categories: (1) *theological* or *scholastic*, as represented by Thomas Aquinas (c. 1224–1274) and the Spanish Thomists of Salamanca, including Francisco de Vitoria (1492/1493–1546); (2) *legalistic*, as represented by Alberico Gentili (*De iure belli* 1588, 1589; revised 1598; printed 1612) and Hugo Grotius (1583–1645); and (3) *humanistic* or *expedient*, as represented by Gentili and Niccolò Machiavelli (1469–1527).[29]

Contemporary commentators typically present just war theory as a unified tradition by distilling the common concerns of just war theorists into lists of requirements for just war (*jus ad bellum*). These lists homogenize the tradition and blur significant differences. Generally, the following conditions are cited, but not necessarily in the order given here[30] (Fiala 2007; Guthrie & Quinlan 2007; Patterson 2007;

---

[27] Walzer calls just war theory a "common moral language" and a "critical theory" that is "doubly critical – of war's occasions and its conduct" (2004a, pp. 7–8).

[28] Bonnie Mann offers an intelligent feminist critique of the Iraqi invasion, and she argues that the "Shock and Awe" language, as well as the 1996 document published by the National Defense University on which it was based, established a basis for the "spectacle" of masculine domination, which played out finally in the "culture of terror" at Abu Ghraib (Mann 2006, pp. 154–159).

[29] Of course, just war theories do not end with Gentili and Grotius, but this chapter is not concerned with the entire just war tradition, only with pinpointing a crucial turning point when pre-emptive war was justified. Legalism prevailed into the seventeenth century, when it "bifurcated into two sub-traditions that prioritized natural law and positive law respectively," the former represented by Samuel von Pufendorf (1632–1694) and Christian Wolff (1679–1754), and the latter, by Emmerich de Vattel (*Le Droit de gens* 1758) and Cornelius van Bynkershoek (1673–1743) (Bellamy 2006b, pp. 76–82). Immanuel Kant (1724–1804) is credited with adding *jus post bellum*, the making of a just peace, to the tradition (Orend 2006, p. 20). Interestingly, with his idea of the "cosmopolitan man" and universal rights (*ius cosmopoliticum*), Kant was a forerunner of modern and post-modern ideas of human transnational identity, which for him were rooted in natural law, the basis also of Aquinas's ideas of just war. But there is a difference between Kant, who starts with a notion of human nature (as does Grotius and others), and today's rights theorists. "Whereas both the scholastics [theologians] and their Hobbesian and Grotian opponents had begun with a notion of humanity from which they had deduced what their natural rights might be, the human-rights charters begin with the notion of rights in order to arrive at the notion of what a person might be" (Pagden 2003, pp. 188, 192).

[30] For an interesting treatment of the just war problem from the perspective of breaking rules rather than following rules, see Bellamy 2006a.

Stover 2004; Wester 2004): (1) legitimate authority; (2) just cause; (3) right intention; (4) proportionality; (5) war as a last resort; and (6) likelihood of success. Two additional conditions speak to just conduct in war (*jus in bello*): (1) discrimination or care towards noncombatants; and (2) proportionality of force.

The first three conditions for just war were enunciated by Aquinas, and he touched on the fourth in relation to his general discussion of self-defense (2002, pp. 262–266).[31] Aquinas was one of the few theorists who did not reason very specifically within a concrete historical set of facts, and his formulations, therefore, read like axioms. He restricted the right to wage war to the "sovereign" and the reasons for waging war to self-defense or to regaining what was wrongfully taken. Aquinas and later Thomists thought that killing, and hence war, should be avoided if possible, nor did they support any notion of pre-emptive self-defense. For how could one repay an injury not yet inflicted? While Aquinas argued generally for a response proportional to the injury received, Vitoria added the conditions of discriminatory and proportional use of force during war, because human beings often erred about which side was right (1991, pp. 304, 320–321).[32]

In the theological view, a just war is undertaken solely to right a wrong, while right from wrong is discernible by correct reason.[33] But no theologian ever claimed that any particular just war was just by divine standards – and this was always Augustine's main point.[34] Just war theories of every persuasion were generally responses to specific acts of aggression or coercion that called for justification or condemnation,[35] and these theories aimed only at containing violence by moral standards and/or the law of nations (*ius gentium*). They are not moral endorsements of any kind. Within the theological framework, war is a strictly political undertaking, which can be conducted with varying degrees of morality.

---

[31] *Summa theologiae* IIaIIae 64 (On homicide).

[32] See Bellamy 2006b, pp. 50–55; Panizza, 2005, October 17, p. 29.

[33] Diego Panizza argues convincingly that the belief in right reason marks a significant difference between the view of the theologians and the legalist–humanist view of Alberico Gentili. Diego Panizza (p. 15).

[34] "[W]e must ascribe to the true God alone the power to grant kingdoms and empires. He it is who gives happiness in the kingdom of heaven only to the good, but grants earthly kingdoms both to the good and to the evil, in accordance with his pleasure" (Augustine 1972, p. 215). "The same may be said of the duration of wars. It rests with the decision of God in his just judgment and mercy either to afflict or console mankind" (Augustine 1972, p. 216). While Augustine's views on war are too complex to be treated of here, he did not think of wars in terms of human justice, but of divine will and justice.

[35] For example, Augustine considered the use of coercive force in relation to the heretics of his time. Vitoria wrote regarding the legitimacy of the Spanish conquests in the Americas, while Grotius wrote the *De Indis* to defend the seizure in 1602 by a private Dutch citizen of a Portuguese trading ship, with goods valued at the "total annual expenditure of the English government at the time" (Tuck 2001, pp. 73–75, 79–94). Trained at the University of Perugia, Gentili was a Professor of Civil Law at Oxford, and his work was a response to the Spanish Thomists, as well as to the imperialistic threats posed by the Spaniards and Turks (Panizza 2005, October 17, pp. 6–9, 22).

Still, many contemporary commentators have associated the just war parameters with a moral endorsement of war.[36] This valuation is suggested by the very phrase "just war" and by the oft-noted fact that just war formulations originated with the theologians. What is said less often is that just war theorizing is part of a long tradition of Christian humanism, marked by very un-Christian acts of coercion, aggression, and imperialistic expansion.[37] While most items on typical lists may be traced to Aquinas's language, the just war tradition has long since been assimilated to the early modern outlook of legalistic thinkers such as Gentili and Grotius.[38] The legalists accepted the same basic premises as the theologians, but adopted an openly political framework of analysis.

One telling point is the inclusion on many contemporary lists of the condition of likelihood of success. No theologian ever considered success a factor. Likelihood of success was added by Grotius, a major proponent of the legalistic school (Grotius 1925, pp. 574–575).[39] Thus, the true bent of contemporary just war doctrine is revealed as diverging from the moral proportionality of the Thomists and inclining towards the legalists' and Machiavelli's practical values of success and statecraft.

Grotius, and Gentili before him, thought of war in precisely the way that has framed both the "war against terrorism" and the Iraqi invasion, where "right" is flexibly construed within both a legalistic and political framework. But Grotius, unlike Gentili, did not support pre-emptive defense; and Grotius also subscribed to the "unilateral" justice of the theologians, in which only one side can be right (Panizza, 2005, p.17). The just war doctrine applied by the United States in the wake of September 11 had its roots, as we shall see, in Gentili's legalistic and expedient humanism, not in the moral scholasticism of the theologians, nor in Grotius's idea of the law of nations. The Bush administration followed the rule-breaking dictates of Gentili's expediency, but it also wanted to portray itself on the right side of a unilateral and absolute justice.

---

[36] Contemporary just war theorists of every stripe fall into the trap of shading "just war" with morality. James Turner Johnson called the "just war tradition a major moral tradition of Western culture, shaped by both religious and nonreligious forces and taking shape in both religious and nonreligious forms within the culture," and that is why he thinks it disintegrated after the Reformation, quoted in Hensel 2008, p. 79. Walzer, with reference to the 2003 Iraqi invasion, asks: "So, is this a just war? This question…asks only if it is morally defensible: just or unjust" (2004a, p. 160). Andrew Fiala is more precise. While focusing "on the morality of the idea that war should be employed as a means for advancing the ideal of democratization," and "approach[ing] this debate as primarily a question of just war theory," he nevertheless adds that "the just war tradition has been reluctant to approve of wars that are fought for such ideological purposes." Fiala (2007, pp. 33, 40). Alex Bellamy is also clear that the "currency that matters most in politics is neither ethics nor law; it is legitimacy" (2006a, p. 14), and that concern, not plain morality, has always been the crux of just war theory, even among theologians.

[37] Brian C. Lockey has shown this admirably in Renaissance England, where natural law tradition, the underpinning of the Thomistic just war theorists, was also the foundation for imperialistic expansionism (2006, pp. 145–146, 158–159). See also Pagden.

[38] Gentili was a professor of the civil law, while Grotius was a humanist without specific legal training.

[39] I owe this observation to Bellamy (2006b, p. 73) and Orend (p. 18).

Just War and States: A Pivotal Historical Moment

In an effort to understand the relationship between just war theory and the war on terror, we should note the historical moment when the pre-emptive strike was legitimated, a moment coinciding with the emergence of the inchoate nation-state in the mid-sixteenth century. This moment is marked by Alberico Gentili's *The Law of War* (*De iure belli*), written in 1588 and revised in 1598. In Bobbitt's schema, this is also the moment when the Machiavellian "princely state" passed into the "kingly state" on its way to becoming the contemporary nation-state (2008, pp. 189–191). Gentili's work, significantly, coincides with the modern shift towards a political and legalistic view of war and away from the theological framework. While Richard Tuck ascribes this modern turning point to Hugo Grotius, writing in the period from 1608 to 1625 (*De Indis* and *De iure belli ac pacis*) (1925, pp. 16–50, 78–108), Diego Panizza agues persuasively that Gentili, and not Grotius, made the decisive break with the theological Spanish school represented by Vitoria and other Thomists (2005, pp. 12–13 & 9n.).[40]

The evolution of the modern state involves a shift in war theory from a moral to a practical schema, from reasons of injustice (*iniuria*) to reasons of state, and from honor to expediency – to use the title of one of Michel de Montaigne's essays ("The Useful and the Honorable"). This means, in essence, that states – not individuals, and not Aquinas's "sovereign" – make war with the paramount aims of self-defense, self-preservation, and imperialistic expansion. The decisive paradigmatic shift from a moral to a legalistic framework, which started in the late sixteenth century with Gentili, was precisely the framework in which the 2003 Iraqi war was initiated and conducted, but this historical precedent went largely unrecognized in contemporary scholarly discussions. Instead, "Operation Iraqi Freedom" was rationalized in the mass media by allusions to the just war tradition originating in Augustine, Aquinas, and the theological framework. In this atmosphere, the Bush administration appropriated the mantle of morality with respect to the right to wage the Iraqi war, while actually conducting both the "war on terrorism" and "Operation Iraqi Freedom" through purely expedient and legalistic moves. To this end, administration spokesmen and policymakers were assisted, wittingly or unwittingly, by just war commentators such as Jean Bethke Elshtain (2003, p. 6) and Michael Walzer (2004a, p. 160), who seamlessly knit together the moral-theological and political-legalistic paradigms, allowing the moral perspective of one to be imputed to the statecraft of the other.

---

[40] An earlier generation of scholars also debated about who was the father of international law. James Brown Scott accorded this honor to Francisco de Vitoria (*Relectio de Indis* and *Relectio de iure belli*, 1539), while Arthur Nussbaum agrees with Richard Tuck in according the honor to Hugo Grotius (*De Indis* 1609; *De iure belli ac pacis* 1625) (Bellamy 2006b, p. 50). Thomas Erskine Holland in 1877 was the first to suggest Alberico Gentili (Panizza 2005, October 17, pp. 5 & 2n).

Alberico Gentili's Legalistic Dilution of Moral Accountability

When the United States and coalition forces invaded Iraq in 2003 as part of the war on terror, talk abounded of "just" and "unjust" war. Commentators focused on the legitimacy of the pre-emptive strike – that is, attacking a purported enemy out of fear of an imminent attack. Augustine, Aquinas, the Thomists, and Grotius never allowed for pre-emptive strikes. For them, the only just war was one to right a wrong (*iniuria*) already committed. Augustine lamented that "it is the injustice of the opposing side that lays on the wise man the duty of waging wars; and this injustice is assuredly to be deplored by a human being, since it is the injustice of human beings" (1972, p. 862, Bk. XIX.7). Under no condition was pre-emptive war allowed. The first foundation of just war doctrine was the natural law principle of being able to repel force with force (*Vim vi repellere licet*), a principle passed down from the Roman legists to the Middle Ages and beyond through its incorporation in Gratian's *Decretum*, c. 1140 (1993, p. 7, Dist. 1 c. 7). This makes defensive war the most just of wars, followed secondly by an offensive war undertaken to redress a prior wrong.

Allowing or not allowing pre-emptive strikes is the benchmark difference between the rationale of Gentili and the views of other legalists, as well as the theologians (Panizza 2005, October 17, pp. 23–28). Panizza points to two other significant differences between Gentili and the Spanish Thomists whom Gentili openly attacked (pp. 11–20, 29–38). First, Gentili thought of war precisely in legalistic terms, as a "duel" or judicial process between two equals, each of whom has an equally plausible claim. For the Spanish theologians, war was, as it was for Augustine, the "unilateral" execution of justice (righting a wrong) (Panizza, pp. 29–38). Second, Gentili viewed war as a process of adjudication to be decided by "bilateral justice" rather than as a conflict between right and wrong (Gentili 1933, p. 32; Panizza, p. 19). In Gentili's case what is right is decided by the outcome of the war, while from Aquinas's perspective what is right is assumed to be *clear beforehand* to human reason.

Vitoria, a Spanish Thomist, was less optimistic. He agreed with Gentili that two parties could go to war, each sincerely believing himself to be in the right. Each would, therefore, be exculpated of any injustice, because one side would be suffering from "invincible ignorance." Otherwise, there could be no just wars, for "[i]f it is agreed that both parties have right and justice on their side, they cannot lawfully fight each other, either offensively or defensively," except out of ignorance (Vitoria 1991, pp. 16–17).

Vitoria was concerned with the rightness of intention, but Gentili repudiated morality as a factor in war. His idea of justice was analogous to a courtroom trial. "Those who contend in the litigation [in a court] justly, that is to say, on a plausible ground, either as defendants or plaintiffs, and lose their case…are not judged guilty of injustice [for contending]. Why should the decision be different in this kind of dispute and in a contest of arms?" (Gentili 1933, p. 32). Gentili subtracts moral right and wrong from the warring sides, because, as a humanist skeptic, he does not believe in the capacity of human reason to know right from wrong invincibly. In fact, the opposite is true:

no one can ever know which side is right. Only the outcome of war determines the side of right, and that "right" is a practical outcome, not necessarily a moral one.

Because war is permissibly undertaken on the basis of imperfect human knowledge, pre-emptive strikes, based on subjective fear and plain expediency, are sanctioned by Gentili. "I call it a defense dictated by expediency," he says, "when we make war through fear that we may ourselves be attacked" (pp. 61–66). Grotius, siding with Vitoria, condemned Gentili's view of pre-emptive strikes – mounted for the sole purpose of weakening a powerful neighbor.[41] To Grotius, a pre-emptive war was one undertaken "on grounds of expediency, not of justice" (Grotius, p. 184), and fear of future attack was not a legitimate reason for war (pp. 173–174). Gentili's twin grounds of expediency and subjective fear needed no justification other than the perception of threat and the calculation of advantage, for they are ultimately justified by reasons of state. And what are those reasons? The state's right of self-preservation. Thus, the perceived threat of WMDs in Iraq would have sufficed for Gentili, although perhaps not without some credible evidence. This differs from the theologians' moral framework for war, rooted in the *necessary* repelling of force with force or the *just* righting of wrongs. Gentili's idea of just war equated war not with moral intentions but with might and expediency. For historical authority to justify the Iraqi invasion, Gentili, not Aquinas and Augustine, should have been invoked.

Gentili's Legacy: The Strike in Yemen and "Unlawful Combatants"

Gentili's paradigm of utterly practical statecraft constituted his prescient understanding of international power relations and war, and it is as relevant to today's market-state as it was to the nascent states of his day. As Panizza shows, one of the most striking consequences of Gentili's approach is that state security trumps any sense of absolute justice. For example, Vitoria spoke of "proportion" and "moderation" – and even of "compassion" – in exacting punishment and restitution from the conquered.[42] Gentili's overriding concern with security and a permanent peace, however, led him to jettison the principles of "moderation" and "proportionality." Against those who would oppose the victor's unlimited right of conquest, Gentili asserts: "I reply that such things [namely the seizure of lands] are just for princes, since in that way they provide for their own victory and security by making their enemies weaker and themselves stronger; so that the enemy may dare less in the future or have less power, and that they themselves may have less cause to fear the same dangers" (Gentili 1933, pp. 304–305).[43]

---

[41] In this sense, not much difference exists between pre-emptive and preventive war, the distinction Walzer proposed in his analysis of the 2003 Iraqi invasion (2004a, pp. 146–148).

[42] I have reproduced only the broad outlines of Panizza's extensive and convincing treatment of the differences between Gentili and the Spanish school (2005, October 17, pp. 28–39).

[43] See Panizza (p. 34).

Gentili's privileging of state security over Vitoria's moral values of "proportion" and "moderation" may have emerged from a discussion of "Exacting Tribute and Lands from the Vanquished," but the framework of that antiquated discussion illuminates the debate surrounding one of the most infamous incidents in the war on terror: the United States' missile attack in 2002 on a car traveling through Yemen that was thought to contain al-Qaeda operatives. In that attack, six people were killed, including an American citizen. If we consider the Yemeni strike an act of war, then the law of armed conflict should come into play. And that law, in the words of one law professor, mandates that "military violence must seek to avoid 'unnecessary' suffering, and violence must be in accordance with the principles of *proportionality* and *discrimination* [as to lawful targets], or else it is not immunized" (Brooks 2004, p. 693). War immunity means that actions, otherwise considered criminal, are exonerated, such as when soldiers kill. What guarantees immunity? One answer: the application of Vitoria's moral principles of care, when acting as an agent of the state. But that was not the administration's response.

Was the Yemeni attack subsequently justified from the perspective of the morality or the expediency of war? Interestingly, in defending the Yemeni attack, the Bush administration did not argue, as it could have, that it had observed proper proportion and discrimination in targeting the "enemy" with little or no collateral damage. National Security Advisor Condoleezza Rice called the Yemen strike a "different battlefield[]" in a "new kind of war" (Witt 2002, November 24), while other officials argued on the grounds of pre-emptive self-defense, because one of the occupants of the car, Ali Qaed Sinan al-Harithi, had assisted in the *USS Cole* attack.[44] Thus, the administration did not align itself with arguments historically belonging to the Thomistic morality of Vitoria and others, but with Gentili's rationale of state security. Taking the strict view of international law, Amnesty International called the missile strike a "summary execution," because a state such as the United States could not declare war on a "non-state actor…should the armed group not form part of the armed forces of a Party to the Geneva Conventions" (Amnesty International 2003, September 23, p. 23). Gentili would have disagreed, because for him the paramount law of war was security. But the strictures of legality are not without ambiguity either, as we shall see.

Not all the wars of the twentieth and twenty-first centuries have been clearly marked by the traditional boundaries of war. For example, Aquinas defined a just war as one: (1) waged by a sovereign authority and not a "private individual," (2) for a just cause (righting wrongs), and (3) with the right intentions (not for personal motives).[45] By these standards, al-Qaeda cannot wage war, because it has no "sovereign authority," that is, no territory, no citizens, and no identifiable combat forces. While accepting al-Qaeda's right to wage war, the Bush administration has also argued, rather disingenuously, that because al-Qaeda is not a signatory "party" to

[44] Dana Priest. CIA killed U.S. citizen in Yemen missile strike; action's legality, effectiveness questioned. *Washington Post*, November 8, 2002: A1. See the excellent discussion in Brooks (pp. 720–724).

[45] Aquinas, *Summa Theologiae* 2a2ae.40 (On War) (2002, pp. 239–247).

the four Geneva Conventions, its combatants are not entitled to the legal protections of the Geneva Conventions' covenants against torture and "degrading treatment."[46] These were the very same legal grounds ironically – al-Qaeda's not being a signatory "party" to the Geneva Conventions – on which Amnesty International had rejected the Yemeni missile strike as a legitimate act of war, because it did not target a legitimate state adversary. Arguing that al-Qaeda's members have no standing as soldiers or prisoners of war, even though we are at "war" with them, the Bush administration has created a new "grey" category of "unlawful combatants" and a new extraterritorial prison in Guantánamo Bay to hold them, in a bold move to circumvent the laws regulating the treatment of both military and civilian detainees. In its most expansive form, the term "unlawful combatants" includes all those who can be construed as direct or indirect supporters, agents, or members of al-Qaeda, including Saddam Hussein's Iraq, the detainees at Guantánamo Bay, and the prisoners at Abu Ghraib.[47] In this "war" without traditional boundary lines, law is confounded by new definitions arbitrarily changing the legal status of the enemy and detainee. Nevertheless, many commentators have condemned the Bush administration's stance on torture and "degrading treatment" as plainly illegal. For whatever the legal framework and whatever the status of the detainee, "international law and U.S. treaty commitments prohibit the use of torture and other forms of cruel, inhuman, and degrading treatment" (Brooks 2004, p. 683).

[46]Brooks (2004, pp. 677–685). The four Geneva Conventions are: (1) Geneva Convention for the Amelioration of the Condition of the Wounded and Sick in Armed Forces in the Field, Aug. 12, 1949, art. 3, 6 U.S.T.3114, 3116–18, 75 U.N.T.S. 31, 32–34; (2) Geneva Convention for the Amelioration of the of the Condition of the Wounded, Sick and Shipwrecked Members of the Armed Forces at Sea, Aug. 12, 1949, art. 3, 6 U.S.T. 3217, 3220–22, 75 U.N.T.S. 85, 86–88; (3) Geneva Convention Relative to the Treatment of Prisoners of War, Aug. 12, 1949, art. 3, 6 U.S.T. 3316, 3318–3320, 75 U.N.T.S. 135, 136–138; and (4) Geneva Convention Relative to the Protection of Civilian Persons in Time of War, Aug. 12, 1949, art. 3, 6 U.S.T. 3516, 3518–3520, 75 U.N.T.S. 287, 288–290. Common Article 3 is contained in all four Conventions, and it prohibits "cruel treatment and torture" as well as "outrages upon personal dignity, in particular, humiliating and degrading treatment." Bobbitt notes that the McCain amendment, Department of Defense Appropriations Act, 2006, Pub. L. No. 109–148, sec. 1003, 119 Stat. 2680, 2739 (2005), sets a dangerous precedent in distinguishing cruel and degrading treatment from torture. This distinction facilitates a "necessity" exemption with regard to cruel and degrading treatment, which the U.S. Supreme Court has recognized in precedents that establish the benchmark for cruel and degrading treatment as a "shocks the conscience" test, which might be absent in cases of state necessity (Bobbitt 2008, pp. 370 & 54n).

[47]Addressing a Joint Session of Congress, Bush declared: "We will drive [terrorists] from place to place until there is no refuge or no rest. And we will pursue nations that provide aid or safe haven to terrorism. Every nation in every region now has a decision to make: Either you are with us or you are with the terrorists. From this day forward, any nation that continues to harbor or support terrorism will be regarded by the United States as a hostile regime" (2001, September 20).

Abu Ghraib Prison: Between Crime and War

Whereas al-Qaeda has "something in common with criminal gangs and something in common with armies" (Brooks 2004, p. 718), this does not apply to Iraq. "Operation Iraqi Freedom" targeted a sovereign state, and Abu Ghraib, a Baghdad prison, was part of that military arena. Both the United States and Iraq signed the Geneva Conventions, although not the two 1977 Protocols,[48] so presumably these Conventions applied to the Iraqi nationals held at Abu Ghraib.

Abu Ghraib was a tremendous defeat in the war for "hearts and minds," because it diminished the United States' moral standing with no corresponding gain on the side of state security. What went wrong? Abu Ghraib was the result of the Bush administration's heightened discourse of "securitization,"[49] which, when combined with absolutist moral claims and rhetorical maneuvers, lowered the bar of moral conduct.[50] The Bush administration's rhetoric of "security," morality, and fear was a way of stifling dissent and escaping accountability. "What is being enacted [by such rhetoric demonizing the enemy] is a subtle but effective game of defence against possible dissent with respect to plans preventatively inserted in governmental agenda" (Ferrari 2007, p. 606).[51] This is the pre-emptive strike played out at the rhetorical level – as evidenced by Bush's linking of Iraq and al-Qaeda as early as January 2002.[52] With rationales similar to those justifying the Yemeni strike and

---

[48] See American Bar Association Report to the House of Delegates 2004, in *The Torture Papers* (2005, pp. 1140–1146).

[49] The discourse of "securitization," as understood by political scientists, is "essentially an intersubjective process. The senses of threat, vulnerability, and (in)security are socially constructed rather than objectively present or absent" (Buzan et al. 1998, p. 57). In fact, "securitization" is a discursive enterprise whereby the "securitizing actors" or spokespersons of a "referent object," often a state, attempt to convince an "audience," such as citizens, of the need to "accept exceptional procedures because of the specific security nature [threat] of some issue" (pp. 40–41). See also Vetlesen (2008, pp. 64–66).

[50] "In the post-9/11 period, the eagerness with which governments around the world have adopted 'security' measures that can render them less accountable to their own people…is indeed troubling" (Andreopoulos 2006a, pp. 155–156).

[51] In this context where "the real justification is not the reason for the war, but the subject that is constituted through it…all critique is an attack on the state, all dissent becomes a threat to identity, to self-expression, and international outcry becomes an irritating misunderstanding of who we are" (Mann 2006, p. 160).

[52] President Bush, in his January 29, 2002 State of the Union Address, clearly linked Iraq with both terrorism and WMDs: "Iraq continues to flaunt its hostility toward America and to support terror. The Iraqi regime has plotted to develop anthrax and nerve gas and nuclear weapons for over a decade…. This is a regime that has something to hide from the civilized world." After suggesting a number of links between Iraq and al-Qaeda in an October 7, 2002, speech, he then said: "Saddam Hussein's regime gleefully celebrated the terrorist attacks on America. Iraq could decide on any given day to provide a biological or chemical weapon to a terrorist group or individual terrorists." The role of rhetoric has been recognized as a significant factor in justifying the Iraqi invasion (Burke 2004). Ferrari quotes P.A. Chilton to the effect that "what constitutes a legitimate concept of 'war' can only be established [linguistically]" (2007, pp. 622 & 8n). See P.A. Chilton (1997, p. 175).

Guantánamo Bay, the administration stripped both Iraq and Abu Ghraib of nation-state status and turned them into "grey" zones of legality.

Traditional wars are marked by clear geopolitical, administrative, and human boundaries, which determine the rules applicable to combatants, civilians, MPs, MIs, and prisoners of war (POWs). All of these boundaries were erased in "Operation Iraqi Freedom" by acts that rewrote, circumvented, or blurred the rules of war conduct. As one Bush administration official said: "We're an empire now, and when we act, we create our own reality" (Suskind 2004, October 17).[53]

First, geopolitical boundaries were undone by the physical invasion itself. After Saddam Hussein's government was toppled, the conditions of Bobbitt's "market-state" prevailed. Iraq was no longer self-governing (Danner 2004, pp. 54–56). The occupying forces, under international law, had no legal standing to govern, but were obliged to observe the Geneva Conventions (Kramer et al. 2005, pp. 67–68).[54] Instead, they appropriated for the Multinational Force (MNF) temporary sovereignty over part of Iraqi territory – the so-called "Green Zone." Second, new law was made by rhetorical fiat. Order 17, signed in June 2004 by Paul Bremer, the head of the Coalition Provisional Authority (CPA), decreed that all civilian contractors in Iraq were immunized from prosecution in Iraqi courts "with respect to acts performed by them pursuant to the terms and conditions of a Contract" with the CPA or any "Sending State."[55] This plainly contradicts international law.

In a June 2008 decision, *Munaf* v. *Geren*, 128 S. Ct. 2207 (2008), the U.S. Supreme Court reiterated that two American citizens held at Camp Cropper in Iraq for crimes committed on Iraqi soil were fully subject to the Iraqi legal process, as mandated by international law.[56] The *Munaf* Court stressed that nations have a "'sovereign right to try and punish [American citizens] for offenses committed within their borders,' unless they 'have relinquished [their] jurisdiction' to do so" (*Id.* at 2222, quoting *Kinsella* v. *Krueger*, 351 U.S. 470, 479 (1956); alterations in original). Of course, the two petitioners in *Munaf* were not shielded

[53] For an analysis, see Michalowski (2009, p. 310)

[54] As an occupying force, the United States and the CPA were also obliged, under international law, to observe the Hague Regulations of 1907, and to assure "public safety and order," while respecting the "lives and property of civilians…at all times" (Kramer et al. 2005, p. 67).

[55] CPA Order Number 17 (Revised), sec. 4 (3). Paralleling this are infringements on the rights of United States citizens, such as those authorized by the Patriot Act, and protections granted domestic companies. On July 10, 2008, President Bush signed into law the Foreign Intelligence Surveillance Act Amendments of 2008, which provides sweeping immunities from lawsuits to telecommunications companies for providing the federal government with information on their customers, without any judicial oversight. The Obama administration supports this immunity.

[56] In *Munaf*, the Court noted: "The habeas petitioners do not dispute that they voluntarily traveled to Iraq…or that they are alleged to have committed serious crimes in Iraq…. Given these facts, our cases make clear that Iraq has a sovereign right to prosecute [petitioners] for crimes committed on its soil" 128 S. Ct. at 2221.

by any contract with the CPA, unlike the six "hired guns" from Blackwater who shot indiscriminately into a Baghdad crowd and killed 17 civilians in September 2007.[57]

Not only was Iraq's sovereignty over criminal matters infringed by Order 17, but under the "market-state" conditions of Iraq's lost geopolitical and national identity, other CPA orders issued in 2003 "rewrote Iraqi law to make the country available for foreign investment and ownership," with United States companies, such as Bechtel and Halliburton, reaping the benefits of this "privatization" (Kramer et al., 2005, p. 69). At Abu Ghraib, even more unscrupulous opportunities were provided.

Abu Ghraib had been an infamous Iraqi prison under Saddam Hussein. During the invasion, it became a visible emblem of the erasure of boundaries in the Iraqi invasion as a whole. Located outside the field of combat, but shelled daily by mortar fire, it was situated in a grey zone between combat and noncombat. Neither a facility for POWs nor for ordinary criminals, its population included a mix of security detainees, hardened criminals, and civilian suspects who had been rounded up in indiscriminate "sweeps" (Kingsbury, 2008, May 20).

At varying times, Abu Ghraib contained anywhere from 2,000 to 7,000 inmates. One estimate is that 19,000 prisoners passed through Abu Ghraib between 2004 and 2006 (Hamm, 2007, p. 282). Army rules mandate that for every 4,000 POWs, one MP batallion be assigned. But at Abu Ghraib, a single battalion was being asked to supervise 7,000 detainees. Thus, if Abu Ghraib had been a regular POW camp, it would have been severely understaffed, with only about one-half of the needed staff (Taguba Report, 2004, p. 433). But in actuality the problem was much worse.

Because Abu Ghraib's detainees were civilians, not only did MPs need a higher grade of training to handle them,[58] but the ratio of guards to detainees also needed to be higher (Mastroianni & Reed 2006, p. 243). Most MPs at Abu Ghraib were lacking even "basic" guard duty training, not to mention the more specialized training to handle non-POW populations.[59] MPs probably would have found POWs relatively unproblematic to guard, because of their identity as fellow soldiers, "who clearly are entitled to humane treatment" (Mastroianni & Reed 2006, p. 243).

[57] See Tom Engelhart (2007, September 24). As of November 2008, the Pentagon had 163,000 contractors in Iraq, while the State Department employed around 5500 (Lee 2008, November 20). On November 27, 2008, the Iraqi Parliament approved a Status of Forces Agreement (SOFA) by a vote of 149 to 35, which rescinded the immunities grated to private contractors by Order 17. Previously, the Iraqi Cabinet and the White House had approved the same measures (Rubin 2007, October 31).

[58] MPs staffing military correctional facilities, such as the one at Fort Leavenworth, require a higher specialty classification, and more specialized training, than MPs guarding POWs, that is, a Military Occupational Safety (MOS) classification of 95C, as compared to 95B for the latter. An MOS of 95C was needed at Abu Ghraib, which was not a POW prison (Mastroianni & Reed 2006, p. 243). But the MPs at Abu Ghraib apparently had neither kind of training: "I find that prior to its deployment to Iraq for Operation Iraqi Freedom, the 320th MP battalion and the 372nd MP Company had received no training in detention/internee operations" (*Taguba Report*, 2004, p. 419).

[59] "There is abundant evidence…that soldiers throughout the 800th MP Brigade were not proficient in their basic MOS skills" (*Taguba Report*, 2004, p. 433).

But in view of the disruptions occasioned by the invasion, Abu Ghraib's inmate population was not shielded by any recognizable identity either as enemy POWs or as noncombatant citizens – or even as human beings.

Many analyses of Abu Ghraib cite administrative faults, and these fall into two broad categories:[60] the "few bad apples" theory, favored by both the Bush administration and the army, which blames low-level soldiers; and the institutional theories, blaming military and prison organizational elements, as well as failures in leadership.[61] In a CBS interview on *60 Minutes II* in April 2004, shortly after the scandal broke, Brig. Gen. Mark Kimmitt, deputy director of coalition operations in Iraq, said: "[Americans] need to understand that is not the Army. The Army is a values-based organization. We live by our values. Some of our soldiers every day die by our values, and these acts that you see in these pictures may reflect the actions of individuals, but by God, it doesn't reflect my army" (2004, April 28). The "few bad apples" theory targets individuals in their personal capacities and not as agents of the state.

In a text cited by contemporary just war commentators, Augustine suggested that a soldier may kill as an "agent" of war, while an ordinary person may not be justified in killing even a highway robber or rapist.[62] This distinction hinges on the difference between one's official and personal identities. Preserving the common weal is a necessity, while preserving one's own life or chastity is optional and, therefore, not exculpable under law.

Whether an individual is acting in an official or personal capacity has legal and moral implications. Singling out and punishing the low-ranking MPs directly involved in the Abu Ghraib scandal, without also punishing their superiors in the chain of command, means that those soldiers were being held accountable in their personal and not official capacities. Only one high-level officer was ever disciplined, and that was Army Reserve Brig. Gen. Janis Karpinski, a career Army reservist, who took over the 800th Military Police Brigade in June 2003 and was in charge of Abu Ghraib when the abuses occurred.[63] In May 2005, after a lengthy investigation, Karpinski was demoted and relieved of her command. Four other top officers were cleared of any wrongdoing (CNN 2005, May 5), although Col. Thomas Pappas was reprimanded and fined $8,000 (Dishneau 2007, January 31). In August 2007, three years after the scandal broke, Lt. Col. Steven Jordan, the only other

[60] Hamm lists three theories: (1) the few "bad apples"; (2) Zimbardo's theory that stress brings out the "latent torturer[]" in all of us; and (3) a governmental policy sanctioned by the "upper echelons" of policymakers (2007, pp. 269–270).

[61] The institutional and failed leadership theories are the most interesting, among which is Hamm's study, as well as Jamieson & McEvoy's (2005). A broader sampling includes Malinowski (2008); Gordon (2006); Monahan & Quinn (2006); Hooks & Mosher (2005).

[62] Augustine (1993, p. 8), *On Free Choice of the Will* (*De libero arbitrio*). Note that these comments are put in the mouth of Augustine's interlocutor, Evodius, not of Augustine himself. See also Aquinas (2002, pp. 262–265).

[63] Bush demotes officer in charge of Abu Ghraib (CNN 2005, May 5). According to the *Taguba Report*, those abuses likely occurred in late October and early November 2003 (*Taguba Report*, 2004, p. 436).

officer prosecuted, was acquitted of all abuse charges (Clifton 2007, August 29). Eleven low-ranking soldiers were tried and convicted, with Cpl. Charles Graner, Jr., receiving the longest prison sentence (ten years). In short, army MPs were being held to the standards usually reserved for domestic policemen, and they were not shielded by a soldier's "following orders."[64]

When the reasons for the Iraqi invasion defaulted to humanitarian goals, "Operation Iraqi Freedom" changed from a war action to one analogous to a domestic policing action, with a prolonged period of occupation. "In humanitarian intervention, as in *domestic law enforcement*, we cannot and we do not forsake our laws and moral principles in order to enforce and protect them."[65] All policing actions, even military ones, unfold within a "moral framework," calling for minimal force, as opposed to a battle context, calling for the "maximum amount of force" (Luban 2007, p. 177).[66] Punishment for the Abu Ghraib abuses was meted out as if it were a policing rather than a military operation, and this reflects a growing trend of "increasing deployment of the military in 'military operations other than war' (MOOTW), which owe as much to policing as to traditional soldiering in their methods and objectives" (Walker 2003, p. 131).[67]

Abu Ghraib was neither an ordinary POW camp nor a civilian prison, and its administrative personnel mirrored that indeterminate status. Viewed in terms of Waddington's distinctions, MPs are neither strictly soldiers, whose aim is "to eliminate the enemy," nor are they strictly police, whose targets are "still citizens" (1999, p. 154).

Counter-terrorism has blurred the military and police distinction even further. The Abu Ghraib inmates were detainees in the broader "war against terrorism." Practically all were civilians; a few were former soldiers.[68] Guarding the Abu Ghraib detainees posed the common problem of counter-terrorism actions generally: that overpowering military forces are providing "aid to the civil power" (1999, p. 154). This is disturbing, especially in light of the United States' response to terrorism, which "disclose[s] a frightening design to overwhelm the state structure of world order from above, imposing global dominance, by fascist means if necessary" (Falk 2006, p. 136).

In this charged context, just war rhetoric helped to create an illusion of moral infallibility, while also justifying responses based on purported reasons of state, or extraordinary "security" considerations, even though the International Red Cross estimates that "nearly 99% of all prisoners held by U.S. authorities in its now-infamous torture cells at Abu Ghraib were arrested 'in error' – that is with no probable

[64] "Soldiers are required to obey superior orders.... Civil police are characteristically individually liable for their actions in using force and cannot claim that they were acting under superior orders" (Waddington 1999, p. 154).

[65] George Lucas, From *jus ad bellum* to *jus ad pacem*, quoted in Fiala (2007, p. 40) (emphasis mine).

[66] In this connection, Luban (2006, p. 18n) credits Lieutenant Colonel Tony Pfaff with making a clear distinction between policing morality and war morality in two articles: "Military ethics in complex contingencies" and "Peacekeeping and the just war tradition."

[67] Walker also notes a preference for the term "transnational" and gives reasons that are analogous to the rationale of Bobbitt's "market state" (2008, p. 111).

[68] The *Taguba Report* mentions only "hundreds of former Iraqi soldiers and officers" (2004, p. 436).

cause" – and hence, unlikely to be "high-value detainees" (Kramer et al. 2005, p. 71; Taguba 2004, p. 410).

The main arguments for torture advanced by some contemporary just war theorists center, unsurprisingly, on legalistic rationales of state expediency. These arguments envision exceptional circumstances, such as Michael Walzer's "ticking bomb" scenario (2004b, pp. 64–65) and Michael Ignatieff's "states of emergency" (2004, pp. 8, 25–53), and they may involve duplicitous definitions of torture, as in Jean Bethke Elshtain's advocacy of "light" torture in a school bomb situation (2004, pp. 87–88).[69]

The problem, many other commentators are quick to point out, is that the exceptional rapidly becomes the institutional norm, so normal, in fact, that, as one observer notes, the Abu Ghraib torturers forgot their task of extracting useful information, yet got carried away by "emotional catharsis and revenge" and tortured anyway.[70] Marnia Lazreg notes that these torture justification theories rely heavily on fictional narratives of necessity (2008, pp. 247–248). Elshtain's argument, for example, makes detailed comparisons between her own fictional scenario of the school bomb and another fiction, the movie *Marathon Man* (2004, pp. 85–87).[71] One must remember that Abu Ghraib and the entire Iraqi invasion were occasioned by what turned out to be the fictional narrative of an Iraq ready to provide al-Qaeda terrorists with WMDs to use against the United States.

What, then, was the trajectory from fictional scenarios to the brutal realities documented in the Abu Ghraib photographs? The short answer is that a culture was created[72] whereby MPs – and Army Reserve Staff Sgt. Ivan L. Frederick, one of the primary offenders, testified to this on *60 Minutes II* (CBS News 2004, April 28) – felt so beholden to the unofficial authority of the army MIs and civilian interrogators (OGA operatives and private contractors) that they violated the duties mandated by their identities as MPs in the chain of command.

---

[69] See Lazreg's excellent analysis and critique of these views, and her point that they are based on rank fictions (2008, pp. 237–252). Danner calls the mélange of fact and fiction at Abu Ghraib a "faintly hysterical absurdity" (2004, p. 39).

[70] The soldiers punished at Abu Ghraib "made two inter-related mistakes: (1) they failed to focus on the instrumental goal of information extraction, and (2) they abused prisoners for reasons of emotional catharsis or revenge. Had they committed the same actions…[and] these abuses yielded information…the horrific actions…would be fully acceptable" (Hooks & Mosher 2005, p. 1641). Exceptional brutality soon becomes a state of normalcy (Gordon 2006, pp. 45–49). Two retired generals note: "Any degree of flexibility about torture at the top drops down the chain of command like a stone – the rare exception fast becoming the rule," quoted in Malinowski (2008, p. 154). Thus, Hooks quotes the *New York Times'* drawing of a "dotted line" from President Bush to Abu Ghraib, via administration lawyers (2005, p. 1634).

[71] For a fine analysis of the pitfalls of taking fiction as a justification of torture, see Luban (2006, pp. 249–262). Luban calls the ticking bomb scenario "an intellectual fraud" (2006, p. 259).

[72] This culture was established not only on-site at Abu Ghraib, but at the highest levels of the administration. Retired colonel Tom Laney, who was a battalion commander in the 1991 Gulf War explains: A pronouncement such as Rumsfeld's about the POWs not being prisoners of war "starts to create a culture of coercion that begins to permeate not just the military but the government…. So people who think they're doing the right thing begin to do the wrong thing. And as a result, efforts to extract intelligence become more important than the strategic objectives for which we are fighting, and that creates a problem" (Halton 2004, May 13).

Army MPs are forbidden to take part in interrogations. In other words, the boundaries between MPs and MIs, as well between MIs and the various civilian interrogators, were erased. While both the MPs and the MI-interrogators are constrained by the Geneva Conventions, the MPs have a specifically moral charge, as distinct from the state expediency guiding the MIs. When interrogators impermissibly enlisted the help of MPs to "set the conditions' for MI interrogations" (Taguba 2004, p. 418), they violated the norms of international law and the U.S. military code, as well as the moral charge of the MPs.

Gary Myers, the attorney for Staff Sgt. Frederick, excused Frederick by saying he was besotted with "the elixir of power, the elixir of believing [he was] helping the CIA…. And so, good guys sometimes do things believing that they are being of assistance and helping a just cause" (CBS News 2004, April 28). This chilling language, "helping a just cause," means, in the words of Neal Puckett, Karpinski's attorney, that Frederick and others "took all their instructions from military intelligence interrogators, who instructed them to bring the prisoners to and away from [interrogations], and sometimes perhaps to soften them up" (Jehl & Schmitt 2004, May 9; Taguba 2004, p. 436). Furthermore, the command was notably silent about the Geneva Conventions (Taguba 2004, pp. 419, 424–425). Copies of these Conventions were not "prominently displayed in all detention facilities," nor were periodic informational briefings held, as the *Taguba Report* deemed necessary (2004, pp. 420, 430). Thus, the rhetoric of unofficial complicity and silence trumped international law and U.S. Army regulations.

Further complicating matters, in August 2003 a team of 27 civilian interrogators arrived at Abu Ghraib, led by Steven Stefanowicz, a former U.S. Navy petty officer and an employee of a company called CACI International, Inc., which had been given a one-year contract to assist the MPs and the MI interrogators (Jehl & Schmitt 2004, May 9). Adding civilians to the military mix was part of the intentional design of "judicial othering," as Ruth Jamieson and Kieran McEvoy argue, whereby civilians – U.S. nationals and non-nationals – are used as interrogators and private security forces, because these personnel elude accountability under present international or domestic law.[73]

[73] This "judicial othering" works two ways, to put harm-doers beyond the reach of the law, and to deprive their victims of any judicial recourse. "Contractors who are American nationals can be tried under U.S. extraterritorial jurisdiction, but non-national contractors cannot and they 'fall into the same gray area as unlawful combatants in Guantánamo Bay.' Private military contractors do not fit the existing definition of mercenaries and have an ambiguous legal status as a basis for enforcing accountability. The employees of private companies are accountable as individuals, as are their superiors in some cases. But attributing responsibility to a private company is much more difficult and, in any case, PMFs as corporate entities do not come under the jurisdiction of the ICC. As for prosecuting the private military companies themselves through national courts, this too is difficult, given their fluid multinational presence and their relationship with their subcontractors. There is less transparency about PMF activities if they are contracted by other government agencies like the CIA…. Also PMFs tend not to have a continuous corporate existence, have 'few fixed assets or permanent employees' and they can 'move relatively easily from one jurisdiction to another' and 'regularly mutate'…. Using private military firms or local proxies is not only more flexible but it also offers the states that use these strategies *greatly enhanced scope for denying responsibility for illegal or abusive activities*" (Jamieson & McEvoy 2005, pp. 513–514; citations omitted; my italics). Compounding these observations is Order 17, which actually protects civilian CPA contractors from prosecution under Iraqi law, a protection that runs contrary to international law.

Just as the detainees were deprived of any identity as citizens or POWs, some of the MI interrogators intentionally blended their identities with civilian interrogators, who were not answerable to the army chain of command: "The intelligence officers' practice of wearing uniforms without insignia made it difficult for soldiers to identify the officers or even to determine which of them were military and which belonged to other agencies, including the C.I.A., whose officers periodically visited Abu Ghraib to participate in interrogations" (Jehl & Schmitt 2004, May 9; Taguba 2004, p. 436). Also, in August 2003, Maj. Gen. Geoffrey D. Miller, formerly in charge of the "gray" Guantánamo Bay facility known as "Gitmo" was sent to Abu Ghraib, purportedly to "Gitmo-ize" it (Halton, 2004, May 13). Finally, in a move which sounded the death knell for the MPs' moral policing mission at Abu Ghraib, in November 2003, Gen. Sanchez transferred command of Abu Ghraib to the 205th MI Brigade under Colonel Thomas M. Pappas (Jehl & Schmitt 2004, May 9). What had been the unofficial culture of state expediency was now formalized by this change of command.

The Dehumanizing Rhetoric of "Othering"

The culture at Abu Ghraib only becomes comprehensible when viewed in the context of the rhetoric of the unbounded "war against terrorism" and of a just war beyond ordinary morality. By designating al-Qaeda members "unlawful combatants," President Bush denied them any cognizable status. By identifying Iraq with al-Qaeda, he similarly stripped the Iraqi people of their identities as sovereign citizens and deprived some of them of all political, legal, moral, and, finally, even ordinary human status.[74] The administration's persistent linking of Iraq and al-Qaeda[75] was part of a wider strategy of "Othering," which vilified and dehumanized the Iraqi enemy, and concluded in erasing the protective strictures governing interpersonal actions, even in war.[76]

---

[74] "In an environment in which terms such as *terrorist* or *war* can be used in an imprecise or loose manner, the risk of rendering a large number of people vulnerable increases" (Andreopoulos 2006a, p. 156).

[75] As late as August 22, 2007, speaking at the Veterans of Foreign Wars' national convention, Bush was linking Iraq and the war against terrorism: "Iraq is one of several fronts in the war on terror – but it is the central front – it's the central front for the enemy that attacked us and wants to attack us again."

[76] No one writes more eloquently than Joan Dayan of the long history in the United States of using the denial or redefinition of legal status as a political tool, from slavery to Abu Ghraib. She speaks of putting certain targeted groups on "enthralled ground.... [T]he ground that is a dead zone, a judicial no-man's land, where region or what is regional can be everywhere. The persons currently deprived of rights, most importantly through labeling, through words in time that that sustain the idea of the wicked or unfit, carry the idea of region with them. They make up a world that has no political boundaries, and where geographical boundaries are dislodged from their proper places. How can I describe the place that becomes synonymous with the incapacitation of the person? In untangling a philosophy of personhood in the rules of law, we ought to understand how two apparently distinct discourses – expulsion and dehumanization – are joined, or, more precisely, operate along a continuum" (2003, p. 95).

First, the political and legal limits on conduct were erased at Abu Ghraib, as discussed above, through rhetorical complicity, in the form of unofficial and illegal "orders," and through an officially sanctioned silence on the Geneva Conventions. In "set[ting] the conditions" for interrogations, a climate ensued that was hospitable to further moral encroachments on basic human identity. Denied any status as Iraqi citizens or POWs, the Abu Ghraib detainees were easily absorbed into the nonhuman identities of terrorists, publicly portrayed since 2001 as evil incarnate. "Once a category of people is defined as existing outside the human community, all obligations to treat them humanely are nullified" (Kramer et al. 2005, p. 72).[77]

From the start, the "war against terrorism" was characterized in Manichean terms of absolute good versus pure evil (Ferrari 2007, p. 607). When Bush first mentioned the "axis of evil," he was appropriating the moral justification of World War II. We were not dealing simply with saboteurs, insurgents, or anarchists, but with agents who were, in Bush's words, "the heirs of all the murderous ideologies of the twentieth century…fascism, Nazism, and totalitarianism" (Burke 2004, p. 334). What we were seeking in Iraq was not simply a regime change and Saddam Hussein's downfall. What we were fighting for, in Jean Bethke Elshtain's just war discourse, was nothing less than a defense of who we are. "We must and will fight – not in order to conquer any countries or to destroy peoples or religions, but to defend who we are and what we, at our best, represent" (2003, p. 6).

While this mission to fight evil has been called "American Exceptionalism" (Fiala 2008, pp. 59–74) and "prime modernity" (Falah et al. 2006, p. 145), these are merely new words for Huntington's and Fukuyama's old narrative of the superiority of the United States' liberal democracy and Western hegemony. European commentators, however, view the Bush administration's rhetoric of "friend" versus "enemy" and "good" versus "evil" as identical to the "typical language of totalitarian regimes" (Ferrari 2007, p. 605).

In this framework of archetypal good and evil, the dehumanization of al-Qaeda terrorists was extended to all Iraqis in general. Worse even, this dehumanization, combined with the prior personalizing of the war on terror, vilified a people rather than the impersonal state. In an August 2009 article on the civilian contractors who helped the C.I.A. develop its harsh interrogation techniques, one of them is quoted as saying that interrogation required "a comparable level of fear and brutality to flying planes into buildings" (Shane 2009, August 12). Finally, this kind of personal vilification is connected to a long history of imperial motivation aimed at Arabs, among others (Lazreg 2008), in which sexual humiliation is part and parcel of imperial domination.[78]

---

[77] "However, as the rights of man became increasingly political rights which could only be held within specific political regimes, so they became increasingly useless as a notion in international or intercultural relations" (Pagden 2003, p. 190).

[78] The relationship among colonialism, sex, and torture is evident in a French intelligence officer's advice to a colleague in Algiers: "An interrogation is like making love. An essential rule is to take your time, know how to hold yourself long enough until you reach the crucial moment, keep up pain until it reaches its climax. Most of all do not go beyond this threshold or your partner will die on you. If you can motivate him, he'll talk. Well, you know, orgasm. Otherwise, he'll pass out. If you love women, lieutenant, you should understand" (Lazreg 2008, p. 125).

Supposedly, Raphael Patai's book *The Arab Mind*, suggested to a "government consultant" that sexually humiliating photos such as those taken at Abu Ghraib could be used to blackmail detainees into spying on their "associates" (Massad 2007, p. 45; Hamm 2007, p. 264). But as Joseph Massad demonstrates – and Edward Said (1978) before him – the Arab was simultaneously romanticized and brutalized by colonizing discourses starting in the nineteenth century (Tétreault 2006, pp. 37–40), and the torture scenarios at Abu Ghraib repeat what happened during the Palestinian anti-colonial revolt in the 1930s (Massad 2007, pp. 43–47).

The culture of permissiveness at Abu Ghraib was not the result of lapses in leadership, but part of a conscious policy of the Bush administration. The sanctions for torture at Abu Ghraib emanated from the highest echelons of the U.S. government. Coupled with the president's public rhetoric championing adherence to law[79] are other speech acts supporting and carving out exemptions to the law.[80] We have already mentioned Order 17 and other legalistic moves by the CPA. With respect specifically to the impermissibility of torture under the Geneva Conventions and international law, the president first exempted al-Qaeda operatives by labeling them "unlawful combatants." Then his administration systematically undid protections for all detainees in Iraq and the worldwide war on terror, by unilaterally redefining the international meaning of torture. In the now-infamous memos by administration lawyers, the limits of torture were changed from the international standards of "severe pain or suffering, whether physical or mental" to that degree of pain "equivalent in intensity to the pain accompanying serious physical injury, such as organ failure, impairment of bodily function, or even death."[81]

The historical tradition of just war theory does not rationalize war with apocalyptic scenarios of good versus evil. The contemporary tendency to justify war with a heightened discourse of security threaded through with moral absolutism is dangerous, because it erases all protective boundaries regulating human conduct. Even an enemy has a legal, moral, and human identity. "Just war theory is particularly dangerous because, even as it claims universal moral validity, it avoids the ultimate moral test of universality [and in] the hands of [someone like] Elshtain, it makes humanitarian arguments for war against Iraq to protect the innocent, but allows for the Iraqi innocent, military and civilian, to be slaughtered" (Burke 2004, p. 352).

Another commentator speaks of the "elasticity of the principle of evil as opposed to the reality or truth principle" (Agozino 2004, p. 81). Truth, or whether there were WMDs in Iraq, "resists elasticity," whereas good and evil have no measurable standards (Agozino 2004, p. 81). The discourse of evil is a dysfunctional discourse and results

[79] See, for example, President Bush's remarks at a June 10, 2004, Press Conference at Sea Island, Georgia, where he uses the word "law" five times in six short sentences, quoted in Danner (2004, p. 46).

[80] Hamm reports an anecdote in which Bush inquires about a severely wounded Abu Zubaydah, who was reportedly unresponsive to questioning: "Who authorized putting him on pain medication?" (Hamm 2007, p. 267), quoting from James Risen (2006, p. 22).

[81] This legalistic maneuvering by the president's lawyers – White House counsel Alberto Gonzales, his associate, John Yoo, and Assistant Attorney General Jay S. Bybee – has been documented and discussed many times (Danner 2004, p. 115; Hamm 2007, p. 266).

in an "elastic" notion of what it or is not allowable in war. To protect an abstract freedom and a democratic identity, the right is asserted to slaughter and torture individuals, all in the name of a higher morality and higher purpose. This is to forget that the realities of human identity begin with a human being in a body. Torture, as Robert Cover brilliantly understood decades before "Operation Iraqi Freedom," takes place between two human beings; and the infliction of the kind of pain allowable under the Bush doctrine invariably reduces one of them to mere "thingness," hardly a way to save the world from undemocratic tyranny:

"The deliberate infliction of pain in order to destroy the victim's normative world and capacity to create shared realities we call torture. The interrogation…is rarely designed to elicit information [but rather to] demonstrate the end of the normative world of the victim – the end of what the victim values, the end of the bonds that constitute the community in which the values are grounded…. That is why torturers always require betrayal – a demonstration that the victim's intangible normative world has been crushed by the material reality of pain and its extension, fearr. (Cover 1986, p. 1603)."

The tyranny of total power, whether it goes by the name of American liberal democracy or Islamic fascism, always devolves upon some confrontation with one's own individual humanity. In hunting terrorists, who act in their personal capacities to promote terrorism, the Bush administration has at least been honest about its aim of destroying the humanity and identity of terrorists. In "Operation Iraqi Freedom" and at Abu Ghraib, however, to claim to be defending national security or the high ideals of freedom and democracy against persons, unproven as either personal or state agents of war or terror, is plainly untenable. How could we be said to have been defending "who we are and what we, at our best, represent"? Unfortunately, part of the answer lies in the mirror that history will hold up – for as long as words and images endure – of those shameful photographs taken at Abu Ghraib. Perhaps that is why the United States had to elect a president in 2008, identifiable both with Khanna's second-world potentiality and America's first-world elitism: a Harvard-educated African-American with the middle name "Hussein," who personifies another face of "American Exceptionalism."

Conclusion and a Look Ahead

The pictures from Abu Ghraib are burned forever into the global consciousness, no less than the twin towers of September 11 and the horrific beheadings connected to al-Zarqawi. If we are truly waging a "war against terrorism," we must hold fast to the outward and inward views, the road of expediency and the path of morality. For otherwise, what will our victory be worth, when we finally do win the war on terror? The discourse of "just war" helped to buttress the Bush administration's claims of moral exceptionalism in the face of extraordinary "securitization" demands. These rationales of righteousness and fear combined to support a culture of moral permissiveness, both at Abu Ghraib and in the American populace.

Historically, "just war" theory is a retrospective doctrine, applied after the fact to justify questionable actions. No purported list of requirements for just war can ever serve as any kind of moral guide to war, and viewing just war theory as a predictive doctrine is dangerous, especially if the facts and motives for undertaking war are elastic or false.

In a global context where the security wars in Afghanistan and Iraq are not succeeding, the unilateral discourse of "war" and particularly of "just war"[82] should be avoided, while the alternatives offered by multilateral international law and authority should be developed. Because military actions today share many of the functions and objectives of domestic policing, clearer guidelines are also needed to regulate status and conduct in complex situations of mixed authority, as at Abu Ghraib.

President Obama has not been in office very long as of this writing. On his second day in office, he issued an Executive Order mandating the closing of Guantánamo Bay within a year.[83] Under President Bush, Abu Ghraib had already been renovated and turned over to the Iraqi government. While Obama's plans for closing Guantánamo Bay's prison may not be realizable, because of difficulties in concluding tainted legal proceedings, or repatriating the detainees, or keeping some incarcerated indefinitely – still, by his executive mandate, he has acknowledged the ill-advisedness of establishing Guantánamo Bay in the first place. Another Executive Order incontrovertibly bans torture and reverses, as a matter of policy, the Bush administration's normalization of torture.[84]

But the Obama administration is also "danc[ing] awkwardly with Bush policies" (Balz 2009, August 26), continuing, for example, the policy of "rendition" or "shipping suspects abroad for interrogation." In his speeches and public statements, however, Obama has intentionally steered clear of the heightened "securitization" rhetoric of the Bush administration, and moved towards a discourse of reconciliation by saying, for example, in his Cairo University speech, that "Islam has always been a part of America's story" and by arguing for a transnational human identity: "[W]hen a financial system weakens in one country, prosperity is hurt everywhere. When a new flu infects one human being, all are at risk" (2009, June 4).

The mistakes of the recent past cannot be reversed instantly. But whether or not additional photographs from Abu Ghraib will be released, whether or not further investigations will be launched or more individuals punished for Abu Ghraib, whether or not Guantánamo Bay will be closed on time – none of these particular actions will be the ultimate measure of future success.

---

82 Walzer trumpets the "triumph" of just war theory (2004a, pp. 3–22), but the very success of just war theory has proved problematic, because this has helped tip the scales away from alternatives offered by multilateral international law and cooperation.

83 Executive Order No. 13492 (signed Jan. 22, 2009). Review and disposition of individuals detained at the Guantánamo Bay naval base and closure of detention facilities. 74 FR 4897 (Jan. 27, 2009).t

84 Executive Order No. 13491 (signed Jan. 22, 2009). Ensuring lawful interrogations. 74 FR 4893 (Jan. 27, 2009).

Reversing past errors necessitates a change in the culture of the United States' transnational actions, especially those taken in pursuit of the "war against terrorism," an undertaking without any boundaries and without any end in sight. A new outlook is needed, one that President Obama seems to be promising, one in which the United States abandons the unrealizable goal of political hegemony, while accepting a world of differences knit together by a shared humanity. The erasing of old boundaries occasioned by market-state conditions must not be allowed to erase the ultimately unifying boundary of human identity. In situations of last resort, under the pressures of a seeming necessity to abandon all rules, the one rule of respect for human dignity must not be cast off. Few are as fortunate as Michel de Montaigne, who served state expediency, while keeping intact some part of his private morality. We must remember, Montaigne cautions, "that not all things are permissible for an honorable man in the service of his king, or of the common cause, or of the laws" (1965, p. 609). A state security that savages human dignity may hardly be worth having.

References

Agozino, B. (2004). The Iraq war did not take place: Sociological implications of a conflict that was neither a just war nor just a war. *International Review of Sociology* **14**(1), 7388.

American Bar Association. (2004). American Bar Association Report to the House of Delegates, August 2004. In: K.J. Greenberg & J.L. Dratel (Eds.), *The Torture Papers* (pp. 1132–1164). New York: Cambridge University Press.

Amnesty International. (2003, September 23). Yemen: The rule of law sidelined in the name of security. Retrieved from http://web.amnesty.org/library/pdf/mde310062003english/$file/mde3100603.pdf.

Andreopoulos, G.J. (2006a). On the accountability of non-state armed groups. In: G.J. Andreopoulos, Z.F.K. Arat, & P. Juviler (Eds.), *Non-State Actors in the Human Rights Universe* (pp. 141–163). Bloomfield, CT: Kumarian Press.

Andreopoulos, G.J. (Ed.) (2006b). *Non-State Actors in the Human Rights Universe*. Bloomfield, CT: Kumarian Press.

Aquinas, T. (2002). *Political Writings* (R.W. Dyson, Ed. & Trans.). Cambridge: Cambridge University Press.

Augustine. (1972). *City of God* (D. Knowles, Ed., & H. Bettenson, Trans.). Baltimore: Penguin. (Original work published in 413–427 CE.)

Augustine. (1993). *On Free Choice of the Will* (*De libero arbitrio*) (T. Williams, Trans.). Indianapolis: Hackett. (Original work published in 391–395 CE.)

Balz, D. (2009, August 26). Obama dances awkwardly with Bush policies. *Washington Post.* Retrieved from http://www.washingtonpost.com/wp-dyn/content/articles/2009/08/25/AR2009082503071.html.

Bellamy, A.J. (2006a). Hard cases, dirty ethics: Rule-breaking in the war on terror. In C. Enemark (Ed.), *Ethics of War* (pp. 7–21). Canberra, Australia: Strategic and Defence Studies Centre.

Bellamy, A.J. (2006b). *Just Wars: From Cicero to Iraq*. Cambridge: Polity Press.

Bin Laden's "Letter to America." (2002, November 24). *Observer Worldview.* Retrieved from http://observer.guardian.co.uk/worldview/story/0,11581,845725,00.html.

Bobbitt, P. (2008). *Terror and Consent: The Wars for the Twenty-First Century*. New York: Knopf.

Brooks, R.E. (2004). War everywhere: Rights, national security law, and the law of armed conflict in the age of terror. *University of Pennsylvania Law Review* 153(2), 675–761.

Burke, A. (2004). Just war or ethical peace? Moral discourses of strategic violence after 9/11. *International Affairs* **80**(2), 329–353.

Bush, G.W. (2001, September 11). Oval office address, available from Lexis-Nexis Academic.

Bush, G.W. (2001, September 12). Statement, available from Lexis-Nexis Academic.

Bush, G.W. (2001, September 20). Transcript of President Bush's address to a joint session of Congress. CNN. Retrieved from http://archives.cnn.com/2001/US/09/20/gen.bush.transcript/.

Bush, G.W. (2002, January 29). Address before a joint session of Congress on the State of the Union. Retrieved from http://www.presidency.ucsb.edu/ws/index.php?pid=29644.

Bush, G.W. (2002, October 7). Address to the American people from Cincinnati. Retrieved from http://archives.cnn.com/2002/ALLPOLITICS/10/07/bush.transcript.

Bush, G.W. (2007, August 22). President Bush attends Veterans of Foreign Wars national convention, discusses war on terror. White House Documents and Publications. Available from Lexis-Nexis Academic.

Buzan, B., Waever, O., & de Wilde, J. (1998). *Security: A New Framework for Analysis*. Boulder, CO: Rienner.

Byrm, R.J. (2008). Religion, politics, and suicide bombing: An interpretative essay. Notes on society. *Canadian Journal of Sociology* 33(1), 89–108.

CBS News (2004, April 28). Abuse of Iraqi POWs by GIs probed. *60 Minutes II*. Retrieved from http://www.cbsnews.com/stories/2004/04/27/60II/main614063.shtml.

Chilton, P.A. (1997). The role of language in human conflict: Prolegomena to the investigation of language as a factor in conflict causation and resolution. *Current Issues in Language & Society* 4(3), 174–189.

Clifton, E. (2007, August 29). Military acquits officer accused of abuses at Abu Ghraib. Interpress Service. Available from Lexis-Nexis Academic.

CNN (2005, May 5). Bush demotes officer in charge of Abu Ghraib. Retrieved from http://www.cnn.com/2005/US/05/05/abu.ghraib/index.html.

Cover, R. (1986). Violence and the word. *Yale Law Journal* **95**(8), 1601–1629.

Coalition Provisional Authority (2004, June 27). Order Number 17 (Revised). Status of the coalition provisional authority, MNF-Iraq, certain missions and personnel in Iraq. Retrieved from http://www.cpa-iraq.org/regulations/20040627_CPAORD_17_Status_of_Coalition_Rev_with_Annex_A.pdf.

Danner, M. (2004). *Torture and Truth: America, Abu Ghraib, and the War on Terror*. New York: New York Review Books.

Dayan, J. (2003). Servile law. In: E. Cadava & A. Levy (Eds.), *Cities Without Citizens* (pp. 87–117). Philadelphia: Slought Books.

Denike, M. (2008). The human rights of others: Sovereignty, legitimacy, and "just causes" for the "war on terror." *Hypatia* **23**(2), 95–121.

Dishneau, D. (2007, January 31). Officer seeks dismissal of Abu Ghraib charges: Defense shows documents that accused officer wasn't in the chain of command. *Richmond Times Dispatch*. Available from Lexis-Nexis Academic.

Elshtain, J.B. (2003). *Just War Against Terror: The Burden of American Power in a Violent World*. New York: Basic Books.

Elshtain, J.B. (2004). Reflection on the problem of "dirty hands." In: S. Levinson (Ed.), *Torture* (pp. 77–89). Oxford: Oxford University Press.

Elshtain, J.B. (2008). Response to Tom Farer's "Un-just war against terrorism and the struggle to appropriate human rights." *Human Rights Quarterly* **30**, 758–766.

Enemark, C. (Ed). (2006). *Ethics of War in a Time of Terror*. Canberra, Australia: Strategic and Defence Studies Centre.

Engelhart, T. (2007, September 24). Order 17. *The Nation*. Retrieved from http://www.thenation.com/doc/20071008/engelhart.

Erlanger, S. (2002, July 21). The world; America the invulnerable? The world looks again. *New York Times*. Available from Lexis-Nexis Academic.

Falah, G-W., Flint, C., & Mamadouh, V. (2006). Just war and extraterritoriality: The popular geopolitics of the United States' war on Iraq as reflected in newspapers of the Arab world. *Annals of the Association of American Geographers* **96**(1), 142–164.
Falk, R. (2006). Global civil society actors and 9/11. In: G.J. Andreopoulos, Z.F.K. Arat, & P. Juviler (Eds.), *Non-State Actors in the Human Rights Universe* (pp. 117–139). Bloomfield, CT: Kumarian.
Farer, T. (2008a). Still searching for engagement: A comment on Professor Jean Bethke Elshtain's response to "Un-just war against terrorism and the struggle to appropriate human rights." *Human Rights Quarterly* **30**, 767–771.
Farer, T. (2008b). Un-just war against terrorism and the struggle to appropriate human rights. *Human Rights Quarterly* **30**, 356–403.
Ferrari, F. (2007). Metaphor at work in the analysis of political discourse: Investigating a "preventive war" persuasion strategy. *Discourse & Society* **18**(5), 603–625.
Fiala, A. (2007). The Bush doctrine, democratization, and humanitarian intervention: a just war critique. *Theoria* (December), 28–47, doi: 10.3167/th.2007.5411403.
Fiala, A. (2008). *The Just War Myth: The Moral Illusions of War*. Lanham, MD: Rowman & Littlefield.
Fukuyama, F. (2006). *The End of History and the Last Man*. New York: Free Press. (Original work published 1992.)
Fukuyama, F. (2008, August 15). Iraq may be stable but the war was a mistake. *Wall Street Journal*. Retrieved from http://online.wsj.com/article/SB121876047023242841.html.
Gentili, A. (1933). *De jure belli libri tres* [On the Law of War], Vol. 2 (J.C. Rolfe, Trans). Oxford: Clarendon. (Original work published 1588, 1589 rev. 1598; this translation based on the 1612 edition.)
Gordon, A.F. (2006). Abu Ghraib: Imprisonment and the war on terror. *Race and Class* 48(1), 42–59.
Gratian. (1993). *The Treatise on Laws (Decretum DD. 1–20), with the Ordinary Gloss* (A. Thompson & J. Gordley, Trans.). Washington, DC: Catholic University of America Press. (Original work published 1582.)
Greenberg, K.J., & Dratel, J.L. (Eds.) (2005). *The Torture Papers: The Road to Abu Ghraib*. New York: Cambridge University Press.
Grotius, H. (1925). *De jure belli ac pacis libri tres* [On the Law of War and Peace], Vol. 2 (F.W. Kelsey,Trans.). Washington, DC: Carnegie Institution of Washington. (Original work published 1646.)
Guthrie, C., & Quinlan, M. (2007). *Just War: The Just War Tradition: Ethics in Modern Warfare*. New York: Walker.
Halton, D. (2004, May 13). The road to Abu Ghraib. *CBC News*. Retrieved from http://www.cbc.ca/news/background/iraq/abughraib_halton.html.
Hamm, M.S. (2007). "High crimes and misdemeanors": George W. Bush and the sins of Abu Ghraib. *Crime Media Culture* **3**(3), 259–284.
Hensel, H.M. (2008). The rejection of natural law and its implications for international relations and armed conflict. In H.M. Hensel (Ed.). *The Legitimate Use of Military Force: The Just War Tradition and the Customary Law of Armed Conflict* (pp. 63–96). Aldershot: Ashgate.
Hooks, G., & Mosher, C. (2005). Outrages against personal dignity: Rationalizing abuse and torture in the war on terror. *Social Forces* **83**(4), 1627–1646.
Howard, M. (2002). What's in a name? How to fight terrorism. *Foreign Affairs* **81**(1), 8.
Huntington, S.P. (2003). *The Clash of Civilizations and the Remaking of World Order*. New York: Simon & Schuster. (Original work published 1996.)
Ignatieff, M. (2004). *The Lesser Evil: Political Ethics in an Age of Terror*. Edinburgh: Edinburgh University Press.
Is it war? The presidential candidates on terrorism [editorial]. (2007, December 23). *Washington Post*.
Jamieson, R., & McEvoy, K. (2005). State crime by proxy and judicial othering. *British Journal of Criminology* **45**, 504–527.

Jehl, D., & Schmitt, E. (2004, May 9). The struggle for Iraq: The military; in abuse, a portrayal of ill-prepared, overwhelmed G.I.'s. *New York Times.* Available from Lexis-Nexis Academic.
Kagan, R. (2002). Power and weakness. *Policy Review.* Retrieved from http://www.hoover.org/publications/policyreview/3460246.htm.
Khanna, P. (2008). *The Second World: Empires and Influence in the New Global Order.* New York: Random House.
Khanna, P. (2008, January 27). Waving goodbye to hegemony. *New York Times*, Magazine Section (pp. 34–41; 62–67). Available from Lexis-Nexis Academic.
Kingsbury, A. (2008, May 20). Recalling the shame of Abu Ghraib: Q&A with Philip Gourevitch, co-author of *Standard Operating Procedure. U.S. News & World Report.* Retrieved from http://www.usnews.com/articles/news/iraq/2008/05/20/recalling-the-shame-of-abu-ghraib.html.
Knauft, B.M. (2007). Provincializing America: Imperialism, capitalism, and counter-hegemony in the twenty-first century. *Current Anthropology* **48**(6), 781–805.
Kramer, R., Michalowski, R., & Rothe, D. (2005). "The supreme international crime": how the U.S. war in Iraq threatens the rule of law. *Social Justice* **32**(2), 52–81.
Lazreg, M. (2008). *Torture and the Twilight of Empire: From Algiers to Baghdad.* Princeton: Princeton University Press.
Lee, M. (2008, April 24). "Jihadist" booted from government lexicon. *Associated Press.* Available from Lexis-Nexis Academic.
Lee, M. (2008, November 20). U.S. contractors lose immunity in Iraq security deal. *Associated Press.* Available from Lexis-Nexis Academic.
Lee, S.P. (Ed.). (2006). *Intervention, Terrorism, and Torture: Contemporary Challenges to Just War Theory.* Dordrecht: Springer.
Levinson, S. (Ed.). (2004). *Torture: A Collection.* Oxford: Oxford University Press.
Lindberg, T. (2002, June 4). The American flag stands for freedom; President's West Point speech gives vision of what to fight for. *Washington Times.* Available from Lexis-Nexis Academic.
Lockey, B.C. (2006). *Law and Empire in English Renaissance Literature.* Cambridge: Cambridge University Press.
Luban, D. (2006). Liberalism, torture, and the ticking bomb. In S.P. Lee (Ed.), *Intervention, Terrorism, and Torture* (pp. 249–262). Dordrecht: Springer.
Luban, D. (2007). Preventive war and human rights. In: H. Shue & D. Rodin (Eds.), *Preemption* (pp. 171–201). Oxford: Oxford University Press.
Malinowski, T. (2008). Restoring moral authority: Ending torture, secret detention, and the prison at Guantanamo Bay. *Annals of the American Academy of Political and Social Science* 616(1), 148–159.
Mann, B. (2006). How America justifies its war: A modern/postmodern aesthetics of masculinity and sovereignty. *Hypatia* **21**(4), 147–163.
Martin, R. (2006). Walzer and Rawls on just wars and humanitarian interventions. In: S. Lee (Ed.), *Intervention, Terrorism, and Torture* (pp. 75–88). Dordrecht: Springer.
Massad, J.A. (2007). *Desiring Arabs.* Chicago: University of Chicago Press.
Mastroianni, G.R., & Reed, G. (2006). Apples, barrels, and Abu Ghraib. *Sociological Focus* **39**(4) 239–250.
Matlock, Jr., J.F. (1999). Can civilizations clash? *Proceedings of the American Philosophical Society* **143**(3), 428–439.
Michalowski, R. (2009). Power, crime and criminology in the new imperial age. *Crime, Law and Social Change* **51**, 303–325.
Monahan, S.C., & Quinn, B.A. (2006). Beyond 'bad apples' and 'weak leaders.' *Theoretical Criminology* **10**(3), 361–385.
Montaigne, M. de. (1965). *Essays* (D.M. Frame, Trans.). Stanford: Stanford University Press.
Murnion, W.E. (2006). A postmodern view of just war. In: S. Lee (Ed.), *Intervention, Terrorism, and Torture* (pp. 23–40). Dordrecht: Springer.
Neier, A. (2001, October 9). Warring against modernity. *Washington Post.* Available from Lexis-Nexis Academic.
Newburn, T. (Ed.) (2003). *Handbook of Policing.* Cullompton, Devon: Willan.

Obama, B. (2009, June 4). Remarks by the President on a new beginning (Cairo University). Retrieved from http://www.whitehouse.gov/the_press_office/Remarks-by-the-President-at-Cairo-University-6-04-09/.

Orend, B. (2006). *The Morality of War*. Peterborough, ON: Broadview.

Pagden, A. (2003). Human rights, natural rights, and Europe's imperial legacy. *Political Theory* **31**(2), 171–99.

Panizza, D. (2005, October 17). Political theory and jurisprudence in Gentili's *De iure belli*: The great debate between 'theological' and 'humanist' perspectives from Vitoria to Grotius (Working Paper 2005/15). Paper presented in the History and Theory of International Law Series, NYU Institute for International Law and Justice. Retrieved from http://www.iilj.org/publications/documents/2005.15Panizza.pdf.

Patterson, E. (2007). *Just War Thinking: Morality and Pragmatism in the Struggle Against Contemporary Threats*. Lanham, MD: Lexington.

Peters, R. (2005). *Jihad in Classical and Modern Islam: A Reader*. Princeton, NJ: Wiener.

Risen, J. (2006). *State of War: The Secret History of the CIA and the Bush Administration*. New York: Free.

Rodin, D. (2007). The problem with prevention. In: H. Shue & D. Rodin (Eds.), *Preemption: Military Action and Moral Justification* (pp. 143–170). Oxford: Oxford University Press.

Rubin, A.J. (2007, October 31). Iraqi cabinet votes to end security firms' immunity. *New York Times*. Retrieved from http://www.nytimes.com/2007/10/31/world/middleeast/31iraq/html.

Said, E. (1978). *Orientalism*. New York: Random House.

Salisbury, S. (2001, September 30). Word "crusade" raises specter of superpower holy war against Islamic world. *Philadelphia Inquirer.* Available from Lexis-Nexis Academic.

Scoblete, G. (2004, September 8). The market-state president. *TCS Daily*. Retrieved from http://www.tcsdaily.com/article.aspx?id=090804C.

Shane, S. (2009, August 12). 2 U.S. architects of harsh tactics in 9/11's wake. *New York Times*. Available from Lexis-Nexis Academic.

Shue, H., & D. Rodin (Eds.) (2007). *Preemption: Military Action and Moral Justification*. Oxford: Oxford University Press.

Simon, S., & Benjamin, D. (2000). America and the new terrorism. *Survival* **42**(1), 59.

Smidt, C. E. (2005). Religion and American attitudes toward Islam and an invasion of Iraq. *Sociology of Religion* **66**(3), 243–261.

Stover, W.J. (2004). Preemptive war: Implications of the Bush and Rumsfeld doctrines. *International Journal on World Peace* **21**(1), 3–14.

Suskind, R. (2004, October 17). Faith, certainty and the presidency of George W. Bush. *New York Times*, Magazine Section. Retrieved from http://www.nytimes.com/2004/10/17/magazine/17BUSH.html.

Taguba Report. (2004). In L K.J. Greenberg & J.L. Dratel (Eds.). *The Torture Papers* (pp. 405–465). New York: Cambridge University Press.

Tétreault, M.A. (2006). The sexual politics of Abu Ghraib: Hegemony, spectacle, and the global war on terror. *NWSA Journal* **18**(3), 33–50.

Tuck, R. (2001). *The Rights of War and Peace: Political Thought and the International Order from Grotius to Kant*. Oxford: Oxford University Press. (Original work published 1999.)

U.S. Congress (2002). Authorization for use of military force against Iraq resolution of 2002 (AUMF). Pub. L. No. 107–243, 116 Stat. 1498. Retrieved from http://frwebgate.access.gpo.gov/cgi-bin/getdoc.cgi?dbname=107_cong_public_laws&docid=f:publ243.107.

U.S. State Department (2002, September 20). National security strategy. Retrieved from http://www.nytimes.com/2002/09/20/politics/20STEXT_FULL.html?page.

U.S. State Department. (2003, February 14). U.S. counterterrorism strategy will enhance national security; strategy calls for frequent, relentless strikes against terrorists. Retrieved from http://www.cia.gov/news-information/cia-the-war-on-terrorism/Counter_Terrorism_Strategy.pdf.

Vetlesen, A.J. (2008). Collective evildoing. In: R. Jeffery (Ed.), *Confronting Evil in International Relations: Ethical Responses to Problems of Moral Agency* (pp. 61–85). New York: Palgrave Macmillan.

Vitoria, F. de. (1991). *Political Writings* (A. Pagden & J. Lawrance, Eds. & Trans.). Cambridge: Cambridge University Press.

Waddington, P.A.J. (1999). Armed and unarmed policing. In: R.I. Mawby (Ed.), *Policing Across the Globe: Issues for the Twenty-First Century* (pp. 151–166). London: UCL Press.

Walker, N. (2003). The pattern of transnational policing. In: T. Newburn (Ed.), *Handbook of Policing* (pp. 111–135). Cullompton, Devon: Willan.

Walzer, M. (2004a). *Arguing About War*. New Haven: Yale University Press.

Walzer, M. (2004b). Political action: The problem of dirty hands. In: S. Levinson (Ed.), *Torture: A Collection* (pp. 61–75). Oxford: Oxford University Press.

Walzer, M. (2006a). *Just and Unjust Wars: A Moral Argument with Historical Illustrations*, 4th ed. New York: Basic Books. (Original work published 1997.)

Walzer, M. (2006b). Regime change and just war. *Dissent* 564(3), 103–111.

Wester, F.E. (2004). Preemption and just war: Considering the case of Iraq. *Parameters* **34**(4), 20–39.

Witt, H. (2002, November 24). U.S.: Killing of al-Qaeda suspects was lawful. *Chicago Tribune*. Retrieved from http://articles.chicagotribune.com/2002-11-24/news/0211240446_1_al-qaeda-killings-terrorist.

Zakaria, F. (2008). *The Post-American World*. New York: Norton.

Policing the Human: Lawfare and Humanitarianism

J. Paul Narkunas

Human rights are founded on adherence to universal principles of rules, rights, and norms by member states and individuals recognizing the sacredness of both the United Nations' 1948 *Universal Declaration of Human Rights* and the functions of international law. And yet, such activist reformers of international law as former Secretary of Defense Donald Rumsfeld in a May 2002 speech described "the war on terrorism as a war for human rights" (Brown 2004, p. 451). Such statements haunt human rights discourses and indeed what can be understood as the always mutating concept of what types of life, and in particular which humans, ought to be granted rights and thereby be subject to protection, and which can be extinguished with legal impunity.

Furthermore, the difficult question of what agency will protect the rights of these subjects from unforeseen contingencies has become all the more pressing given that the primary legal organizing unit since the Treaty of Westphalia, the sovereign nation-state, is in flux. Sovereign states increasingly compete with global nongovernment organizations (NGOs; e.g., Amnesty International, Human Rights Watch), think tanks (e.g., American Enterprise Institute, Brookings Institution), the Bretton Woods institutions, the United Nations, transnational corporations, and other regional elements in light of what has been called both an emerging global civil society or, more crudely and erroneously, the decline of the nation-state.

Furthermore, the proliferation of nonstate actors, including terrorists and rogue states, has created a situation where legal legitimacy becomes increasingly politicized with powerful international actors such as the United States defining human rights despite its own spotty record. To address the gaps in universal positive law, UN agencies and NGOs have tried to universalize institutional norms of the "right to intervene" in sovereign countries in order to remove local laws or lack thereof to create a common legal *lifeworld* by promoting universal human freedom, often by

J.P. Narkunas (✉)
Department of English, John Jay College of Criminal Justice/CUNY, 619 W. 54th Street, 7th Floor, New York, NY 10019, USA
e-mail: jnarkunas@jjay.cuny.edu

G. Andreopoulos et al. (eds.), *International Criminal Justice: Critical Perspectives and New Challenges*, DOI 10.1007/978-1-4419-1102-5_3,
© Springer Science+Business Media, LLC 2011

way of natural law tenets.[1] But as international humanitarian law (aka war law) becomes increasingly a measure for claiming the right to intervene, particularly in the war on terror, how can human rights become mere instruments for neocolonial and neoimperialistic projects?

This chapter will focus on two aspects of the human rights equation. First, the legal tension between natural and positive law regarding the subject of rights will be analyzed. In other words, can the expansion of rights, based as they generally are on systems of property, still operate at a moment when state and nonstate agents are unstable, and territoriality is itself being rethought by informational, cultural, and economic technologies, and their legal machinery?

Second, by highlighting that the law of going to war and humanitarian law are the same thing, I will show how the categories of personhood, the expansion of rights, and the flexible boundary between rules of engagement *jus in bello* and rules for going and legitimating war *jus ad bellum* has left humanitarians and military strategists less at odds and more closely aligned. To that end, articulating opposition to the war on terror and United States, global imperialism and militarism is made more complex given how human rights have been used for strategic political gains, particularly by the United States during the Bill Clinton and George W. Bush administrations.

To argue the latter point, I will highlight a curious phenomenon represented by Samuel Huntington's (1993) "clash of civilizations," whereby culture is granted de facto legal status that can work to regulate ultimately the limits of the human as culture. By considering how easily culture has been naturalized, I claim that arguments for establishing a human rights culture of universalizing particularist norms must consider how fluid these operations can be so that human rights are not merely a tool for the oppressed, but also an oppressive tool.

Method

I will mix critical legal theory, legal discourses, and recent attempts by literature and law theorists to argue the commonality of the emergence of the human subject and the topic of human rights. Joseph Slaughter (2008) in *Human Rights, Inc.*, for example, has traced the relationship of the rise of the novel and human rights, with particular focus on the novel of character formation, or *bildungsroman*, and liberalism's emphasis on individual rights. Indeed, perhaps the entire concept of self-consciousness,

---

[1]Here would be an instructive moment to mark a distinction between positive law and natural law. Natural law according to the law.com law dictionary is standards of conduct derived from traditional moral principles (first mentioned by Roman jurists in the first century AD) and/or God's law and will. The biblical Ten Commandments, such as "thou shall not kill," are often included in these principles. Positive law, natural law's opposite, is defined as created by mankind through the state (retrieved from http://www.dictionary.law.com/default2.asp?selected=1552&bold=%7C%7C%7C%7C)

which is so essential to critical judgment, emerges with the *bildungsroman* and the development of human interiority through the act of reading.[2] Slaughter highlights the figurative aspect for establishing the "enabling fiction" of the person and individual, and how it is tied to the production of the subject of rights. To become a legal person entails being both sovereign and subject; subjectivity incorporates differing and chaotic human identities and practices into a field of intelligible subjectivities.

What we call figurative language in literary studies actually creates and multiplies legal classifications that de facto and de jure determine who is of the law (including state and nonstate actors, acts of aggression, and acts of protection) and, likewise, who is an outlaw, rogue state, or bearer of human rights, if you will. Rather than merely representing reality, acts of law are productive forces that create the very limits of understanding through the same products of imagination, thought, and image-making used in acts of literature. Unfortunately, the obsession in literary studies on limiting political acts to representations whereby victims' stories of atrocities are the *sine qua non* of human rights, seems utterly bereft of knowledge about how the law functions as a formalized exercise of force and violence.

Indeed, many literary critics appear to forget their own training in the metaphorical and figurative dimensions of language – in sum, the nontransparency of language's communicability – and suggest that the mere telling of stories or "bearing witness to the event" will ensure that the victims will not be suppressed by states and/or oppressive power. In the process, storytelling itself becomes the major political act for fostering debate and a culture of human rights. Nevertheless, as any attorney knows far too well, storytelling merely provides the means to a possible legal judgment and legal subjectivity, using multiple levels of mediation from the work of translators to the legal system's privileging of coherent narratives. Even if the refugee or victim has suffered and needs legal protection, an unstructured and incoherent narrative that defies European conventions of narration (beginning, middle, end) may be usurped by a fake but organized story. In short, no story or representation can be controlled after it enters a court of law or any public sphere of debate.

Results

Law professor Duncan Kennedy (2002) has diagnosed how a certain faith in rationality translates in the United States to a societal belief in individual rights, which are accepted as ontological. A similar faith in legal reasoning to mediate disputes between parties in contracts can extend to any subject of individual rights.[3] Kennedy challenges the dismissive legacies of Burke on human rights as simply the rights of

[2]Slaughter builds on important work done by Nancy Armstrong (1990) in *Desire and Domestic Fiction*, and by Franco Moretti (2007).

[3]A telling example of this incorporation includes the move within "animal studies" and post-humanist discourses to extend rights to nonhuman agents including animals and inanimate objects.

Englishmen and Frenchman, as well as Jeremy Bentham's damning of all human rights as "nonsense upon stilts." Faith in law and judgment, Kennedy asserts, operates within the daily context of the law itself when judges attempt to balance damaged parties in immanent relations (the specifics of the case), while simultaneously claiming a transcendent position of interpretive objectivity able to uphold the law regardless of political concerns or the specifics of the case. By emphasizing the law as a dynamic immanent process, Kennedy traces dominant rights discourses used by liberals and conservatives and how they frequently borrow from each other in the U.S. context.

Kennedy gives as an example the liberal arguments for conferring rights to victims as property rights that need to be expanded to marginalized identities. By the same token, however, these same property rights are then deployed by conservatives who now speak of the damages done to whites by affirmative action in *Bakke v. Regents of California*. Both privilege the subjectivity in question not because of their actions, but because of who they are. This move from practice, epistemology, and constructed historical subjectivity to ontology sets up some dangerous precedents, while evacuating contestations of power or social/legal inequity because ontology is purportedly natural. The political left and right thereby converge, beneath the all-encompassing shrine of security and discourse of property as the domain of legal rights and human subjectivity.

Extending Kennedy's argument on legal rationalities to another site of engagement – the faith in extending property rights in a national context – also operates in human rights on an international scale. Humanitarians argue for universal protections within the law by expanding individual rights to a global arena. The focus on individual rights leads to a limited perception of "bad" governments that exercise wrongs that can be put right by an emerging global civil society, led by NGOs deemed "free" merely because they are not statist. The centrality of the state or governmental forces leads to two paradoxical positions for human rights advocates: a hatred of state organizations presumably by illegitimate, rogue, or immoral forces; and a need for "good" state forces to be mobilized to protect individual rights: "By consolidating human experience into legal entitlements, human rights strengthens the national governmental structure, and equates the structure of the state with the structure of freedom" (Kennedy 2004, p. 16).

In addition to Kennedy, Julie Mertus (2004) and Upendra Baxi (2008) have critiqued the professionalization of humanitarianism and human rights discourses and the overreliance on legal measures for promoting and extending human rights and human rights resources to the detriment of other forms of advocacy. Among these arguments, debates between universalist and particularist ethical claims for human rights monopolize human rights strategies and pit civic and political rights (universalist) against cultural and societal norms (particularist).

Universalist claims generally emerge as norms from particular communities and become universal, as the western European Enlightenment legacy suggests with human rights. The universalist position is represented institutionally and intellectually by the United Nations preamble and the so-called English School after Hedley Bull, which assumes an ordered set of norms in a society of states (Mertus 2004).

Universalists recognize how circumstances and norms change, allowing local interpretations for reconfiguring rights, and, despite the universalist claims, promoting dynamic changes, for example, in the capacity for victims to become claimants through legal measures. However, universalists from all political persuasions contend that international human rights laws are expansive, working in a complex machinery of incorporation within the international system and its purported claims to equal protection because every human has natural dignity. In addition to its legalism and its love and hatred of states and their emphasis on expansion, the universalist mode of thought may work too efficiently, but dangerously, with neoliberal economics. The individual freedom of rights holders could be extended even to nonhuman entities such as the corporation when, neoliberals allege, they are shackled by state regulations.[4] As Baxi warns: "[T]he paradigm of the Universal Declaration of Human Rights is being steadily, but surely, supplanted by that of a trade-related, market-friendly human rights" (2008, p. 132).

The particularist position, on the other hand, suggests that humans acknowledge their individual relationship to others and therefore make ethical and moral distinctions because of a network of interests and obligations. Every society/culture has independent and unique practices that it normalizes from the bottom up, either through manufacturing consensus or constructivism, namely constructing socio-cultural contexts and identities through habituation, which institutionalizes cultural norms. Constructivism has been particularly important for protecting indigenous rights and cultural practices. It has also ironically been deployed by the United States in its declaration of legal exceptionalism. Moreover, constructivism may again work too comfortably with neoliberal economics because of the ambiguous relationship of cultural practices to the law, and because norm creation follows the same techniques of habituation and branding as advertisers in the manufacturing of consent around identities, whether it be for a culture or a commercial product.

The domestic and international politics of the United States offer an interesting particularist legacy regarding universalist human rights and the use of humanitarianism for strategic power politics. The United States has deployed human rights when trying to usurp the sovereignty of specific nation-states in representing other atrocities, but claims specific sovereign exceptions when its own interests or atrocities are at stake. As Julie A. Mertus argues, the United States in the post-Cold War era has used the rhetoric of human rights to punish regimes during trade negotiations, as the Clinton administration did in the 1990s with China's most favored nation status. This reached a pinnacle with the American exceptionalist messianism of George W. Bush in invading Iraq and Afghanistan. The United States waltzes gingerly with human rights, making rhetorical claims to liberate Afghani women from the

[4]The precedent for this appears in the United States where the equal protection of the Fourteenth Amendment may cover corporations as legal persons due to the decision in *Santa Clara County vs. Southern Pacific Railroad*. This is the subject of some debate, but may indicate that an expansive model of rights can achieve absurdities when the particularities of politics, economics, or more generally the ability to exercise power are overlooked in legal decisions.

tyranny of the Taliban to lobby and mobilize a divided public for war, while avoiding UN treaties on landmines, economic rights, or withdrawing from the International Criminal Court because it may affect its own sovereign interests. The unwillingness even to entertain demands or protocols of economic rights, while contending tenuously that the "war on terror" secures human rights, indicates how the United States articulates its particular interests or goals as universal due to its social organization around liberty and entrepreneurship.

At the same time, the United States uses NGOs both as "a rights or humanitarian service provider," or funds, works with, or works against NGOs in order to stall or frustrate reform if they go against U.S. interests – an important effect of humanitarian structures and relationship to states. Mertus contends that Bush's theological dictates use human dignity and freedom and liberty for all as powerful humanitarian slogans while undermining any state entities that might try to enforce rules and regulations or laws: "Far from reflecting a universal consensus, the Bush catalog of rights is a random rendition of the administration's current priorities. The listing omits nearly all of the human rights deemed 'nonderogable' in international human rights treaties…including the right to life, freedom from torture, and freedom from slavery" (2004, p. 59).

The one exception was the law of property, as U.S. trade and investment became the only form of dignity the United States seemed willing to enforce (Mertus 2004). Beginning with the Clinton administration, but formalized in the Bush administration in the 2002 National Security Strategy document, the right to property, so pertinent to neoliberal economic policies, seemed to usurp the rights bestowed on humans or protected for them. The right to free markets is the universal human right worth fighting for, not the alleviation of human suffering. These examples show how powerful governments take measures to ensure their particularist priorities regardless of culture or societal norms in order to perpetuate war in the name of human rights.

An effect of this dance between constructivism, the English School, and universalism and particularism is that ever-more specific identities and human subjectivities become incorporated into the general legal matrix of property, law, sovereign subject, and ultimately faith in the reformist possibilities of law with or without state actors. Amy Gutmann (2003) put it in a different context: the "idolatry of rights" can lead to a fetishization of legal solutions for securing property and human freedom and neglect other avenues for protecting humans. Despite the universal claim to law and human rights, the proliferation of nonstate actors in power politics, including the NGOs of the purported global civil society, paradoxically normalizes extraterritorial legal formations and flexible norms-based systems of incorporation.

While human rights NGOs are part of an emerging global civil society working for "good," they offer information storehouses and are lobbying entities or "educating organs" for more powerful sovereign states (such as the United States) that could enact legal or military force. NGOs, however, can exercise little power of their own. In sum, the majority of human rights work entails negotiating with states to alter their behaviors should they engage in inhuman acts against members of their populations or against those whom they confront in war, or to lobby states to deploy force in the name of protecting other humans. What about the human rights claims from those who do not have access to state forces, often called the human rights deficit? How does statelessness affect the "human status" of those who seek human rights?

When wars take place, the tensions between state and nonstate actors identify who can be included and who can be excluded for protection by access to a state. The prison on the military base at Guantanamo Bay and the process of extraordinary rendition, whereby the U.S. government outsources the job of housing and torture, calls into question the relationship of territory and law. This disjuncture offers a particular conundrum for natural rights, which have served as the foundation for human rights. Natural rights at least require some space or property of legitimacy to ground them and a geographical terrain on which the law can be exercised.

Historically, Hugo Grotius, seventeenth-century theorist of "just war," evoked some transcendent entity, like God or human reason, to legitimate natural justice and "just" reasons for going to war, including the right to self-defense, reparation for injury, or for punishment. In *On the Law of War and Peace*, Grotius (2009; first published 1625) indicated that war should be an exceptional event when negotiations fail between legitimate actors; moral principles and the purportedly human capacity for reason should operate when weighing war between state actors. These processes are formalized through the *jus ad bellum*, the rules for going to war, and the *jus in bello*, the rules for waging wars and protecting combatants and noncombatants alike. War law, known as the test case for "armed conflict" or international humanitarian law, provides legal protections for people who are engaged in war, but also must be assessed any time force is used for humanitarian purposes.

As a critical legal theorist, Nathanial Berman (2004), argues, the normalization of war has occluded the stable boundary between a state of war and a state of peace (more on this later). Contrary to popular belief the proliferation of laws to stop war may have "been directly involved in the construction of war" (2004, p. 4). Indeed, Berman describes how war law is less a device of limiting or controlling violence and instead is used to "channel" violence (2004, p. 5), which also normalizes war to such a degree that the war/not-war distinction may be difficult to formalize and has been deployed both for humanitarian and imperial reasons.

Humanitarian interventions work through humanitarian–military alliances with such state-actors as the United States increasingly using human rights arguments to legitimate military intervention. David Kennedy (2004) contends that this is nothing new; sailors aboard the aircraft carrier *USS Independence* have a better sense of humanitarian and human rights law than most other transnational entities. According to Kennedy, who served as a civilian instructor with the U.S. Naval Justice School Detachment for International Training, an organization educating 53 countries on humanitarian law, "It turns out that the American military is by far the world's largest human-rights training institution. Across the globe, engagement with the U.S. military – purchasing our weapons, participating in joint exercises with out forces – comes with training in the international norms and regulatory practices of humanitarian law and human rights" (2004, p. 294). Indeed, the military speaks the language of human rights. Lawyers often determine the very field of possibility for war, what targets are bombed, who is a combatant, and numerous cost–benefit analyses on targets of opportunity. (This may be where the sovereign decision of the exception [who lives and who dies] is now exercised, as the lawyer exercises the decision on the limits of force for strategic ends without regard to a military or state goal.)

As Kennedy points out, humanitarians who oppose war and judge advocates/military lawyers speak the same language of rights, even if from different perspectives. Both use the law as a commercial asset to influence and plead the case of the most imprecise rules and procedures. Indeed, it marks what Kennedy (2006) has called lawfare, the management of war and law – a strategic assessment of various assertions and productive strategies by military and humanitarian actors to frame a situation to their advantage. As a result, the transcendent claim of justice and the abstractions of human dignity are rarely weighed in light of the immanent and imminent strategic needs of lawfare and the fear of bad publicity and press.

The duty to intervene leaves the question unanswered of how humanitarian structures may unwittingly contribute to further misery. Political liberals such as Samantha Powers (2002) and Michael Ignatieff (2003) argue that the risks of committing harm are worth risking to protect large swathes of humanity by drawing attention to their suffering. Human rights discourses can serve as a beacon of representation of atrocity; they represent the horrors enacted against individuals in order to mobilize shame for populations with the will and military might to intervene. The mobilization of shame claim, however, is generally argued by journalists who will reveal and potentially profit from the atrocities.[5] The assertion also assumes the truth claims of representation and atrocity, bringing atrocity from darkness into the light of day and the good of representation in itself.

As media theorist Tom Keenan (2003) has shown in numerous articles, in a society where the flux of the ubiquitous media event and global culture of celebrity are the norms, people commit the most heinous atrocities only when the cameras start rolling. In short, unless the atrocity is documented by the camera's gaze it will be anonymous and senseless, rather than the action of an individual taking pride in his/her killing. As a result, the mobilization of shame presumes that humans have a sovereign consciousness, universal morality, and uniform human reaction to atrocity, which will lead said subject de facto if not de jure to use any legal and economic forces to assuage human suffering. This assumption neglects to consider

[5]Here the debates on whether seeing atrocities leads to action, moral repugnance, or merely habituates humans to death as another form of entertainment are instructive. Susan Sontag's *Regarding the Pain of Others* (2004) and Tom Keenan's work (2003) remain the most provocative, if depressing, analyses of these debates. Let me be clear: atrocities should not be forgotten or left in the darkness of a faraway prison, torture chamber, or rural village; nevertheless, the revelation of atrocities does not, in itself, provide for the possibility of justice. The virtual absence of outrage or communal repugnance at the Abu Ghraib photos, except from the usual suspects on the left, serves as recent evidence that torture can be normalized or accepted as an unfortunate side-effect of a utilitarian need. Indeed, the fact that terms such as *torture porn* emerge as subgenres in film for the *Saw* movie series, and the Abu Ghraib photos themselves shows that human degradation can be a form of "infotainment."

the ethically repugnant but rational argument of atrocity committers lacking shame and basking in the media glow of their "15 min of fame."[6]

Human rights advocates have been forced to acknowledge that the cozy relationship with powerful militaries has resulted in humanitarian interventions using the language of rights to justify neocolonial projects and often intensify human suffering. According to Kennedy (2004), reliance on the fetishization of action in using large militaries for good or just causes fails to consider the ramifications of these proliferating humanitarian structures. He contends that they can become their own self-legitimating bureaucracies without consideration for actual human suffering. The humanitarian structure, thereby, regularizes the relationship of war and law and can police the human.

As I described above, human rights, which operate as the embodiment of a free human subject, are equated with property rights. These rights are secured only with the protection of property by powerful state actors, such as the U.S. military. Nevertheless, both the U.S. military and nonstate actors, including the privatized military mercenaries to whom the United States outsources conflicts, may also lay claim to human rights protections in engaging in humanitarian invasions, for noble or imperial reasons.

While human rights laws try to alleviate human suffering and provide the conditions of possibility for oppressed peoples to seek legal redress by extending legal structures, they also create through lawfare the legal architecture and subjectivities of those exceptions to equal protection. Ironically, state actors, those viewed as legitimate in international law and who can monopolize force to enforce rights, are themselves undermined by these procedures of lawfare because they must now compete with other nonstate actors, including corporations and privatized armies and militias, which render the lines of legitimate and illegitimate, "good and bad," force-permeable. The creation of new legal subjectivities and identities within positive law, as well as forms of human life outside them, have been readily used by the U.S. legal teams and military in its endless "war on terror."

War on Terror and Lawfare

The "war on terror" and the wars in Afghanistan and Iraq demonstrate a strategic mixing of the *jus ad bellum* and the *jus in bello*. Indeed, the George W. Bush regime extended certain humanitarian goals begun under the Clinton administration to more horrific ends after September 11, 2001. Legal precedents multiply figures and

[6] "With a simple gesture of the hand, not simply cynical or ironic, not simply nihilistic, no matter how destructive, these policemen announced the effective erasure of the fundamental axiom of the human rights movement in an age of publicity: that the exposure of violence is feared by the perpetrators, and hence that act of witness is not simply an ethical gesture but an active intervention. Mobilizing shame presupposes that dark deeds are done in the dark, and that the light of publicity – especially the television camera – thus has the power to strike preemptively on behalf of justice. With a wave, these policemen announced their comfort with the camera, their knowledge of the actual power of truth and representation" (Keenan, p. 215).

subjectivities of inclusion within human rights law due to the purported "givenness" of the human species, but the "war on terror" shows the human status both within and outside the legal system. This section will explore whether changing concepts of the human may be as important for thinking human rights as the legal category of rights.[7]

The transcendent model of international law upheld by the statements and principles of the Articles of the United Nations Charter forbids the use of force across borders except:

1. When approved by nine members of the Security Council;
2. When the right to self-defense is evoked;
3. When customary rules, treaties, and formalized *jus cogens* rules (nontreaty rules that have achieved "preemptory" character including genocide, slavery, torture, and use of force) are deployed (Byers 2005).

The numerous exceptions to these covenants, especially by Security Council members, indicate that the categories of universal justice and rights, even if perpetually extended, do not protect humans unless they can connect to a sovereign power to enforce them.

More and more conflicts today lack the previously followed distinctions of international armed conflict that we see in *jus in bello* legal rubrics because of the proliferation of nonstate actors, and because most wars now are discontinuous (marked by periods of direct military engagement and then policing actions). In other words, many current wars do not follow the prolonged sense of protracted wars between states, resulting in a treaty to end hostilities, but a perpetual state of war with sporadic incidents of the use of force. So, there has been a shift to policing actions rather than a diminishment of atrocity or human suffering due to fewer declared wars as Berman (2004) indicated. In the realm of lawfare, the rules, norms, and laws for state actors may be used to limit what are deemed legitimate and illegitimate networks of force and to determine which norms establish who can be considered a legal party. In sum, these decisions determine the limits of political agents and ultimately police the human and individual rights to decide who will be recognized as a subject and subjected to the law.

The war on terror effectively highlights the Unites States' simultaneous deployment of several legal categories, types of law, as well as their limits in order to police the human. The distinction between whether a particular intervention is an armed conflict, and is thereby subject to war protections, or not a war is a major stratagem states orchestrate to avoid culpability. States complicate matters by exploiting the characteristics between a state of war and a state of peace because they are based on identifying and classifying the actors.

As critical theorists Giorgio Agamben (2005), Jacques Derrida (2004), and Human Rights Watch director Kenneth Roth (2004) have argued, the war on terror has literalized war as no longer being a state of exception, but the rule. In sum, what began as a metaphor for a policing action became the means for legitimating wars globally.

---

[7] I argue this point more elaborately in my book, *The Ahuman: Thinking Beyond the Global Human.*

Roth focuses on the Bush legal team's claim that the war on terror is a preemptive effort at self-defense, one of the UN's recognized stipulations for war. Indeed, before the formal declaration of war, law enforcement rules offer protections for individual rights, including due process protections. The International Committee of the Red Cross advocates that enforcement rules take precedent, and a state of war should not be declared unless the hostilities are "intense," there is a political motive, and those being tried for crimes are major participants in the hostilities. However, as Roth puts it, the simultaneous ambiguity of these classifications and the strategic use of these categories by the United States has rendered criminals and those protected by international criminal law as warriors or combatants, and thereby subject to the more permissive laws of war. If a state actor initiates conflict, the use of international criminal law instead of war law could kick in, precisely to process these "criminal" figures as subjects of law, who have committed vile crimes against humanity and need to be punished or reformed. For example, during the Bush regime the United States acknowledged the importance of the Geneva Conventions, particularly for its own troops, but then employed legal categories to claim that the people it held were "enemy combatants" who were not subject to the Geneva Conventions. At the same time, it used humanitarian law's right to self-defense for a pre-emptive strike to legitimatize the invasion of Iraq.

In the war/not-war instance, it is terribly important to mark the distinction between combatants and noncombatants who are protected by war law, instead of international criminal law. I will not enter into the multidimensional complexities of criminal law, but virtually any agent who has defied a rule or law and has some party willing to prosecute these "crimes" can be criminalized, including individuals who are citizens of state actors and subject to criminal law.

Nevertheless, because the categorization of a combatant in the wake of the decolonization movements and the creation of the 1949 Geneva Conventions and the Nuremberg trials, the role of nonstate actors has increasingly become recognized even by war law (Berman 2004). These follow some of the statements outlined by Krishna Menon, the Indian Defense Minister in the early 1960s, which allowed for anticolonial struggles and national independence movements to be recognized legally, leading eventually to Additional Protocol 1 of 1977. The proliferation of nonstate actors, particularly in the wake of the decolonization movements after World War II, created a set of actors who in their struggles for self-determination could not declare war because they lacked a recognized government. Menon's efforts were in part to challenge colonial powers' usage of human rights during the Cold War to avoid any guidelines during hostilities with decolonizing forces, and to challenge the colonial powers' practice of destroying whatever infrastructure or provisions (Article 56) were in place to decimate the decolonizing power.

According to Berman, "Menon's formulation, intended to provide *jus ad bellum* legitimacy for recourse to force at any time by the colonized, could also bring a wide range of actions by both colonizers and colonizer under the *jus in bello* for the duration of colonization.... One could easily imagine anticolonial activities claiming that the colonizers should not be able to invoke *jus in bello* to justify repressive actions that should be handled under 'normal' law restricting 'police' actions"

(2004, p. 28). In other words, Menon's argument, which was made initially to foster the self-determination of certain peoples, may also lead to more and more policing actors (including paramilitary organizations), regardless of their connection to particular states.

What Menon's argument and lawfare also highlight, however, is that more and more "armed conflicts" take place as policing actions without formal declarations of war. Policing actions, bureaucracy, and administrative law all work by establishing norms that carry the force of law as the primary mechanism for maintaining the security of populations by normalizing them; they police them due to pervasive threats to the body politic. And due to the proliferation of nonstate actors, policing actions proliferate by both fully actualized states (such as the armed excursions in Grenada) or the privatized military organizations of Blackwater and DynCorp, which follow a different set of control dynamics than calls to justice. To avoid possible human rights violations in the war on terror, the United States has deployed certain private military companies, which need not follow the same Uniform Code of Military Justice (Singer 2003). Human rights must deal with changing concepts of sovereignty so important to maintain a rule of law for recognizing and potentially honoring treaties and to designate a combatant and a civilian beyond a simple colonial worldview.

The war on terror exploits the fluid distinction between aggressors and peacekeepers (or restorers of order). The distinction between aggressors and peacekeepers frequently entails factual, immanent, and episodic judgments, rather than a claim to a transcendent authority or body, regardless of the International Criminal Court. We see this especially between the United States and al-Qaeda since the 2003 invasion of Iraq, where lawfare has taken on its central status. Al-Qaeda is not a legitimate state actor because it does not control a nation-state and has no legal claims to territoriality as it is not a government in control of a territory. Indeed, the pervasiveness of al-Qaeda in Iraq, where before the invasion there was no substantive al-Qaeda population, shows that the organization is itself more like a franchise or military construction than a unified sovereign entity. Yet, the United States claims that it needs to perpetuate its presence in Iraq precisely to defend U.S. citizens ("fight the terrorists abroad so that they do not come here") and purportedly Iraqi lovers of freedom from the terrorists in their midst. The former aggression to remove the "criminal" Saddam Hussein having ended with his capture and death sentence, has extended because the aggressor force is now a peacekeeping operation, maintaining order until a legitimate government that can lay claim to an extended space of territory is able to consolidate itself. After 6 years, this still seems elusive despite the United States' evacuation of the Green Zone; the war on terror continues in Iraq and intensifies in Afghanistan where pursuing terrorists seems to fulfill both peacekeeping and "hunting down aggressors" functions.

Lawfare has created a situation whereby the rules of engagement and legitimization for war claim a democratic rationale and often market their own means and ends as freedom. The very mechanisms for changing the law to protect human rights can be used to throw more and more people into the condition of statelessness. By the same token in the lawfare realm, if NGOs had access to vast swathes of money, they theoretically could cut out the middlemen of nation-states and hire privatized militias to engage in the process of peacekeeping or intervention. Indeed, this may be a future possibility for sovereign states as the United States privatizes vast swathes of its public sphere including the military, and this might lead to some dramatic reconceptualization of how human rights operate and who is subject to and subjected by the law.

The war on terror uses human rights as a mechanism to justify penetrating the sovereignty of nation-states to, for example, free populations in Iraq or oppressed women in Afghanistan by bringing more places into "the civilized world." In the process, decisions on who is human and who is not are made. At the same time, maintaining the integrity of sovereignty can be invoked to create legal policies such as "extraordinary rendition" or to deny *habeus corpus* statutes to those in Guantanamo Bay who are considered to be combatants and who, in effect, have been rendered stateless. They may no longer have the natural rights justifications of being human. Human rights and humanitarian law can serve the political function of a sovereign state, such as the United States – despite its own Constitution – or the media fiction known as the so-called "international community," in order to police which particular humans are to be recognized as stateless or normatively human.

Cultural Programming

Given all these legal conundrums and statelessness, it is not surprising that the desire has emerged for some agent to keep things together to protect universal humanity. The UN system does provide an interesting attempt to do so, even if according to Michel Feher's argument (2000), it is "powerless by design," because individual states will always put their own self-interests before the abstraction of universal humanity. More dangerously, the heinous incarnations of civilizational discourse deployed by political realists, like Samuel Huntington's "clash of civilizations" (2004) and the neoconservative idealism of what the Bush administration called "freedom-loving people," demonstrate how easily racial, ethnic, and cultural hatred in Bosnia, Rwanda, Kosovo, Iraq, and among minorities and immigrants to the US can be mobilized through the free-floating concepts of "civilization," "culture," and "freedom."

Civilizational discourse relies, nonetheless, on the ground of culture, as well as the "givenness" of cultural difference as the mode for organizing life and human multiplicities. In other words, Huntington uses the discourse of cultural difference in order to justify the collapsing of difference between, I think, two poles, the human and the nonhuman, or what used to be called the civilized and the barbarian. Huntington deploys the language of lawfare to justify the policing of the human within normative, albeit reductive, cultural categories and practices that substitute for political and legal categories. While generalized cultural arguments about law, politics, and human rights usually fall apart upon any intellectual or historical reflection, they do show how the process of establishing norms can be used for the most oppressive forces, as exemplified by the Bush administration's distinction between war and not-war. This norm production needs to be addressed by human rights activists who argue for rights from below and around cultural identity (constructivism), as we see powerful factions in sovereign states making the same claims as the dispossessed.

The concept of culture as a form of programming has historically been a useful tool of the nation-state to organize and arrange life within intelligible patterns. Nevertheless, the nation-state is in open competition with other forces of capital and power for monopolizing force in organizing collectivities and pluralistic societies. In Samuel Huntington's *Clash of Civilizations* (1993), he describes a series of cultural and religious blocs: Western, Islamic, Orthodox, Latin American, African, Sinic, Buddhist, Hindu, and Japanese. To make this argument, he celebrates human cultural difference, but regionalizes religion and culture at a geographical level, evoking perhaps economic trading blocs.[8] The historical struggles of capitalism versus communism, power between sovereign nation-states, rich and poor, colonialism and decolonization, freedom and unfreedom, are emptied of power and instead will be organized at the local or regional level of "cultures" and "civilizations."

Huntington stages global Hobbesian culture wars through his clash of civilizations. These will in many ways determine what civilizations will persevere amidst these "wars of all against all," culminating in a "state of culture," rather than a "state of nature." According to Huntington, politics and states no longer matter because cultures are de facto states at a regional level. His analysis utilizes a Francis Fukuyama/Daniel Bell political ideology argument and the rise of general culturalism to indicate that only

[8]His text appeared at a moment of emerging bourgeoisies throughout East Asia and the Middle East, and, I would contend, competing methods of economic development. Indeed, the rise of East Asian economies – what the World Bank called the East Asian miracle in 1993 – was based on strong interventionist states that would frequently use import substitution methods, aka protectionism, in order to protect emerging local industries (Krugman 1997). Their success flew in the face of the dominant faith in Milton Friedman's and Friedrich Hayek's concept of neoliberal economics. However, rather than indicate Keynesian economic policies throughout the region in the 1990s, Senior Minister Lee Kuan Yew and Mohathir Mohammed of Malaysia argued that Confucian capitalism and cultural legitimations were responsible for their economic success. Cultural explanations played well for controlling their own populations in nations with authoritarian rulers in Singapore, Malaysia, and China who seemingly might argue for greater political and legal rights, including human rights. Culturalism seemed a strategic way to include parts of Communist China into this sphere, which was heavily controlled by an authoritarian state in disciplining workers, while capital flowed freely as it embraced neoliberal economics initially through Special Economic Zones, Hong Kong, and later the country (Harvey, 2007; Klein, 2007). (Huntington included Sinic culture to take account of Singapore, though the large Muslim population in Malaysia left it out despite Mahathir's argument.) This pre-emptive cultural argument, in many ways, used cultural nationalism, to forestall any inchoate domestic political or legal reforms, as emerging middle classes might demand freedom beyond the purely economic sphere. At the same time, it provided a wedge for the United States to deploy human rights discourses to mask economic protectionism in trade relations with China and maintain the neoliberal status quo.

Western European culture (thereby excluding Russia, Eastern Orthodox Christianity, and all Slavs) has a universal commitment to freedom and the rule of law. Cultures cannot possibly coexist within specific territories because of Huntington's biologism and social Darwinism – natural selection read through culture. Politics and statecraft are thereby eliminated in light of a "cultural struggle for existence," which emerges due to finite resources and a Malthusian fear of population flows.

As a result, Huntington contends that the West and its theories of human rights and democracy will need to revitalize itself if it is to save its political legacy from extinction by vanquishing those who threaten it. These cultural attributes are both abstract enabling fictions (liberty, equality) and legal ones of democracy, rights, and rule of law. In short, the "culture of the West" for Huntington will have a unique legal status due to its universalism in relationship to the rest of the cultural blocs.

Western ideas of individualism, liberalism, constitutionalism, human rights, equality, liberty, the rule of law, democracy, free markets, the separation of church and state, often have little resonance in Islamic, Confucian, Japanese, Hindu, Buddhist or Orthodox cultures. Western efforts to propagate such ideas produce instead a reaction against "human rights imperialism" and a reaffirmation of indigenous values, as can be seen in the support for religious fundamentalism by the younger generation in non-Western cultures (1993, pp. 40–41).

"Liberty, equality, democracy, civil rights, nondiscrimination, rule of law" are reconfigured for Huntington as European localisms that can no longer conceive themselves as universal: they are culturally determined legal categories rather than political legal categories. The only possibility will be perpetual war, both to consolidate the cultural blocs and to retain the West's identity through its particularist concerns of human rights. As a result, competing cultural blocs of China and Islam are precisely the sites of future warfare: cultural, legal, epistemological, and, ultimately, where force and possible lawfare will be used in the name of human rights. In short, Huntington transposes *realpolitik* political and legal formations to the stuff of culture and suggests that lawfare becomes merely the legitimating tool.[9]

For Huntington, religious or cultural nationalisms seemingly are the greatest threat to the integrity of universal values that would include the principles on which human rights are founded. His arguments (1993, 2004) are tautological and paradoxical: he claims that the primary impetus of world politics will no longer be driven by universal economic, political, or ideological attempts to speak for humanity. In sum, there can no universal humanity on which human rights are based except in those Western spheres of influence because there is no universal concept of the species. Consequently, the normative political and legal structures that human

---

[9]Huntington's cultural zero-sum game, a clash of civilizations through competing cultural dominants leads to the West needing to shore up its culture even as it faces assault from other cultures within its own geographical borders. Huntington's final book, *Who Are We? The Challenges to America's National Identity* (2004), describes the "dangers" of multiculturalism and unmitigated and unassimilated immigrants and sees the clash of civilizations on U.S. territory.

rights advocates argue for will not work outside of the Western European echo chamber because of cultural differences and the focus on cultural values outside of the West.

With extraordinary oversimplification and generalization, Huntington portrays no political or legal rubrics other than cultural values and norms; the only commonality between cultures can happen in the global market. It is surprising how his generalist culturalist claims are taken seriously, particularly given his reductive concepts of culture, based on geographical blocs, reducing cultural complexity and human difference to a set of quantifiable values dominated by religion and geographical values.

Huntington's replacement of nature by culture for the ontology of the human provides, however, an interesting conundrum for natural rights. Human rights are conferred to humans by the pure fact of their existence; culture is destiny. Huntington's creation of reductive cultural blocs shows how easy it is to establish normative processes with a legal basis and accountability, the very procedure that human rights implement. The Bush administration's actions during the war on terror provide further evidence of how instituted norms may always struggle for universal acceptance even if they are applied widely by different, often opposing, powers. In neocolonial fashion, Huntington and Bush conclude that the human is coterminous with Europe and the United States, so only these are worthy of conferring or protecting rights. In sum, we have a particularist normative concept of the human vying for universal status, which uses human rights discourse in order to police its concepts of the human.

While these claims are, of course, historically dubious, they can take on a normative status and create the self-fulfilling prophecy that Huntington diagnoses with other cultures needing to create competing concepts of the human in religion or the economy rather than in the political. The danger of envisaging competing nonstate actors as civilizations that are devoid of any political force is a nightmare from which humanitarians would undoubtedly like to awaken. Yet, it also shows that conceiving of the human is a political act that should not be forgotten when advocates argue for human rights.

Let me conclude with a possible image of what lawfare, human rights, and humanitarianism could produce through an ironic design concept by philosopher Peter Sloterdijk, and designer Gesa Mueller von der Haegen (2005). Their German/American joint venture, "Instant Democracy, the Pneumatic Parliament," provides an interesting critical commentary on the synergy of humanitarian structures, market desires, and how the law of universal claims to human rights can be exercised far from any concepts of justice. The Pneumatic Parliament is a registered design concept to market the "architectonic prerequisites" for a democracy to come "after liberation" from the forces of tyranny that currently rule sovereign territories. With help from the U.S. Air Force and an unwavering faith in "high technology" as an end in itself, democratic structures will be air-dropped into "'sponsors of international terrorism' (Libya, Iran, Cuba, North Korea, Sudan) or former 'outposts of tyranny' (Belarus, Zimbabwe, Myanmar)...[to begin] work on 'Instant Democracy.'" Sloterdijk adds: "A further target group of customers are the so-called 'failed states,' countries whose own attempts to democratize have failed, but now with 'democratization from the top-down' get a second chance to erect a proper state system" (2005, p. 952).[10] Countries "newly liberated" by the humanitarian presence of the U.S. Army or those future 80–100 "failed states" "targeted" to join what Sloterdijk (2005) following Huntington (1993, 2004) ironically calls the universal "Community of Values" can benefit from the technical expertise of the United States. The air can also be colored to emphasize the mood of the country, simultaneously using local knowledge to "make… a contribution to spreading the political culture of the west" (Sloterdijk and von der Haegen 2005, p. 952).[11]

Sloteridjk's Pneumatic Parliament provides a corollary to rethink the policing function of space and the normative regimes of Enlightenment political concepts to create newly emergent "sovereign subjects" and give them "the choice" of humanity through markets and human rights, underwritten by Kantian ethics. His ironic commentary may be instructive for thinking about the instrumentalization of human rights and Huntington's blocs of cultural normative structures (1993) that could affect the very concept of humanity. Sloterdijk also highlights the market's capacity to turn human rights and democracy into commodities in what Oliver Wendell Holmes called in a differing context the "marketplace of ideas"; perhaps lawfare could expedite the efficiency of turning human rights into a marketing slogan or a lot of hot air.

References

Agamben, G. (2005). *State of Exception* (K. Attell, Trans.). Chicago: University of Chicago Press.

Armstrong, N. (1990). *Desire and Domestic Fiction: A Political History of the Novel*. New York: Oxford University Press.

Baxi, U. (2008). *The Future of Rights*. Oxford: Oxford University Press.

Berman, N. (2004). Privileging combat? Contemporary conflict and the legal construction of war. *Colum. J. Transnat'l L.* **43**(1), 1–71.

Brown, W. (2004). The most we can hope for: Human rights and the politics of fatalism. *S. Atl. Quart.* **103**(2/3), 451–463.

Byers, M. (2005). *War Law: Understanding International Law and Armed Conflict*. New York: Grove.

Derrida, J. (2004). *Rogues: Two Essays on Reason* (M. Naas, Trans.). Stanford, CA: Stanford University Press.

[10] The design concept was originally broadcast at the Center for Art and Media, Karlsruhe. For a representation of the Pneumatic Parliament, see http://www.g-i-o.com/pp5.htm

[11] Pneumatic logic is a reliable and functional control method for industrial processes. In recent years these systems have largely been replaced by electrical control systems, due to the size of the logic units and the cost versus their electrical counterparts. They are still in use in processes where compressed air is the only energy source available or where the cost, safety, and other considerations outweigh the advantage of modern digital control.

Feher, M. (2000). *Powerless by Design: The Age of the International Community*. Durham, NC: Duke University Press.
Grotius, H. (2009). *On the Law of War and Peace*. Ithaca, NY: Ithaca University Press. (Originally published 1625).
Gutmann, A. (2003). Introduction. In: A. Gutmann (Ed.), *Human Rights As Politics and Idolatry by Michael Ignatieff*. Princeton, NJ: Princeton University Press.
Harvey, D. (2007). *A Brief History of Neoliberalism*. Oxford: Oxford University Press.
Natural law. In: *Law.com Dictionary*. Retrieved from http://dictionary.law.com/Default.aspx?selected=1307.
Huntington, S. (1993). The clash of civilizations. *Foreign Aff.* **72**(3), 22–49.
Huntington, S. (2004). *Who Are We? The Challenges to America's Identity*. New York: Simon & Schuster.
Ignatieff, M. (2003). Human rights, sovereignty and intervention. In: N. Owen (Ed.), *Human Rights, Human Wrongs*, Oxford: Oxford University Press, pp. 49–88.
Keenan, T. (2003). Mobilizing shame. In: E. Cadava & A. Levy (Eds.), *Cities Without Citizens*, Philadelphia, PA: Slought Foundation, pp. 201–218.
Kennedy, D. (2002). The critique of rights in critical legal studies. In: W. Brown & J. Halley (Eds.), *Legalism/Left Critique*, Durham, NC: Duke University Press, pp. 178–228.
Kennedy, D. (2004). *The Dark Sides of Virtue: Reassessing International Humanitarianism*. Princeton, NJ: Princeton University Press.
Kennedy, D. (2006). *Of War and Law*. Princeton, NJ: Princeton University Press.
Klein, N. (2007). *The Shock Doctrine: The Rise of Disaster Capitalism*. New York: Metropolitan Books.
Krugman, P. (1997). *Pop Internationalism*. Cambridge, MA: MIT.
Mertus, J.A. (2004). *Bait and Switch: Human Rights and U.S. Foreign Policy*. New York: Routledge.
Moretti, F. (2007). *The Novel 1: History, Geography, and Culture*. Princeton: Princeton University Press.
Power, S. (2002). *A Problem from Hell: America and the Age of Genocide*. New York: Basic Books.
Roth, K. (2004). The law of war and the war on terror. *Foreign Affairs* (January/February 2004). Retrieved from http://www.Foreignaffairs.com/articles/59524/Kenneth-roth/the-law-of-war-in-the-war-on-terror.
Singer, P.W. (2003). *Corporate Warriors*. Ithaca, NY: Cornell University Press.
Slaughter, J.R. (2008). *Human Rights, Inc.: The World Novel, Narrative Form, And International Law*. New York: Fordham University Press.
Sontag, S. (2004). *Regarding the Pain of Others*. New York: Picador.
Sloterdijk, P. & von der Haegen, G.M. (2005). Instant democracy: The pneumatic parliament. In: B. Latour & P. Weibel (Eds.), *Making Things Public: Atmospheres of Democracy*, Cambridge, MA: MIT, pp. 952–957.

The Big Chill: First Amendment Protections and the War on Terror

Martin Wallenstein

Introduction

The debate over how the criminal justice system in the United States should deal with the terrorist threat is best understood when viewed in the light of Herb Packer's (1968) notion about the dynamic tension between advocates of crime control and advocates of civil liberties. Perhaps nothing widens the ideological divide between crime control advocates and civil liberties advocates as dramatically as discussion of the "war on terrorism." The very language used is open to question. The definition of *terrorism* is amorphous. Moreover, acceptance of the war metaphor holds implications for public policy.

Packer's Model

Packer claims that crime control advocates want to see the criminal justice system operate as an efficient factory, while civil liberties advocates want to put strong quality-control measures in place keep the running of that system in check. Crime control advocates, according to Packer, see the greatest threat to our nation as coming from law-breakers and therefore generally trust governmental institutions, while civil liberties advocates see the greatest threat to the country in unchecked governmental power (1968, pp. 154–173; Kaplan et al. 1991, pp. 130–140). Those advocating crime control are not necessarily against civil liberties. They simply value crime control more. Likewise, civil liberties advocates are not pro-crime. They simply are unwilling to allow what they view as unreasonable encroachments on civil liberties in order to stop it.

M. Wallenstein (✉)
Department of Communications and Theater, John Jay College of Criminal Justice, New York, NY, USA
e-mail: mwallenstein@jjay.cuny.edu

G. Andreopoulos et al. (eds.), *International Criminal Justice: Critical Perspectives and New Challenges*, DOI 10.1007/978-1-4419-1102-5_4,
© Springer Science+Business Media, LLC 2011

Purpose

This chapter attempts to explore the effect of the war on terror on the balance between coping with the terrorist threat and preserving First Amendment rights.

Method

Herb Packer's paradigm of the "crime control" and "civil liberties" models is applied to a humanistic exploration of the tensions created by our choices in the war on terror.

Implications in Revamping Criminal Justice Systems to Fight Terror

The criminal justice system is not set up to deal effectively with the prospective threat that terrorism poses. Crime control advocates have pushed successfully for changes in the system to facilitate control and capture of terrorists. These changes have challenged traditional notions of civil liberties in areas both important and diverse. Free speech, free press, free assembly, *habeas corpus*, speedy trial, accepted notions about right to counsel, the nature of reasonable interrogation, search and seizure, and even accepted notions about burden of proof in criminal proceedings – have all come into play. New techniques and technologies at the disposal of terrorists and at the disposal of governments for fighting terrorism have both been evolving, and these have made the issues both more important and more complex.

In the end, the greatest terrorist threat may be its potential to provoke governments to respond by curtailing the very civil liberties that governments are charged with protecting.

The Shock! The Horror!

It was a day we will never forget. The proudest building of a proud city lay in rubble, the people inside it buried alive and presumed dead. The feeling of invulnerability was gone forever. The grief was unimaginable. That so many innocent Americans could be killed by one callous and deliberate act of destruction was an unthinkable horror. From the first there was suspicion of Arab extremists being responsible. After all, they had tried it before.

No, this was not September 11, 2001. This was the April 19, 1995, bombing of the Oklahoma City Federal Building, and the terrorists were homegrown and not Muslim. Indeed, domestic terrorism goes back a lot further than that. The early labor movement in this country had an extremely bloody history, with management bringing in "scabs" to do the jobs of striking workers, while hired thugs beat up and intimidated strikers. Labor struck back, sometimes violently. At the turn of the twentieth century, it was anarchists who were the object of fear. They were replaced in the following decades by communists. In each case, there were mass arrests and a trampling of civil liberties.

While international terrorism is relatively new to the United States, we have had plenty of our own terrorist organizations representing both the right and the left. The Ku Klux Klan, The Order, Aryan Nations, and Arizona Patriots. These groups have tended to be right-wing anti-communist Christian organizations, and they have usually targeted federal law enforcement agencies and racial or religious groups. Left-wing terrorist groups in America have include the Symbionese Liberation Front (SLA), the Weathermen, and the Black Panthers. These groups flourished in the 1960s and early 1970s. They tended to be opposed to capitalism as a political/economic system. They targeted seats of capitalism and government buildings.

The point here is that terrorist incidents only appear unique, when in truth they are part of a long history. Yet it is the apparent uniqueness of the threat at a particular time and place that crime control advocates use to argue for a temporary rollback of civil liberties. They argue that we must curtail free speech in the time of crisis. Civil libertarians, on the other hand, argue that a war on terror will in fact be a war without end.

Defining Terrorism

When the Red Coats were being shot at by colonists from behind trees, and when the people of Boston protested the tax on tea by throwing boxes of tea into Boston Harbor, the British would probably have labeled them as terrorists. South Africa jailed advocates against apartheid, such as Nelson Mandela, and they were labeled terrorists as well. The Taliban do not consider themselves terrorists. Osama Bin Laden considers himself a "freedom fighter." A Pakistani religious party wanted Michael Jackson and Madonna tried as terrorists because "they are the torch bearers of American society" and "the cultural and social values" that they encourage "are destroying humanity" (Snowden & Whitsel 2005, p. 188). In fact, there is no internationally accepted definition of terrorism, but the U.S. Code, Title 22 Section 2656, defines terrorism as "premeditated politically motivated violence perpetrated against noncombatant targets by sub-national groups or clandestine agents, usually intended to influence an audience."

Terrorism and Burdens of Proof

Benjamin Franklin once said: "Better that a hundred guilty men go free than that one innocent man languish in prison." When one changes this to, "Better that a hundred World Trade Center bombers go free than that one innocent man languish in prison," it has a much different response. That changes the equation (Simondsen & Spindlove 2004).

Crime control advocates argue that technology has raised the stakes too high to let things stay as they are. Bioterrorism (such as anthrax or smallpox), "dirty bombs" which spread radioactive material, and even nuclear weapons (not to mention risks such as poisoning the water supply or destroying a port or shutting down the electricity to a region or the Internet to the entire country) are threats too big to risk. The civil liberties equation needs to be changed. Simondsen and Spindlove (2004, pp. 407–435) give a chilling list of horrible possibilities. A graduate student in criminal justice said of the possibility of individuals being wrongfully convicted, that if the burden of proof shifts to make it easier to convict terrorists, "They [the wrongfully convicted] just have to take one for the team."

Civil liberties advocates point out that one of the worst forms of terrorism is state-sponsored terrorism and that this often starts with governments grabbing power to deal with alleged terrorist threats. For example, the Nazis came to power by burning down the building that housed the German legislature, and blaming it on the communists. The Chinese crackdown in Tiananmen Square was supposedly for the purpose of restoring order. Norman Abrams (November 2006, November 1) discusses concerns about failures to protect civil liberties by courts, legislatures, and the executive branches in the war on terror.

This subtle shift in the relative burden of proof cannot help but chill expression of radical ideas. No person wishes to be branded an inciter to riot or a terrorist conspirator/recruiter, when the burden shifts to the accused to prove himself not guilty.

Is the Criminal Justice System Set Up to Deal with Terrorism?

There are several factors in the workings of the criminal justice system that make it less than ideal for dealing with terrorist threats. Unfortunately, changing the system to make it better suited to fight terror may seriously impact free expression.

1. The criminal justice system is designed to be reactive rather than proactive.
2. The criminal justice system relies on respect for law to deter criminal behavior by law-abiding citizens.
3. The criminal justice system's deterrence is based on the assumption that the criminal will change behavior to avoid being punished.
4. The criminal justice system is based on the assumption that seeing people punished will likely deter others from crime.

Let us go back to the first assumption: the criminal justice system is designed to be *reactive* rather than proactive. We do not punish before crimes happen. We do not throw people in jail because we think that they *would* commit a crime. The whole machinery of the criminal justice system kicks into gear only after a crime has been committed. In England, Tony Blair proposed a law making it illegal to advocate terrorism. The First Amendment clearly prohibits that kind of a law unless one can show that the person doing the advocating has created an *imminent threat* and that there is no way to deal with it that abridges freedom of expression less than the one proposed.

Many look at terrorist acts and say this is too late. We need to be proactive and not reactive. We must take action before the damage is done. The goal of the terrorist is to do the terrorist act, not necessarily to get away with having done that act. Does the suicide bomber or hijacker care what happens after she explodes the bomb or after he's crashed the plane? Can we stop terrorism in the act before the damage is done? Those who say yes point to the fact that no major attacks have succeeded in the United States since September 11, 2001. They point to foiled attempts at airport and airplane bombings, and the attempt to destroy the Brooklyn Bridge, each plan stopped before it could accomplish its destruction.

Arrest for Future Crime: *Minority Report* Redux

In the 2002 movie *Minority Report*, and in the short story by Philip Dick (1956) upon which it was based, people were arrested for future crimes that they might commit. This would certainly help to solve the problem that a reactive criminal justice system holds. While this was a work of science fiction, we might not be as far from this as you might think.

On September 25, 2007, on the BBC World Service program *Newshour*, Neil Bowdler reported that the U.S. Department of Homeland Security is hoping to set up scans in airports and other public places equipped with new technology for sensing hostile intent of potential attackers – newly developed computer software that can measure something called "micro-expressions." These are facial expressions that are too fleeting to be registered by the naked eye, but which can be detected by computers that can "sense" emotions such as anger or hostility. So people who registered the wrong emotions on the sensors in the ticket line might be singled out for preventative arrest before evidence of any criminal activity.

The potential First Amendment and due process issues raised by arrest for *potential* crimes, if this policy were ever implemented, should keep scholars in several disciplines busy for a long time! Crime control advocates anticipate this as a major breakthrough, while civil liberties advocates view it as a major break with the requirement of probable cause for arrest.

First Amendment Guarantees

The First Amendment states: "Congress shall make no law respecting an establishment of religion, or prohibiting the free exercise thereof; or abridging the freedom of speech, or of the press; or the right of the people peaceably to assemble, and to petition the Government for a redress of grievances."

The New York Times reported that in 2002 the New York Police Department (NYPD) had used pre-emptive arrests to prevent rioting during the World Economic Forum held in New York, as well as in 2004 during the Republican National Convention. During the Republican National Convention, thousands of protesters were arrested. So many people were arrested that they were warehoused in, well, converted warehouses turned into makeshift jails. Arraignment in New York is supposed to take place within 24 h. These people, however, were deliberately detained for days until after the convention had adjourned. The courts threw out thousands of these cases.

Crime control advocates say "So what?" This is a small price to pay when compared to the worst of the risks of a terrorist attack. According to the civil liberties advocates (and the protesters who sued the City of New York for these illegal detentions) the "what" is that this is a direct violation of the First Amendment guarantees of free speech, free press, and the right to free assembly for redress of grievances. They say that these rights go directly to whether we have a true democracy or a repressive regime where protest is not tolerated.

Academic Freedom for Foreign Nationals

Diminished academic freedom for foreign nationals is inextricably tied to this First Amendment issue. The big chill has already been placed upon foreign-born professors teaching in the United States. They might tell you that they feel constrained to be a lot more careful about what they say in class and in their writing now than they were before 9/11. Colleagues tell me that they will never openly express disagreement with the U.S. government because they fear that their status will be challenged and they will be forced to leave.

Their fears may not be irrational. The Nalini Ghuman case is illustrative (Bernstein 2007, September 17). Dr. Ghuman was a 34-year-old scholar from Oxford with a Ph.D. from the University of California at Berkeley who was teaching at Mills College. She had been living in this country for 10 years. Her mother was a British homemaker and her father an emeritus professor of Educational Psychology at the University of Wales. He was a Sikh from India who had lived in Britain for over 25 years. After a research trip to Britain, Dr. Ghuman returned to San Francisco airport on August 8, 2006. Airport security met her at the door of the plane and took her into custody for the next 8 h. They tore up her American visa (which was supposed to be valid until May 2008); they defaced her British passport; subjected her to a body search; and told her that if she moved during the search she would be considered to be attacking the armed female searcher, who she claimed was groping her. After hours of questioning, Dr. Ghuman was threatened with removal to a detention center unless she got back on a plane to Great Britain. She asked to speak with the British Consul. Her requests were denied. When the British Consul (who had been alerted to this situation by her fiancé) attempted to intervene, he was stonewalled.

In her own words: "They told me I was nobody, I was nowhere, and I had no rights.... For the first time I understood what the deprivation of liberty means" (Bernstein 2007, September 17, p. B5).

Perhaps it was that her scholarly interest posed a threat – although I have a hard time imagining how general musicology or her specific study of the British composer Sir Edward Elgar threatened national security. She was told that it could have been a poison pen letter from a jealous colleague or a jilted lover that set this in motion. More likely, it was what one of her guards told her – a simple mistake.

Dr. Ghuman's case became a cause in the musicology community. The president of the American Musicological Association protested her treatment and exclusion to the State Department; Mills College wrote on her behalf. There was an inquiry in the British Parliament; several U.S. congressmen and Senator Richard Durban of Illinois attempted to intercede on her behalf. But to this day, she has never been given an explanation – and to this day, she is still barred from returning to the United States and has been forced to take an unpaid leave from Mills.

Dr. Ghuman is not alone. There are other foreign national scholars who have been denied entry or re-entry into this country with no reason given. In fact, the American Civil Liberties Union claims that the government under the Bush administration repeatedly violated the First Amendment "by using heightened security measures to keep out foreign scholars with whose ideology it disagree[d]" (Bernstein 2007, September 17, p. B5).

Joined by the American Association of University Professors, the American Academy of Religion, and the PEN American Center, the American Civil Liberties Union has sued the government to allow Tariq Ramadan to enter the country to speak. Ramadan is a Muslim scholar who has been barred from entering the United States for 5 years (Schwartz 2009, March 18, p. A19).

While the current Obama administration has retreated from many of the Bush-era policies, it has not retreated from this one. The policy of censorship by exclusion of foreign nationals continues; they are still being refused entry into the United States based upon their political positions (Fischer 2009, April 24). This causes an incredible chill on expression even for those foreign nationals who have gained entry. As one foreign national said to this writer, as a result of this policy: "Oh, if anybody asks me, the United States is the greatest country in the world and it has no flaws. Yes, sir, no flaws – until my immigration status changes."

Let us examine the second point: the criminal justice system relies upon respect for law to deter criminal behavior. When legendary FBI agent Eliot Ness was asked what he would do if Prohibition was repealed, his answer was that he would get a drink. The assumption is that individuals who respect the law will not engage in unlawful behavior. However, the whole point of terrorism is to bring down the system for which the terrorist has no respect. When it comes to terrorism, the law becomes like the late comedian Rodney Dangerfield and "gets no respect."

Let us examine the third point. The criminal justice system's deterrence is based on the assumption that the criminal will change behavior to avoid being punished: *specific deterrence*. The terrorist who gets caught becomes a hero to those whom he cares about. He may not wish to be caught, but avoiding punishment is not his primary goal. He is inflicting damage on a system he despises. The terrorist is not an unprincipled weak-willed person or one with poor impulse control. The terrorist is a person on a mission. Zacarias Moussaoui could not wait to take the stand to brag about his role in the 9/11 attacks. Many claim that he took more credit than he had actually earned. Others say most terrorists don't want to go to jail; most don't want to be martyrs; the criminal justice system will deter potential terrorists. Nevertheless, this perceived ineffectiveness of specific deterrence may contribute to the desire for secret trials.

Let us examine the fourth point: the criminal justice system is based on the assumption that seeing people punished will likely deter them from crime: *general deterrence*. If seeing the terrorist put to death makes him a martyr and thus inspires two terrorists to take the place of the one that you have caught, then this is not going to be a very effective deterrent. Still, advocates of general deterrence say that the jailed or dead terrorist might be admired, but not many will want to step forward into his shoes. In short, the effectiveness of this policy is a big question mark.

How Should Courts React to Terrorism?

There are two theories about how courts should react to terrorism, war, or any threat. The crime control approach says that when the country is in peril, we ought to be willing to subordinate our rights and liberties. The Constitution, after all, was never intended to be a suicide pact. If the country goes down in flames, its borders are invaded, its economy is wrecked, its people are sickened from bio-terrorism (anthrax or smallpox) – what good is the Constitution then?

The civil liberties advocates would say just the opposite. In times of crisis or peril, they argue, the courts must be even more vigilant. What will we have saved if, in response to terrorism, we adapt to the methods and values of the terrorists. We will have destroyed everything that we were trying to save. When terrorists are able to get us to reject our basic values as embodied in the Bill of Rights, in many ways they may have already won. Certainly, we will have already lost.

So, which way do the courts go?

The *New York University Law Review*, in April 2005, published its lead article on just this subject (Epstein et al., 2005). This study looked at whether decisions made in wartime were given greater weight in peacetime using quantitative methodology. Their study looked at all civil liberties decisions spanning 60 years. They found that the U.S. Supreme Court's decisions in wartime were a mixed bag, but they tended to support the will of the legislature and to sacrifice minority rights for the safety of the majority when collective security was at risk.

The finding of this study that, in times of perceived crisis, civil liberties suffer, is neither startling nor new. However, if the perceived crisis is chronic, such as the war on terror appears to be, then it is not as easy to comfort one's self with the assumption that the pendulum will swing back either far enough or fast enough to preserve any interim losses to individual liberty.

The Patriot Act

Polls suggested that after September 11, 2001, a majority of the nation supported significant expansion of governmental power including wiretapping telephones, intercepting e-mail, intercepting ordinary mail, examining Internet activity, examining students' educational records, examining telephone records, examining bank records, tracking credit card purchases, examining tax records, and detaining suspects for up to a week without charging them (currently, in New York, suspects must be charged or released within 24 h). The public was split down the middle on detaining terrorists indefinitely without charging them. The public was certainly much more willing to go along with racial profiling, and racial profiling was rampant (Cole & Dempsey 2002, p. 168).

The public got its wish with passage of the Patriot Act. This act was quickly passed with great bipartisan support after the September 11, 2001, attacks; both Democrats and Republicans supported it. This act allowed greater coordination between governmental agencies that previously were deliberately kept separate. For example, the CIA and the FBI previously were not allowed to participate in joint operations and had limited ability to share information, but that was no longer true under the Patriot Act. Also, the White House was able to gain access to information (including telephone and e-mail interceptions, and grand jury records) that it previously could not easily access.

However, happiness with this broad expansion of governmental power was far from universal. In 43 states, 379 towns and cities approved resolutions opposing provisions of the act. The major concern of these localities was the potential for civil liberties abuses. For example, Section 215 of the Patriot Act (the so-called "library" provision) allowed the government to investigate library records using secret warrants for business records including "books, records, papers, or other items." It also allowed the government to seize entire databases (e.g., all the medical records of a hospital or all the files of an immigration group). This section of the act also included a "gag rule" that made it illegal for the person who owned the records to talk about the search.

In fact, the University of Wisconsin at Whitewater started to distribute a message to students saying: "In accordance with the Patriot Act, we may disclose your health information to authorized Federal Officials who are conducting national security and intelligence activities or providing protective services to the president or other important officials. By law we cannot reveal when we have disclosed such information to the government."

Section 213 of the act was the so-called "sneak-and-peek" provision. This allowed the government to search a person's home and delay telling them about it. Some of the sections of the Patriot Act were set to expire. The sneak-and-peek provision was not.

In the past, the government would have to seek a warrant for a secret search from a magistrate. But this warrant would have to specify what was being investigated and what was being sought. The government would have to show one of the five following as a reason to get a secret hidden warrant: (1) risk to life or physical safety; (2) flight from prosecution; (3) evidence tampering; (4) intimidation of witnesses; or (5) seriously jeopardizing an investigation or unduly delaying a trial.

Under the Patriot Act, all these checks are gone.

Search and Surveillance Under the Patriot Act May Be Unconstitutional

The search and surveillance changes under the Patriot Act may be unconstitutional. At least one judge has ruled that the changes violate the requirement of probable cause. On September 26, 2007, Judge Anne L. Aiken, a federal district court judge in Oregon, ruled that the relaxed standard for search and seizure of American citizens under the Patriot Act was both unconstitutional and unwise. Specifically, she ruled that the change in an article from "the" to "a" invalidated the law.

Originally, the Foreign Intelligence Surveillance Act allowed surveillance and searches if "the purpose" was foreign intelligence gathering. The Patriot Act changed this language to read if "a significant purpose" was foreign intelligence gathering. Judge Aiken said: "In place of the Fourth Amendment the people are expected to defer to the Executive Branch" (Keller 2007, September 27, pp. 1, 29).

The case that led to this decision was a civil suit by Brandon Mayfield, a Portland, Oregon, attorney who had converted to the Muslim religion and who had represented Leon Battle, a convicted terrorist, in a custody suit. He was arrested after the Madrid train bombing of March 2004, one of the worst terrorism incidents in Europe. Police investigating the bombing had found a plastic bag with detonator caps in it, and the bag had a fingerprint on it. Initially, there was no match to the print when the FBI ran it through the system. Then they tried to enhance it using computer technology and they found 20 possible matches, including Mayfield's. The Spanish investigators had serious doubts about the match, but the U.S. officials began surveillance on Mayfield and his family and jailed him for 2 weeks before a federal judge threw out the case. The government apologized and agreed to a $2 million settlement with him, but Mayfield only settled on the condition that he could contest the constitutionality of what had been done.

Still, Congress passed laws making it easier for the government to extend wiretapping surveillance before submitting it to the special judge's panel, although it affirmed the policy of requiring the special judge's panel to approve the surveillance. Needless to say, it can easily be argued that free association and free speech are stifled when people know that Big Brother may be watching. While President Obama is clearly more sympathetic to civil liberties than was the Bush administration, these laws relaxing requirements for surveillance remain on the books.

Habeas Corpus and the War on Terror

Habeas corpus is called the "the great writ." It literally means "to produce the body." It is the process for getting a determination of the legality of an individual's detention by the government. Congress has legislated away the right of ordinary courts to rule on *habeas* petitions for the detainees in Guantánamo and other enemy combatants in the Detainee Treatment Act. Instead, this will be ruled on by a military court with the president appointing the court and the president having ultimate authority on appeal.

In fact, the U.S. Supreme Court heard legal arguments by the attorneys for Salim Ahmed Hamdan, Osama bin Laden's driver, in the case of *Hamdan v. Rumsfeld*. Hamdan is charged with conspiracy. One of the questions is whether the Congress has suspended the right of *habeas corpus*. The Constitution says that it can only be suspended in "cases of rebellion or invasion." Congress has only suspended this right four times since the nation's founding.

In another case, Jose Padilla, an American citizen, was held as an enemy combatant without trial for over 3 years. The federal authorities, who originally said that he would be handled by a military tribunal, switched him over to civil authority in order to make a dead issue out of the question of whether the handling of his case by a military court was constitutional. The court refused to hear the case (coming one vote short of the number needed to review it). But the Court warned that if the federal authorities transferred this back to the military – something that they claimed that they had the right to do – the Supreme Court would revisit the case (Greenhouse 2006, April 4, pp. 1, 19). *See, Rumsfeld v. Padilla* (2004). To avoid having the Court rule on the legality of his trial before a military commission, Padilla was tried was tried in a civilian court. Whoriskey, P. & Eggan, D. (2008, January 23).

In 2006, Congress passed the Military Commissions Act, which suspended the right of *habeas corpus* and created special military tribunals for the trial of foreign nationals that the president labels as enemy combatants. The use of these military courts is controversial. In September 2007, a special military court ruled that the detainees at Guantánamo could be tried by the military tribunal if the prosecutors can show that they are "unlawful" enemy combatants (Glaberson 2007, September 25, pp. 1, 26).

Crime control advocates see suspension of *habeas corpus* as perhaps unfortunate but certainly a necessary by-product of the war on terror. Civil liberties advocates see this as a most serious threat because *habeas corpus* is the vehicle that allows a defendant to bring a claim of illegal governmental action before a court and forces the government to deal with that claim.

Warrantless Domestic Surveillance of U.S. Citizens

Back in the 1960s and 1970s, the U.S. government spent lots of tax dollars and intelligence resources spying on political dissidents. In fact, it came out in the Watergate hearings that President Nixon had developed an "enemies" list that included the late television and radio reporter, Daniel Schorr. In reaction to this, Congress passed FISA, the Federal Intelligence Surveillance Act of 1978 (Burton 2006, pp. 381–401). This act set up a streamlined procedure for conducting surveillance and obtaining warrants. In the original bill, the attorney general could authorize surveillance if he or she determined that the "factual basis" for the surveillance existed. The attorney general then had to obtain a warrant from 1 of 11 judges on the Foreign Intelligence Surveillance Court within 24 h. In 2002, this time to get a warrant was stretched out to 72 h. If the judge failed to approve, the government could appeal to a separate three-judge panel. The way it would work is that the field agent would fill out the warrant request form including:

1. The target individual.
2. Facts establishing probable cause that the target was involved in terrorism or spying.
3. Details of the facilities and communications to be monitored.
4. Procedures to minimize the collection of information about people in the United States.

This request would then go:

- From the field agent (who had filled out the request)
- To the field office supervisor (who verified and approved it)
- To the agents and lawyers at headquarters (who ensured that the request had all the required information and who polished it)
- To the director of the agency (who certified that the information sought was necessary to protect the United States against actual or potential terrorism, attacks, or spying, and that it could not be obtained by normal investigative techniques)
- To the Justice Department lawyers at the Office of Intelligence Policy and Review (OIPR) who would draft a formal request based upon the application and finally
- To the attorney general who would review and approve the application, determine whether emergency surveillance was necessary before the warrant was obtained, and who then, finally, would send it on to a judge of the special Foreign Intelligence Surveillance Court (How FISA process works. 2006, February 7, p. A18).

In January 2006, a story broke that President Bush had authorized hundreds of wiretaps of U.S. citizens. He was not using FISA, nor was he seeking warrants from the Foreign Intelligence Surveillance Court or any court. The president claimed authority under the War Powers Act issued by Congress in response to 9/11. This resolution authorized the president to "use all necessary and appropriate force against those nations organizations or persons he determines planned, authorized, committed or aided the terrorist attacks that occurred on September 11, 2001, or harbored such organizations or persons, in order to prevent any future acts of international terrorism against the United States." Alternately, the president claimed that he had this power as commander-in-chief.

The civil liberties view of all this is that FISA does not cover domestic surveillance and that these actions clearly violate the U.S. Constitution's Fourth Amendment warrant requirement. One member of the U.S. Senate, Russ Feingold (D-Wisconsin), argued that this was such a serious breach of conduct that the president should have been impeached. In fact, the ease which the giant ear of the government can now enter private conversations is likely to deter free association and to pose an even greater pall on free expression.

Detention of Suspected Terrorists

After the September 11 attacks, the government arrested almost 1,200 individuals, most Moslem, most Arabs, most eventually released without being charged with anything. They were held without charges for an average of 80 days. An internal FBI report, the findings of which found their way into a *Newsday* article on June 3, 2003, said that the FBI had failed to distinguish between detainees with connections to terrorism and those who lacked these connections.

In fact, the Patriot Act allows for detention of immigrants suspected of terrorism for up to 7 days and additional renewable 6-month periods if the alien's release would threaten the national security of the United States or the safety of the community or any person. In effect, this allows indefinite detention. The courts have since rejected this.

According to "What Is the Greatest Evil," a book review by Martha Minow of Michael Ignatieff's *The Lesser Evil: Political Ethics in an Age of Terror* (2005, May), there were at the time of that writing, about 1,000 individuals in the United States in long-term detention without having being charged, 550 of them in Guantánamo Bay, Cuba. Many of those released claimed that they were tortured or coerced in their interrogations, a claim supported by the Red Cross.

Crime control advocates say that this was necessary to prevent terrorists from remaining at liberty to plan future attacks on the United States. Civil liberties advocates point out that these detentions could radicalize not only those held in detention but their friends and family as well.

Interrogation by Torture

Methods of interrogation in the fight against terror get the crime control advocates and the civil liberties advocates screaming at each other. In Afghanistan, a captive who had never had contact with Western music would be thrown into a room and subjected to an audio assault with acid rock playing at full blast. (To some, that sounds cruel and unusual at any volume.) From Abu Ghraib prison in Iraq, we all saw pictures of nude, humiliated prisoners. No one on either side claims that this was acceptable. However, nudity, slapping, slamming prisoners against false walls, sleep deprivation, threats, and other techniques that civil liberties advocates say violate treaties prohibiting torture and the Geneva Conventions have all been used (Baker & Shane 2009, April 21; Johnson & Tate 2009, April 9, p. A2).

Maureen Dowd (2005, January 30, p. C17) wrote an op-ed piece in the *New York Times* on arguably perverse techniques of seduction and sexual humiliation allegedly used in Guantánamo as well. There have long been stories about prisoner hunger strikes and ordered forced feedings as well as bizarre and inhumane interrogation techniques that have included the use of dogs, and having female interrogators in skimpy outfits do lap dances on prisoners or smear fake menstrual blood on suspects and then not allow them to wash – which would be offensive in Muslim culture.

More recently, the Justice Department has disclosed details about interrogators threatening death and rape of prisoners and their family members, threatening prisoners with handguns and power drills, water boarding that went beyond the government's own guidelines, and blowing cigar and cigarette smoke into prisoners' faces until they vomited (Johnston 2009, August 24 & August 25; Donadio et al. 2009, November 5).

The United States is a signatory to the United Nations Convention Against Torture and Other Cruel, Inhuman, or Degrading Treatment or Punishment – although, unlike Canada, Russia, Great Britain, and every nation in Western Europe, as well as almost 30 other nations, we have not ratified it. In a report issued on February 15, 2009, that runs over 50 pages, the United Nations Economic and Social Council's Commission on Human Rights found that the United States has engaged in torture and other violations of human rights in Guantánamo Bay.

Crime control advocates say that we are only doing what we need to do. Civil liberties advocates say that we are acting like a rogue state and that our policies endanger our own citizens when they travel abroad (Santana 2009, April 18, p. A4). Ironically, it has recently surfaced that the interrogation techniques advocated by the CIA and military intelligence are based on a memo detailing techniques for eliciting false confessions used by Communist China during the Korean War. Attorney General Eric Holder has appointed a special prosecutor to investigate those who carried out these interrogations, although there is no plan to investigate those who promulgated the policy that permitted and encouraged these techniques. However, even the report to Attorney General Holder found that these techniques may have helped to obtain crucial information (Mazzetti & Shane 2009, August 25).

Lynne F. Stewart and Attorney–Client Privilege

One of the issues raised by terrorism is what the relationship should be between the attorney and the accused terrorist. In 2003, Lynne Stewart, a defense counsel, was not allowed to see her client, Sheikh Omar Abdel Rahman – who plotted to kill President Mubarak of Egypt and was the brains behind the first World Trade Center bombing in 1993 – unless she agreed not to convey any communication from him to the outside world. Attorney General John Ashcroft had given himself the authority to eavesdrop on conversations between prisoners and their lawyers if he had reason to believe the lawyers were being used to facilitate further acts of violence or terrorism. Ms. Stewart was then accused of passing information from the Sheik to the press. She was convicted on five felony counts, was disbarred, and was sentenced to 28 months in prison, which was appealed. There was no evidence that the information she passed on resulted in any terrorist act nor that her purpose was to aid any terrorist cause. Nevertheless, in July 2010, she was resentenced based on additional charges of perjury at the original trial, and is now serving a 10-year sentence Susman, T. (2010, July 16).

The crime control advocates say, "She deserved it"; she should have lived up to her end of the bargain. By passing information, she potentially put people at risk. The civil liberties advocates say that this case raises grave constitutional concerns involving the First Amendment as well as the Sixth Amendment. How can an attorney effectively represent a client if the attorney cannot reveal to anyone what the client says? This case, the civil liberties side claims, was intended to have a chilling effect on zealous representation of clients accused of terrorism.

This issue has intensified since the Lynne Stewart case. In fact, several defense attorneys who represent prisoners at Guantánamo filed suit, claiming that they have reason to believe that their conversations are being bugged. One attorney in the group claims that he is now compelled to tell clients that their conversations may not be confidential. Another has begun to refuse new clients because he does not believe he can provide them with adequate representation when he cannot guarantee their confidentiality.

The restrictions placed on Lynne Stewart and the sanctions that she faced impact not only the right to counsel but also the right of free expression as well.

Secret Trials

Should there be secret trials of terrorism suspects to prevent them from communicating to other terrorists? Congress has proposed military trials for the suspects in Guantánamo. In fact, some of these trials have already taken place. What about for U.S. citizens? Do we allow secret trials? Remember, the U.S. Constitution *prohibits* them.

In the Winter 2006 issue of *The News Media & the Law*, Kirsten B. Mitchell and Susan Burgess reported that 18% of federal criminal cases on the Washington, DC, docket are shielded from the public through a secret docketing system. "Over a 5-year period, 450 out of 2,600 criminal cases were indicted, tried, prosecuted and sentenced to jail in complete secrecy." These cases involved mainly drugs and gangs where the government felt that it needed to protect cooperating witnesses and negotiate plea deals, but the government could employ this same rationale to justify secret prosecution of terror suspects.

Lucy Dalglish, the executive director of the Reporters Committee for Freedom of the Press, the group that broke the story, says that she believes that this is going on all over the country. She assumed that these were terrorism cases as well as high-stakes drug cases. Secret dockets have been kept in Florida and Connecticut as well (Reporter's Committee 2003). Crime control advocates say that we are in a war and we have to use methods of wartime against terrorists. Civil liberties advocates point out that secret trials are the hallmark of anti-democratic regimes, a major tool for repression, and argue for a First Amendment right to access to trials (Thomas 2006, October, p. 1537). If trials are hidden from press and public view, then there is no chance for First Amendment protections to act as a check on governmental abuses.

Ethnic Profiling

Before the war on terror, the courts frowned on ethnic profiling as a means of singling people out for questioning, searches, or arrest. The civil liberties types were backed by the courts when they claimed that ethnic profiling was unconstitutional discrimination based on race or religion or national origin. This was based both on First Amendment and Equal Protection clauses of the Constitution. The war on terror seems to have changed this.

Partly because of these kinds of principles, before September 11, 2001, there were serious restrictions on surveillance of (or in) mosques. In February 2003, a federal judge in Manhattan, Judge Charles S. Haight, Jr., lifted many of these restrictions in New York. He based this decision on an affidavit by the New York City's Deputy Police Commissioner for Intelligence, David Cohen (a former high-ranking CIA official). Cohen claimed that there were "changed circumstances" after 9/11. Cohen claimed that American mosques had become radicalized and that mosques and other Moslem institutions were being taken advantage of "to shield the work of terrorists from law enforcement scrutiny by taking advantage of restrictions on the investigation of First Amendment Activity" (Rashbaum 2006, April 24, pp. 1, 4). While a veil of secrecy covers how anti-terrorism forces work, we know that the NYPD Intelligence Division has hired informants to go into mosques to check out the people there. According to a defense counsel in the case of the attempted Herald Square bombing case, informants reported on who the imams were, what their travel plans were, who the board members were, which members looked suspicious – and all of this ended up in police files (Rashbaum 2006, April 24, pp. B1, B6).

Crime control advocates may point to the recently foiling of the plot to target subways, stadia, and other places in New York City (Rashbaum & Baker 2009, September 23) as just one example supporting the necessity for ethnic profiling to counter the threat of extremist Muslim terrorists. Civil liberties advocates argue that this is the kind of mistreatment of minorities that make religious and community leaders in those communities reluctant to cooperate with authorities.

Entrapment Issues

If an undercover officer goes up to someone on the street and says, "I'll give you $100 if you'll come have sex with me" and the person replies "Sure! Lead on, MacDuff," is the person who agreed to have sex guilty of soliciting? No. This is entrapment. It was the officer's idea and but for the officer, the would-be prostitute would not have engaged in the transaction.

Some civil liberties supporters like to talk about agent provocateurs back in the "bad old days" of the 1960s and 1970s. These FBI agents would infiltrate political organizations and agitate until the members took radical illegal action. Then the undercover officers would have the members arrested for conspiring to carry out the plots that the undercover officers themselves were responsible for hatching (Strassfeld 2004, June, p. 1892).

In the trial of Shahawar Matin Siraj for conspiring to blow up the Herald Square subway station, similar issues came up. Apparently, the case was based largely upon secret audio and video conversations made by one Osama Eldawoody, an Egyptian naturalized citizen who was an unemployed engineer who tried to make ends meet as an ice cream vendor, a cab driver, and finally as a restaurant worker. The police first came into contact with him when an anonymous informant told them that Eldawoody was a suspicious character after 9/11. He was picked up and questioned first by the FBI and later by the NYPD. They ended up hiring him as a paid informant. He received almost $100,000 in less than 3 years!

The defense claim was that their defendant was little more than a dupe, being egged on by Eldawoody who claimed to be a member of a nonexistent terrorist organization, had engineer's expertise, and promised to supply backpacks and explosives. While the jury found Siraj guilty, the troubling questions of entrapment remained.

Extraordinary Rendition: The New Silver Platter

The United Nations claims that the United States has been engaging in a new kind of silver platter doctrine. Before the Bill of Rights was applied to the states, federal law enforcement would hand cases with questionably obtained evidence to state authorities for trial, giving them these cases on a "silver platter." We have, critics claim, been moving prisoners out of places that don't allow torture to places in the world where torture is allowed. While the government denies this, there are some prisoners who have been released who claim that this happened to them.

One such case, reported in *The New Yorker* (Mayer 2005, February 14), was that of Maher Arar, a Canadian engineer born in Syria. Arar was apprehended in New York in September 2002 at JFK Airport. His name appeared on a terrorism watch list. First, American authorities held and questioned him for 13 days. Then he was placed in handcuffs and leg irons and transferred to an executive jet. The plane stopped in Washington, DC; Portland, Oregon; Rome, Italy; and then landed him in Amman, Jordan. Arar claims that he heard pilots and crew identify themselves during radio conversations as "the Special Removal Unit." Arar was then taken from Jordan to Syria where after a day of threats, he was beaten with 2-in.-thick electrical cable and kept in a windowless underground cell. He was later released. During this entire time, he had been charged with no crime.

According to Mayer, the most common destinations for rendered suspects are "Egypt, Morocco, Syria, and Jordan, each one cited by the U.S. State Department for human-rights violations. Masked U.S. operatives would grab suspects throughout Europe and whisk them away in jets to places with a more relaxed view on what questioning techniques were acceptable" (p. 106).

Khaled el-Masri was a terrorist wanted for murder. The CIA arrested el-Masri on New Year's Eve of 2003. He was pulled off a bus that had crossed the Serbian border into Macedonia. He was questioned for days by agents who refused to contact the German authorities; El-Masri was a Lebanese-born German citizen. He was beaten by about eight men in black wearing masks. There was only one problem. This was the wrong Khaled el-Masri. The one they arrested was a car salesman and father of four and not a terrorist. After 5 months of torture and imprisonment, Khaled el-Masri was released.

In 2005, after a meeting with Secretary of State Condoleza Rice, German Chancellor Angela Merkel said that the Bush administration had admitted that el-Masri had been taken by mistake. Rice later denied that she had said that. In January 2007, German prosecutors put out arrest warrants for 13 CIA agents for their role in el-Masri's kidnapping. El-Masri tried to sue the U.S. government, but in order for him to sue, he needed reports from the U.S. government. Relying on an old case, *United States v. Reynolds* (1953), where the government refused to allow access to governmental reports to the widow of someone who had died in the crash of a B-29 bomber, the U.S. Supreme Court refused her access to the papers she needed to prove her case based on state secret privilege. If this sets the pattern, nobody who suffers from extraordinary rendition will ever be able to sue in this country (Savage 2007, October 8; Weiss 2007, October 9).

Crime control advocates say that if these tactics save lives, then we should use them: sometimes there just isn't time for other tactics. Ironically, civil liberties advocates can cite Dan Coleman, an ex-FBI agent who worked on investigating the bombings of U.S. embassies in Kenya and Tanzania. He was able to help get confessions from four suspects that revealed important information about al-Qaeda without torture. Rather than using torture, Coleman forged relationships with detainees. He says that you can't rely on the information you get from tortured suspects. If you deprive someone of his clothes, Coleman argues, "he's going to be ashamed, and humiliated, and cold. He'll tell you anything you want to hear to get his clothes back. There's no value in it" (Mayer 2005, May 2, p. 6). Nevertheless, the process of rendition continues under the Obama administration, although there are some plans to make this process more open than it had been under the previous administration (Johnston 2009, April 25, p. 8).

Still, when the victims of extraordinary rendition have tried to sue the United States, the government, relying on the Reynolds case, has claimed that the documentation they would need to release to allow the suits to go forward remain privileged as governmental secrets. The U.S. Supreme Court has refused to force the government to produce those documents and the cases cannot go forward as a result. In the first months of the Obama administration, the Justice Department has been making the same arguments restricting plaintiff's rights to information necessary to proceed with their lawsuits that were made under the Bush administration.

In September 2009, the Justice Department announced plans to make it more difficult to claim that material should not be released under the governmental state secret privilege. All such assertions will require a memorandum from the agency requesting the privilege to the Assistant Attorney General handling the lawsuit. If that attorney approved the request, it would then be handed on to a review committee composed of upper-level officers of the Justice Department. This committee would be charged with determining whether the disclosure risked "significant harm to national security." It would also be charged with seeking ways of avoiding shutting down the lawsuit if the information was deemed to be covered by the privilege; it would forward its recommendation to the attorney general who would then make the final determination (Savage 2009, September 23, p. A16).

Discussion of Findings

No issue is more polarizing than how we should deal with the threat of terrorism. Crime control advocates say we are in a war and it is not a metaphorical war but a real one evidenced by the presence of Ground Zero at the World Trade Center site. The physical stakes are potential death or injury of thousands, possibly millions, of Americans, economic disruption, and devastation of our infrastructure. Unless we recognize the tremendous threat that terrorism poses, we will fall victim to that threat.

The civil liberties advocates say that this is not an actual war with a foreign place where we can march to victory. The government already has sufficient weapons to deal with the terrorist threat, and they were there before 9/11. They point to the 9/11 Commission's report as evidence that we had the information we needed to stop the attacks without instituting measures that threatened liberty. They look at the hallmarks of liberal democracy: free press, free speech, freedom of religion, openness in government, respect for civil liberties in the criminal justice system, and limits to governmental power to investigate and arrest, and see all of them threatened, and they argue that there is no terrorist threat quite so chilling as that of the terrorist state.

They point to Germany under the Nazis, the former Soviet Union under Stalin, Argentina under Peron, or Iraq under Saddam where people were snatched from the street, kept secretly for years, tortured, and convicted in secret trials by highly political courts. The loss of civil liberties, they say, is the hallmark of a terrorist state or a rogue nation and the justification is always the threat that the dissident poses to society. No dissident group has the power to seriously curtail liberty in the way that an overly zealous government can.

Implications for Future Research

Packer's paradigm of crime control and civil liberties models offers a framework to examine the political, philosophical, and legal questions raised by the war on terror. Following the rhetorical strategies of the advocates of these two world views offers a fertile field for communication scholars in the humanities to analyze. What if any metaphors are shared? What language is unique to the advocates of each view? What evidence appears most salient to the advocates of each side? Social scientists might study the shifting tides in this battle through content analysis of the language used by politicians and newspapers and court decisions in discussing the war on terror. Legal scholars might study the shifting tides in the battle of crime control advocates and proponents of the civil liberties paradigm.

Conclusions

All of these issues bring to the surface a basic conflict in values between advocates of crime control and civil liberties, particularly where First Amendment concerns come into play. Crime control advocates see the government as a guardian against external threat. Civil liberties advocates see the greatest threat to freedom as coming from an overzealous government. Perhaps the best test for the proper balance between the two is this: When one side's arguments become easy to make, then the balance has slipped too far to one side or the other. After the measures taken to prevent terrorist attacks in the wake of 9/11, it would appear that the scale shows the balance shifted far to the crime control side. While President Obama has pulled back on some of these policies, he too is committed to the war on terror and some of the changes instituted by the Bush administration (such as the slackened requirements for surveillance, the restrictions on foreign nationals, the use of extraordinary rendition, and, although to a considerably lesser extent, the reluctance of the government to reveal information about extraordinary rendition) still remain in place.

While the winter chill on First Amendment protections seems to be thawing, we have not yet returned to the summer warmth in which freedom of expression most thrives.

References

Abrams, N. (2006, November 1). The developments in U.S. anti-terrorism law: Checks and balances undermined. *J. Int. Crim. Just.* **4**(5), 1117.

Baker, P., & Shane, S. (2009, April 21). Pressure grows to investigate interrogations: Obama assures C.I.A. it won't be blamed. *NY Times* pp. 1, 18.

Bernstein, N. (2007, September 17). Music scholar barred from U.S., but no one will tell her why. *NYTimes* pp. B1, B5.

Bowdler, N. (2007, September 25). Hostile intentions. *The BBC World Service Newshour.*

Burton, A. (2006). Fixing FISA for long war: Regulating warrantless surveillance in the age of terrorism. *Pierce L. Rev.* **4**, 381.

Cole, D., & Dempsey, J.X. (2002). *Terrorism and the Constitution: Sacrificing Civil Liberties in the Name of National Security*. New York: The New Press.

Deflin, M., & Maybin, L. (2005). Interpol and the policing of international terrorism: Developments and dynamics since September 11. In: L.L. Snowden & B.C. Whitsel (Eds.), *Terrorism: Research, Readings, and Realities* (pp. 175–195). Upper Saddle River, NJ: Pearson.

Dick, P. (2002). *The Minority Report*. New York: Pantheon Books. (Original work published 1956).

Donadio, R., Mazzetti, M., & Shane S. (2009, November 5). Italy convicts 23 Americans, most working for C.I.A., of abducting Muslim cleric. *NY Times*, p. A15.

Dowd, M. (2005, January 30). Torture chicks gone wild. *NY Times*, p. C17. Retrieved from Proquest Historical Newspapers, *The New York Times* (1851–2006).
Enmund v Florida, 481 U.S. 137 (1982).
Epstein, L., Ho, D., & Segal, J. (2005, April). The Supreme Court during crisis: How war affects only non-war cases. *N. Y. Univ. Law. Rev.* **80**, 1.
Federal Intelligence Surveillance Act of 1978 (FISA).
Filisko, G.M. (2006, April 6). Moussaoui sentence debated: Allowing the death penalty for failing to warn could lead to its expansion some scholars say. *ABA J. E-Report*, p. 3.
Fischer, W. (2009, March 24). Censorship seen in exclusion of foreign scholars. *Interpress Service*. Retrieved through Lexis/Nexis.
Glaberson, W. (2007, September 25). Court advances military trials for detainees. *NY Times* pp. 1, 26.
Greenhouse, L. (2006, April 4). Justices decline terrorism case of a U.S. citizen: Padilla falls vote short; results leave detention intact – one opinion warns government. *NY Times* pp. 1, 19.
Hamdan v. Rumsfeld 548 U.S. 557 (2006).
How FISA process works. (2006, February 7). *The New York Times*, p. A18.
Hudson, D., Jr. (2006, April 7). Padilla question leaves unanswered questions: Supreme Court denies review but the issue of detainee status still alive. *ABA J. E-Report*.
Johnson, C., & Tate, J. (2009, April 17). Newly released Bush documents detail torture tactics; Obama: C.I.A. officers won't be prosecuted. *Boston Globe* p. A2.
Johnston, D. (2009, August 25). Rendition to continue, but with better oversight, U.S. says. *NY Times* p. 8.
Kaplan, J., Skolnick, J., & Feeley, M. (1991). *Criminal Justice: Introductory Cases And Material*, 5th ed., Westbury, NY: Foundation Press.
Keller, S.J. (2007, September 27). Patriot Act sections on search and surveillance are ruled unconstitutional. *NY Times* pp. 1, 29.
Mayer, J. (2005, February 14). Outsourcing torture: The secret history of America's "extraordinary rendition" program. *New Yorker*, 81. Retrieved from Platinum Periodicals Document I.D. No. 831855781.
Mazzetti, M., & Shane, S. (2009, May 24). Rendition to continue but with better oversight. *NY Times* p. 1.
Minow, M. (2005, May). What is the greatest evil? [Review of the book *The Lesser Evil: Political Ethics in an Age of Terror*, by Michael Ignatieff]. *Harv. L. Rev.* **118**, 2134.
Mitchell, K., & Burgess, S. (Winter 2006). Disappearing dockets: When public dockets have holes, the public's right to open judicial proceedings is jeopardized. *News Media & Law* **30**, 4–6.
Packer, H. (1968). *The Limits of Criminal Sanction*. Palo Alto, CA: Stanford University Press.
Rashbaum, W.K. (2006, April 24). Terror case may offer clues into police use of informants. *NY Times* pp. B1, B4.
Rashbaum, W.K. (2006, April 25). Police informer in terror trial takes stand: Recorded a defendant accused in a bomb plot. *NY Times* pp. B1, B6.
Rashbaum, W.K., & Baker, A. (2009, September 23). How using imam in terror inquiry backfired on New York police. *NY Times* pp. A1, A4.
Reporter's Committee for Freedom of the Press (2003). *Secret Justice: Secret Dockets*. http://www.rcfp.org/secretjustice/secretdockets/index.html
Rumsfeld v. Padilla, 542 U.S. 426 (2004).
Santana, R. (2009, April 18). Groups disappointed U.S. not prosecuting CIA agents. *Boston Globe* p. A4.
Savage, D. (2007, October 8). "State secrets" case may get airing. *Los Angeles Times*. Retrieved from http://www.latimes.com.news/nationworld/nation/la-na-secrets8oct08,0,644302.story?col
Savage, C. (2009, September 23). Justice department planning to limit government's use of state secrets privilege. *NY Times* p. A16.

Schwartz, J. (2009, March 18). U.S. urged to lift antiterror ban on foreign scholars. *NY Times* p. A18.
Simondsen, C., & Spindlove, J. (2004). *Terrorism Today: The Past, the Players, the Future*, 3rd ed., Upper Saddle River, NJ: Prentice-Hall.
Snowdon, L. & Whitsel, B. (2005) *Terrorism: Research, Readings, and Realities.*, Upper Saddle River, N.J.,Allyn & Bacon/Prentice Hall.
Strassfeld, R. (2004, June). Symposium: Law, loyalty and treason: How can the law regulate loyalty without imperiling it? Lose in Viet Nam, bring the boys home. *N.C.L. Rev.* **82**, 1891.
Susman, T. (2010, July 16). Judge adds years to ex-attorney's sentence; Lynne Stewart was convicted of helping her terrorist client contact his followers. Susman, T (2010, July 16) *The Los Angeles Times* Part AA; p. 8. Retreived from Lexis/Nexis.
Swarns, R. (2009, August 31). Cheney offers sharp defense of CIA tactics. *NY Times* pp. 1A, 9A.
Thomas, M. (2006, October). The First Amendment right of access to docket sheets. *Calif. Law. Rev.* **94**, 1534–1580.
Tison v. Arizona, 481 U.S. 137 (1987).
The United States Code, Title 22 Section 2656.
United Press International (2004, January 8). Group challenges court's hidden docket. Retrieved from UPI.com.
U.S. Constitution, Amendments 1, 4, 5, 6, 8.
United States v. Reynolds, 345 U.S. 1 (1953).
Weiss, D.C. (2007, October 9). Supreme Court rejects CIA detention case. *ABA J.* Retrieved from http//www.abajournal.com/news/supreme_court_turns_down_cia_detention_case/
Whoriskey, P. & Eggen, D. (2008 January 23) Judge sentences Padilla to 17 years, cites his detention, *The Washington Post, Washington Post.Com*, Retrieved from Lexis/Nexis.

Terrorism: The Dilemma of Response

Elena Pokalova

Introduction

The fight against terrorism has been on the agenda of policymakers and academics for a number of decades. And while numerous efforts have been attempted to fight terrorism, the puzzle remains: What constitutes the most appropriate response, equivalent to the threat? Numerous research projects have been carried out with the goal of assessing the effectiveness of anti-terrorist initiatives. A lot of rich data on terrorism has been produced or is currently being collected, as can be exemplified by the Study of Terrorism and Responses to Terrorism (START) project of the U.S. Department of Homeland Security. However, more research in the field of anti-terrorism is needed in order to prompt corresponding government policy decisions targeted at the elimination of the threat of terrorism.

Terrorism poses a challenge for all states in the global arena. However, in the context of a liberal democracy, governments face numerous constraints on the types of policies they can implement in the fight against terrorism. Democratic governments are obliged to protect not only the security of their citizens but also their rights and liberties, carefully guarding the democratic principles of governance. Unlike autocratic regimes, liberal democracies are not free to wipe out the threat of terrorism by all means possible. Instead, anti-terrorist measures have to be compliant with the democratic values held by the citizens.

In this respect, measures to fight terrorism implemented in a liberal democracy have to be legitimate. In addition, such measures have to be effective. A lot of efforts have been dedicated to assessing the effectiveness of anti-terrorist measures and provisions. However, most of the time, anti-terrorist initiatives have been treated as a unified pool of responses, guided by the single goal of eradicating the threat. Distinctions between the different approaches behind specific policy responses have been left unresolved. In this respect, the current analysis makes an

E. Pokalova (✉)
Department of Political Science, Kent State University, Kent, OH, USA
e-mail: elena.pokalova@gmail.com

G. Andreopoulos et al. (eds.), *International Criminal Justice: Critical Perspectives and New Challenges*, DOI 10.1007/978-1-4419-1102-5_5,
© Springer Science+Business Media, LLC 2011

attempt to look deeper into the nature of anti-terrorist measures and place them into two categories of responses: counter-terrorism and law enforcement. Even though the majority of states today employ a combination of these two approaches, delineating between specific anti-terrorist legislation and the criminal justice framework would allow us to better assess the effectiveness of anti-terrorist measures and provisions and tailor a better response to terrorism, based on the principles of effectiveness and legitimacy.

Examining both counter-terrorism and law enforcement, this chapter analyzes the role of civil liberties in the fight against terrorism. The discussion demonstrates the importance of civil liberties in diverting the threat of terrorist attacks. Because increased civil liberties decrease the probability of terrorist attacks, they need to be enhanced, and not abridged, which is often the case with an ever-expanding scope of counterterrorist legislation.

Previous empirical findings have demonstrated that many anti-terrorist policies remain largely ineffective, if not counter-productive. And while the pure impact of anti-terrorist efforts is hard to distill, existing evidence suggests that counter-terrorism can exert a negative effect on civil liberties enjoyed by citizens in a liberal democracy. Taking into consideration the questionable effectiveness of both counter-terrorism and law enforcement against terrorism and the negative impact of counter-terrorism on democratic freedoms, I suggest that law enforcement might be a more appropriate approach for fighting terrorism.

The chapter proceeds as follows. The first section discusses the evolution of anti-terrorist measures and provisions and looks at the challenges that liberal democracies face in elaborating on the most appropriate response. The second section outlines counter-terrorism and law enforcement as the two frameworks for categorizing anti-terrorist measures. Country examples are cited to illustrate the substantive features of these approaches, and the advantages and drawbacks of each approach are analyzed. Next, the two approaches are contrasted on the principles of effectiveness and legitimacy. Finally, I analyze empirical data on incidences of terrorism in order to examine the role civil rights and liberties play in terms of predicting the future probability of a terrorist attack in a country. The concluding section elaborates on the findings and discusses further policy implications.

Preventing Terrorism: Evolving Response

A wide variety of policy responses have been institutionalized to target terrorism. Addressing the roots of terrorism, deterrence, security screening, cutting financial assistance, intelligence gathering have been all employed as means of reducing the probability of further attacks. The problem with the choice among these strategies is that policymakers operate in extreme conditions of uncertainty, as it is problematic to predict when and where terrorism will strike next. And even though some may argue that the United States' response to terrorism after 9/11 has ensured the absence of further attacks on the American soil, we cannot trace the direct links between the absence of attacks and specific anti-terrorist measures. Such factors as terrorist planning, financing, and the simple proximity of targets can affect the decision to strike. Thus, for instance, Britain, a staunch U.S. ally in the fight against terrorism, has been pursuing similar strategies following September 11, 2001. And yet, these measures did not safeguard Britain against the bombings of 2005, 2007, and 2008.

The response to the challenge of terrorism has been subject to many shifts in paradigms and ideology over the years. The ad hoc measures and provisions against terrorism started to change after the attacks at the Munich Olympics in 1972, when the response to terrorism started to encompass internal security measures, expanded police capabilities, diplomacy, and military means of addressing the problem. Throughout the years, anti-terrorist measures and provisions expanded dramatically. The most recent paradigm shift was brought about by the focusing event of September 11, after which the global campaign against global terror began. Terrorism today is treated not only as a serious crime, but also as a threat to national security.

The U.S.-led "war on terror," however, ushered in heightened concerns over effectiveness and legitimacy of various anti-terrorist policies. Questions regarding the impact of anti-terrorist provisions on civil rights and liberties and the effectiveness of instituted measures have come into focus. Government policies against terrorism have been oftentimes criticized as ineffective in fighting such a vague and amorphous threat as terrorism (Cauley & Im 1988; Enders & Sandler 1993, 2002; Faria 2006; LeVine & Salert 1996). As Doron Zimmermann and Andreas Wenger (2007) note, a controversial trend has emerged in recent years: "The balance between efficiency and legitimacy in the fight against terrorism has been tilted in favor of efficiency for the sake of perceived short-term gains" (p. 221). Such perceived short-term benefits can affect our understanding of the threat of terrorism. As a result, the soft-on-terrorism position becomes unattractive, which leads to numerous political outcomes – John Kerry's loss to George W. Bush in 2004 being one of them.

In the long term, many anti-terrorist policies present certain dangers as well. Even though most anti-terrorist policies are introduced as temporary provisions immediately following a terrorist attack, they rarely get reversed and gradually build up. The expanding body of anti-terrorist provisions, in turn, has an adverse effect on citizens and creates a more intrusive government, which can eventually lead to the establishment of a police state. Such a scenario can be illustrated by the events in Peru in the 1990s, when the repressive anti-terrorist measures ushered in the dictatorship of Alberto Fujimori.

Traditionally, liberal democracies are at a bigger disadvantage when fighting terrorism than their authoritarian counterparts. According to Walter Enders and Todd Sandler (2006), "the political and civil freedoms that define a liberal democracy provide a favorable environment for terrorists to wage their terror campaign" (p. 24). Thus, the very democratic principles of governance make democracies an easy target for terrorism. At the same time, liberal democracies are constrained in their choice of strategies to fight terrorism: anti-terrorist measures have to be deemed effective and perceived as legitimate – considerations that do not restrict autocratic governments.

Freedoms of liberal democracies inadvertently place them at a disadvantage, because their design demands that they "tolerate the intolerable" (Schmid 1992). A liberal democracy is not at liberty to start a "dirty war," such as the one in Argentina against the People's Revolutionary Army in the 1970s. There, the government of Juan Domingo Perón granted the military expanded rights to fight the terrorists. In the course of the war, many innocent citizens were killed or "disappeared." In contrast, in a liberal democracy, if the response to terrorism is deemed as too harsh and measures as too expansive, the government can lose popular support (Enders & Sandler 2006). Thus, in Spain, protests against the involvement in the "war on terror" in Iraq brought the victory to Jose Luis Zapatero in 2004. Unlike his predecessor Jose Maria Aznar, Zapatero promised to pull the Spanish troops out of Iraq, which he did, once elected.

And while the very freedoms of a liberal democracy place it at a disadvantage while fighting terrorism, civil liberties can be a crucial component for preventing terrorist attacks. The manifold nature of the relationship between democracy and terrorism is demonstrated in Quan Li's (2005) recent analysis. Li's findings indicate that democratic institutional constraints reduce the effectiveness of a liberal democracy in the fight against terrorism, while democratic participation brings down the number of terrorist attacks in a country. This suggests that while anti-terrorist measures might be oftentimes ineffective against terrorism, they should closely adhere to the democratic principles of governance and avoid placing additional constraints on the level of civil liberties. Taking into consideration the recent trends of expanded policy mandates and the broadening scope of policy responses, it is imperative to reconsider our approaches to the threat of terrorism and revise policy alternatives according to the criteria of effectiveness and legitimacy that they are intended to meet.

States have a number of policy choices at their disposal when addressing the threat of terrorism. As Gregory Miller (2007) summarizes, these choices range from doing nothing (which might not be the most popular alternative – because a liberal democracy is obliged to protect its citizens) – to the restriction and violence as the more extreme responses to terrorism involving a greater level of coercion. While considering the choice of an appropriate strategy, policymakers need to answer the question of what deters terrorism. This involves the question of whether coercive government policies eliminate the threat, or simply contribute to the cycles of violence. Moreover, the question remains of which response is the most effective alternative that does not have a harmful impact on the founding pillars of democracy – civil rights and liberties.

Counter-Terrorism and Law Enforcement Models of Response

While the number of strategies available to a state to fight terrorism is virtually limitless, two approaches to terrorism can be delineated. They are counter-terrorism and law enforcement. The two approaches offer two distinct points of view for addressing terrorism, and each possesses advantages and disadvantages. The dichotomy between the two approaches is similar to the very tension that exists in criminal justice between due process and crime control, where each strives for primacy. And while most states employ a combination of counter-terrorism and law enforcement, outlining the constituent features of each would allow us to dissect anti-terrorist policy responses and examine further how each strategy fits the principles of effectiveness and legitimacy. Further, distinguishing between these two approaches would help us estimate their effect on freedoms in a democratic regime, which in turn leads us to more conclusions about effectiveness and legitimacy of anti-terrorist measures.

Counter-Terrorism

The term *counter-terrorism* is often used to define a broad range of anti-terrorist policies and initiatives. In this sense, the term encompasses the whole entirety of responses introduced to address the threat of terrorism. For the purposes of the current study, however, counter-terrorism is defined narrowly as legislation introduced to specifically address the issue of terrorism. Thus, counter-terrorism refers to anti-terrorist laws and provisions that came into being in response to the terrorist threat and/or terrorist attacks.

In Christopher Hewitt's (1984) typology of policies against terrorism, counter-terrorism coincides with the category of "emergency powers, and other anti-terrorist legislation" (p. 35), as opposed to ceasefires and negotiations, improvement of economic conditions, initiation of reforms, and the employment of security forces. Under this approach terrorism receives much more attention than a regular subcategory of crime, and it often entails the establishment of insulated government bodies or departments whose primary goal is to address the challenge of terrorism.

Counter-terrorism, as represented by anti-terrorist laws and provisions, has been widely implemented around the world. An increasing reliance on counter-terrorism has been registered following the attacks of September 11, because the realm of addressing terrorism has expanded from criminal law to the fields of national and international security. As demonstrated by the U.S. House of Representatives Hearing (2004), in the wake of 9/11 the United States assigned anti-terrorist strategies to the spheres of national and homeland security. The issue of terrorism was subsequently addressed in the 2002 National Security Strategy, 2002 National Strategy for Homeland Security, 2003 National Strategy for Fighting Terrorism, and a number of other initiatives, which fall into much broader categories than criminal law.

Counter-terrorism in the United States can be traced back to the Antiterrorism and Effective Death Penalty Act of 1996 (AEDPA), which was introduced largely in response to the 1993 World Trade Center Attack and the 1995 Oklahoma City bombings. This piece of legislation considerably expanded the notion of terrorism, as well as revised penalties for existing offences. AEDPA was among the first acts to expand beyond the borders of the traditional criminal law. Thus, it allowed the government to intervene in financial flows of suspects of terrorist activities and cut material support to those accused of terrorist activities. Another indicator of the broadness of the AEDPA mandate was the power to forcefully remove individuals suspected of terrorist activities from the territory of the United States or deny them entry into the country. The Act of 1996 initiated substantive and structural changes in the ways of addressing terrorism in the United States. These provisions allowed the executive branch to expand its powers over judicial processes under the banner of the "war on terror," and have since raised concerns among the general public, academics, and policymakers.

A recent piece of legislation that provoked heated debates in the United States was the Patriot Act (2001), signed into law within weeks of the terrorist attacks of September 11. The Patriot Act is rather lengthy, incorporates an overwhelming number of terms and definitions, and greatly expands the authorities of the government in the fight against terrorism. It outlines search provisions, communication monitoring, release of financial records, deportation procedures for immigrants suspected of terrorism, etc. The act, as a document enhancing the powers of the government to investigate and prosecute individuals suspected of terrorist activities, has been subject to severe criticisms as violating a number of constitutional amendments (Banks 2004).

Russia presents another example of a country implementing the counter-terrorism approach. In 2006, Russia adopted a law "On Counteraction of Terrorism," followed by a presidential decree "On Counterterrorist Measures" (Putin 2006a). The law defines terrorism as "the ideology of violence and the practice of influencing the adoption of a decision by state power bodies, local self-government bodies or international organizations connected with frightening the population and (or) other forms of unlawful violent actions" (Putin 2006b, Article 3), and a substantial part of the legislation is dedicated to the conduct of anti-terrorist operations in response to terrorist attacks. In this respect, as compared to the previous 1998 law "On the Fight Against Terrorism" replaced by the new legislation, the 2006 act is a much broader formulated piece, which elevates the Armed Forces of the Russian Federation to a prominent position in the fight against terrorism.

In addition to the law, the presidential decree established Russia's National Counter-Terrorism Committee under the auspices of the Federal Security Service (FSB) Director. The committee is responsible for coordinating federal, regional, and local anti-terrorist operations and initiatives, developing anti-terrorist policy proposals, overseeing the implementation of policies by executive agencies, and coordinating anti-terrorist activities and operations domestically and internationally. The committee represents an insulated agency solely dedicated to the issue of terrorism and thus elevates the status of terrorism above other categories of crime in Russia.

Counter-terrorism as an approach to the fight against terrorism offers certain advantages. Firstly, counter-terrorism allows for a swift response. As illustrated by the Patriot Act, legislation can be in place within weeks of a terrorist attack. In this respect, anti-terrorist legislation can provide a much timelier alternative than such measures as conciliation, installation of security devices, or police operations.

Next, this response is highly visible. Newly introduced anti-terrorist legislation can be widely publicized and is therefore easily accessible to the public, who expect the government to take action in response to terrorist attacks.

W. Kip Viscusi and Richard J. Zeckhauser (2003) argue that the desire for anti-terrorist policies is at its highest level immediately following a terrorist attack, when the public perceives its vulnerability to be at a maximum level. When introducing specific terrorism legislation, a government is seen as taking action in response to the threat, which is what is expected of a government in a liberal democracy. Finally, the counter-terrorism approach deals exclusively with terrorism, and the response here is not inhibited by specificities of other groups of crime. Thus, in case terrorism justifies a unique intervention, different from responses to other criminal categories, counter-terrorism offers a venue for policymakers to elaborate on this response and introduce the most appropriate legislation.

The main critique of counter-terrorism, on the other hand, is the ever-growing concern over infringements of anti-terrorist legislation on civil rights and liberties. As David Charters (1994) summarizes on the basis of country case studies prior to 9/11, the expansion of government powers mostly affected such areas as search-and-arrest, detention periods, deportation powers, and actions of lawyers representing individuals accused of involvement in terrorism. This list has recently expanded further to increased secrecy in intelligence data gathering, lower standards of search-and-seizure, commingling of criminal and intelligence investigations, and a vague designation of a group of people as enemy combatants – considerations that today undermine the constitutionality of counter-terrorism provisions.

Additional concerns around counter-terrorism focus on the definition of terrorism and the discretion in the application of anti-terrorist laws and provisions. Thus, definitions employed in the legislation can be rather vague and imprecise (Crelinsten 1998), while discretional application of anti-terrorist legislation exacerbates the definitional problem even further through discriminate identification as terrorists of individuals who in reality might have little connection to this crime (Chalk 1998).

Law Enforcement

An alternative response to the threat of terrorism falls into the law enforcement framework. Law enforcement designates the use of criminal law to combat terrorism and does not treat the crime of terrorism differently from other criminal activities. The rationale behind using criminal laws to combat terrorism is similar to that behind efforts to reduce deviant behavior. According to Henry (2002), "the primary mission of law enforcement is the prevention of crime, and this mission ultimately extends to the prevention of terrorist crimes" (p. 324). Successful prosecution of offenders is believed to create disincentives to commit crimes in the future – this principle is transferred to terrorist activities. Under this model terrorists are prosecuted within the existing judicial system without the establishment of special courts or facilities. Essentially, under the law enforcement model, measures targeted at crime reduction are applied to the fight against terrorism and therefore do not extend beyond the criminal justice system as counter-terrorism does.

Disruption of terrorist activities, deterrence of future attacks, and prosecution of individuals found guilty of terrorist activities are all inherent goals of both counter-terrorism and law enforcement. The difference between the models, however, lies in ways of achieving these goals. Thus, while counter-terrorism relies on specific anti-terrorist policies and regulations, law enforcement is dependent on intelligence, technology, and the community – which are all pillars of effective policing. As Vincent E. Henry (2002) points out, the institution of police is located at the heart of law enforcement, and the effectiveness of its operations determines the level of preparedness to face the threat of terrorism.

Ronald V. Clarke and Graeme R. Newman (2007) identify the main roles of the police in the fight against terrorism are intelligence-gathering, protection of potential targets, and readiness to respond to attacks. In this respect, "intelligence-led policing" is crucial in combating the threat. The assumption behind intelligence practices of the police is that a small number of individuals are responsible for a large share of crimes and that crime can be best targeted through intelligence units investigating and prosecuting offenders (Clarke & Newman 2007). These intelligence units are of paramount significance for information-gathering on terrorist activities, organizations, and networks.

Technology presents another tool for the police to fight terrorism. Samuel Nunn (2003) points out that "technologies are seen as a major tactical component of civilian law enforcement charged with identifying, locating, apprehending, and prosecuting hidden terrorist cells" (p. 454). New technological advances, such as the global positioning system (GPS), offer increasingly sophisticated means for fighting crime, and have a great potential for combating terrorism. Finally, apart from intelligence and technology, recent years have witnessed a shift towards what came to be known as community policing, a practice promoting strong ties between the police and the communities they serve.

Community policing exploits new potential in efforts to combat crime because it encompasses the capabilities of the police, local authorities, and members of the community. Community policing is a joint effort of the community and the police, where the community itself is the ultimate source of information on crime patterns and needs of addressing criminal offences.

Rachel Briggs et al. (2006) argue that the necessity to integrate the community into the fight against terrorism is justified for several reasons. Thus, the community is an important source of information, it offers signs for early interventions, and community cooperation is key for the success of government initiatives to protect the society. Terrorism, Briggs rightly observes, has local roots. Therefore, the work done at the community level is capable of nipping terrorism in the bud, since community policing is oftentimes combined with social programs of community building and social stabilization.

The law enforcement model is based on criminal justice foundations and is therefore largely reliant on the police forces, which in turn depend on intelligence-gathering, technological advances, and the community in their operations. In addition, the law enforcement approach implies utilization of the existing network of criminal courts and institutions, as opposed to creating new structures that solely target terrorism. The application of the law enforcement model to fighting terrorism can be seen in Japan.

Japan faced a serious terrorist threat in the late 1960s and early 1970s coming from Japan's Red Army and a number of growing social movements such as Chukaku-ha. In response to these attacks Japan relied on the police to ensure the country's internal security. In this case the government utilized the long-standing ties between the police and society, which in the Japanese culture have been traditionally strong (Katzenstein 1993). In Japan, local police stations have historically served as the source of intelligence, and annual house calls by policemen and regular interviews with citizens have been common practice. When faced with the terrorist threat, Japan resorted to the existing surveillance system and was reluctant to take a more proactive stance on the issue.

As Peter Katzenstein (1993) elaborates, Japan's position on terrorism is dictated by its legal norms, which are "embedded in social norms rather than constitutive of them" (p. 278). Social norms here, in turn, dictate that the police remain the main defender of societal safety. This is the reason why Japan did not assume a more activist viewpoint on the fight against terrorism and remained rather aloof in the international efforts for cooperation. Instead, the police has implemented extensive search techniques, combined with the creation of wide networks of police support organizations and individual community contacts supplying the authorities with information. In addition, the Japanese society has performed the function of informal control over the police operations, which ensures accountability and transparency of the justice system.

The United Kingdom can be cited as another case where the state has extensively relied on law enforcement techniques. The UK has gained vast experience in dealing with terrorism and has implemented a variety of measures ranging from anti-terrorist legislation to military responses to the imposition of emergency powers. At the same time, in the course of its long-lasting fight against terrorism the UK has implemented a full range of law enforcement measures, which can be placed in two categories, those of "prospective" and "retrospective" (Innes 2006), and encompass extensive use of the police forces.

According to Martin Innes (2006), the "prospective" aspect of the police work refers to measures aimed at prevention, deterrence, and disruption of terrorism. These activities are carried out on a regular basis as part of the police routines. The "retrospective" aspect, on the other hand, focuses on the post-crime response, and involves criminal investigation and prosecution. The Metropolitan Police Service carries the largest responsibility among other police agencies in terms of anti-terrorism in the UK, and these two aspects of anti-terrorist initiatives are integrated into the functions of the Special Branch police officers (Innes 2006). Additionally, the British National Criminal Intelligence Service, founded in 1992, supplements the police in the sphere of intelligence-gathering. The agency was initially set up to collect and process high-level criminal intelligence, but has since expanded its mandate and today processes intelligence on both organized crime and terrorism.

The law enforcement model of addressing the crime of terrorism holds certain strengths. Firstly, treating terrorism as a subcategory of crime does not overly exaggerate the nature of the threat. Terrorism as a tactic is designed to have wide psychological repercussions, meant to create the feelings of fear and vulnerability among the population (Crenshaw 2000). At the same time, the probability of being a victim of a terrorist attack remains rather low. In this respect, law enforcement undermines the intended psychological consequences of a terrorist attack and addresses it as an act, which pertains to the characteristics of most acts of crime, with the only differences being "merely ones of degree" (Clarke & Newman 2007).

Further, policing terrorism offers a constitutional response to the threat, which is embedded in the justice system. In this respect, the police as an institution of public service are designed to protect public safety and security, and can be an effective means of fighting terrorism (Murray 2005). Finally, the police are usually the most trained existing institution in a state, with experience of addressing societal crises and disasters. Here, law enforcement presents venues for addressing the challenge of terrorism through established functioning agencies, instead of creating and training new bodies of response forces.

On the downside, the law enforcement responses to terrorism might not be very visible, and the public might not perceive this type of reaction on the part of a state as active counteraction to the immediate threat. Police operations are usually time-consuming, with investigation and prosecution at times taking years to accomplish. Prosecution itself has a questionable effect on deterrence, and prosecuting an individual does not necessarily destroy the respective terrorist network or organization. Further, terrorism arguably presents a substantively different criminal offense and, as such, might require a qualitatively different counteraction than the majority of criminal offences deserve. Finally, as Samuel Nunn (2003) points out, there always remains a probability of the police abuse, be it the power of arrest, detention, or technological surveillance.

Counter-terrorism and law enforcement are oftentimes used to supplement each other (as in the example of the UK). However, looking at the two as distinct anti-terrorist approaches allows us to better understand the advantages and disadvantages of each of them in the fight against terrorism. Further, analyzing the strengths and weaknesses of the two approaches in terms of effectiveness and legitimacy can lead to some conclusions regarding the best response strategies.

Counter-Terrorism Vs. Law Enforcement: Effectiveness

Assessment of the effectiveness of anti-terrorist measures presents a significant problem for researchers and policymakers. The concept of effectiveness is extremely hard to operationalize and measure. And even despite a growing number of studies investigating the effect of anti-terrorist measures and provisions, there is no consensus on what constitutes the most effective response to terrorism.

A large number of anti-terrorist policies have been found ineffective in addressing the threat of terrorism. As Hewitt (1984) concludes, "some policies do not work at all, and some policies are successful in certain situations but not in others" (p. 92). However, before accepting this predominantly pessimistic conclusion, we need to look at what effectiveness stands for, what constitutes success, and what criteria have to be met before announcing a policy effective.

Charters (1994) approaches this endeavor by delineating four criteria in order to assess the effectiveness of anti-terrorist provisions:

1. The rate of terrorist incidents in the country concerned.
2. The number of casualties resulting from terrorism.
3. The number of terrorists captured, convicted, and jailed as a result of due process, and not replaced in the terrorist group.
4. The number of terrorists "neutralized" as a result of attrition (i.e., killed or wounded), and not replaced (p. 214).

While these criteria might seem self-explanatory, they are hard to trace and measure. First, it is problematic to attribute the receding number of incidents to policy success. The absence of terrorist attacks might be caused by a multitude of factors, including but not limited to reforms, regime change, shifts in terrorist tactics and demands, etc. (Miller 2007). Secondly, the number of attacks might diminish, but the number of casualties can increase. As exemplified by the attacks of September 11, terrorists can carry out compact high-impact attacks claiming lives of thousands of people. Finally, characteristics of terrorist groups present another problem for quantification. Not only is it hard to gain access to representatives of a terrorist organization, but it is also unlikely to obtain reliable data on the number and demographics of its members. These issues highlight the problems of evaluating the criteria for effectiveness and carrying out policy evaluations.

However, the absence of common criteria for effectiveness has not stopped scholarly investigations into the effect of anti-terrorist policies and provisions. What has been found supports Hewitt's (1984) point of view. For instance, Jon Cauley and E.I. Im (1988), in their analysis of such measures against terrorism as the 1973 U.S. Airport Security Act, the 1976 U.S. Embassy Security Act, the 1977 U.S. proclamation of adherence to the U.N. Convention on the Prevention and Punishment of Crimes against Internationally Protected Persons, Including Diplomatic Agents, determined that effectiveness of anti-terrorist policies is significantly thwarted by a substitution effect. And while substitution effects are complex, securing some targets forces terrorists to invent alternative means of attack, which leads to more innovations in the arsenal of terrorists. Thus, João Ricardo Faria (2006) points out that terrorists often resort to innovating techniques while the government lags behind trying to catch up with the perpetrators. This undermines the effectiveness of anti-terrorist policies.

Enders and Sandler (2002) arrive at a somewhat similar conclusion. In their analysis of policy interventions, the authors look at how anti-terrorist policies affect incidents of transnational terrorism. Grounding their research in the assumption that attack–counterattack dynamics allow us to predict patterns of transnational terrorism, and, therefore, come up with the most effective policy alternatives, Enders and Sandler conduct an extensive empirical investigation. The results of their analysis, based on the 1970–1999 International Terrorism Attributes and Terrorist

Events (ITERATE) data indicate that the most effective measure of deterring terrorism seems to be a simultaneous reduction of all kinds of resources available to terrorists. Enders and Sandler come to the conclusion that piecemeal anti-terrorist measures do not work.

Thus, the overall effect of anti-terrorist measures seems to be rather insignificant irrespective of the shape or form of anti-terrorist provisions. The overall conclusion of Cynthia Lum et al. (2006) supports this observation. On the basis of a meta-analysis of interventions studies they state that no consistent indication of the success of anti-terrorist policies exists. Accordingly, "in many cases, effects are not statistically discernible from a null effect, or can be harmful and increase the likelihood of certain types of terrorism" (p. 32). Until now, research that has been carried out on the issue of effectiveness of anti-terrorist policies indicates that anti-terrorist measures and provisions largely fail to meet their goal of reducing incidents of terrorist attacks.

This discussion on the issue of effectiveness of anti-terrorist measures outlines the considerations behind comparisons between counter-terrorism and law enforcement. While we cannot conclude with confidence that one of these approaches is better, empirical evidence seems to suggest that law enforcement should be favored over counter-terrorism. Imposition of new anti-terrorist policies is predicted to spur terrorist innovations and lead to the implementation of alternative modes of terrorist operations, which negates the very purpose of institutionalizing additional anti-terrorist measures. These findings caution us against the counter-terrorism approach. On the other hand, measures that seem to work, even though often only temporarily, can be best implemented under the law enforcement approach. They include screening installations, security screening, covert operations, and watch lists (Bremmer 1992), and are routinely performed by police forces worldwide.

Counter-Terrorism Vs. Law Enforcement: Legitimacy

Anti-terrorist measures and provisions have raised numerous criticisms in regards to their impact on civil rights and liberties. While the threat of terrorism requires a response, the question remains whether freedom should be sacrificed in the name of security and, therefore, whether anti-terrorist provisions are legitimate. Democratic governments are obliged to protect the well-being of their citizens. However, because civil rights and liberties remain at the heart of the institution of liberal democracy, it is of paramount importance to sustain their level, and not give in to terrorists by abridging them. Terrorists target not only the well-being of citizens, but also the very principles of a liberal democracy. In their efforts to fight terrorism, governments impose anti-terrorist policies, which, in turn, restrict civil rights and liberties of citizens, thus jeopardizing the justifiability of introducing new anti-terrorist measures.

Anti-terrorist provisions produce a wide impact on the freedoms citizens enjoy in a liberal democracy. Searches without warrants, questioning without detention, expanded powers of arrest and deportation, severe penalties for terrorist offences, trials in special courts – all undermine the due process foundations of liberal democracies. These measures indicate the sacrifice of freedom for security in today's world where concerns over terrorism are constantly growing. However, as Enders and Sandler (2006) note: "As attacks escalate, liberal democracies will sacrifice further freedoms as their constituencies become more willing to exchange liberties for a greater sense of security" (p. 51). This, in turn, questions the nature of an emerging regime – is a state that is wiling to infringe on civil rights and liberties of its citizens still a democracy?

Answering this question, Alex Schmid (1992) argues that democracy should not forfeit freedoms in the fight against terrorism, as in his view, the sacrifice of civil liberties symbolizes the victory of terrorists in the fight over legitimacy. Fernando Reinares (1998) pursues the issue of democratic principles of governance and their interrelation with terrorism even further. His analysis stems from the assumption that terrorism presents a threat to the stability of democratic regimes and might disrupt the legal guarantees enjoyed by citizens through newly imposed anti-terrorist policies. Thus, he argues that democratic regimes are entitled to follow the established legal rules and procedures and utilize political, judicial, and enforcement measures available to fight the threat of terrorism.

Further, analyzing the controversies of courts set up to specifically address the issue of terrorism, Reinares finds that technicalities of anti-terrorist legislation might render these institutions unconstitutional due to their imprecise and vague formulations. In this respect, he strongly advocates for the law enforcement approach in addressing terrorism. He criticizes the structure of special courts, as well as provisions of emergency legislation, which disrupt the nature of existing political arrangements.

The detrimental effect anti-terrorist policies can produce on democracy is a significant factor weighing against counter-terrorism. Peter Chalk (1998) argues that by undermining the very principles of liberal democracy, counter-terrorism loses its legitimacy. He notes that when the response to terrorism is not limited, thoroughly defined, and controlled, the institutionalized anti-terrorist policies may pose an even greater threat to democratic principles than terrorists themselves. Analyzing anti-terrorist provisions in Italy, Spain, and Peru, Chalk illustrates how anti-terrorist policies, originally imposed by a democratic state, came to very much resemble institutionalized terror from "above," instead of eradicating terror from "below." Consequently, the very possibility for a government to start using anti-terrorist policies in an unconstitutional and arbitrary manner might lead to the failure of the state legitimacy, which greatly jeopardizes democracy.

This section outlines the perils that anti-terrorist measures and provisions pose for liberal democracies. I illustrate how counter-terrorism often can undermine the civil rights and liberties of citizens. Special anti-terrorist interventions impinge on societal freedoms without firm proof of having a positive effect on the reduction of the terrorist threat. At the same time, these measures alienate members of community from the government – the very elements a state needs to engage in cooperation against the threat in order to achieve success (Briggs et al. 2006). Again, empirical observations offer evidence in support of law enforcement, which does not disrupt the legal guarantees of citizens in a democratic regime. Indeed, as I argue in the next section, civil liberties are crucial for the success of endeavors against terrorism, and counter-terrorism is neither effective nor legitimate enough to prevail over law enforcement as a way of fighting terrorism.

The Role of Civil Liberties in the Fight Against Terrorism

While elaborating on the appropriate response to terrorism, a liberal democracy is bound to justify the choice of strategies according to the principles of effectiveness and legitimacy. While doing so, democracies need to pay specific attention to the preservation of the democratic principles of governance and have to safeguard civil rights and liberties inherent in a democratic regime. By protecting civil rights and liberties, democracies can avoid giving in to terrorists, who target the foundations of democratic societies. In addition, as the analysis below illustrates, enhancement of civil liberties can in fact decrease the probability of terrorism in a country. Thus, civil liberties should be preserved not only as a crucial element of democracy, but also as a tool in the fight against the threat of terrorism.

Anti-terrorist measures are targeted at decreasing the probability of terrorism. In this respect, the goal of this project is to investigate whether civil liberties have an impact on the probability of terrorist attacks in a country. While sacrificing civil rights and liberties is detrimental to democracy, if such infringements decrease the probability of terrorist attacks in the future, such measures can be justified as a necessary concession to ensure security. On the other hand, if a reduction in the level of civil liberties actually induces the population to resort to terrorism as a way of political advocacy, then curtailing rights and liberties is not legitimate for combating terrorism. If the latter is true, then the counter-terrorism approach becomes less attractive than law enforcement due to its negative impacts on civil liberties. With these speculations in mind, I analyze the significance of civil liberties as a predictor of the probability of a terrorist attack in a state and hypothesize that the probability of terrorist attacks in the future will be negatively correlated with the level of civil liberties in a state.

In order to investigate the probability of terrorist attacks I use logistic regression analysis. The ordinary least squares technique would not be appropriate in this case, because it would reflect fluctuations in the numbers of attacks in a specific state. Logit analysis, on the other hand, is a powerful tool for predicting probabilities (Liao 1994). As a result, the probability of terrorist attacks serves as a dependent variable for the current analysis and is coded as a 0/1 category, with 0 representing the absence of terrorist attacks in a given state and 1 indicating the presence thereof. The total number of observations constitutes 134 states, which were the starting location for terrorist attacks. The data for the years 2003–2004 on terrorism was obtained from the ITERATE database (Mickolus et al. 2004). This time period was chosen to investigate the current, post-9/11 trends in terrorism, and the choice was restricted by the data availability for more recent years.

Civil liberties in the model stand for the ability of citizens to exercise democratic freedoms, such as freedom of expression, freedom of speech, freedom of association, etc. The data for this variable comes from the Freedom House data set (2006), and observations for the year 2004 were recoded so that 1 represents the lowest level of civil liberties and 7 the highest. The level of civil liberties is treated as a predictor of the future probability of a terrorist attack, and I suspect that states with higher levels of civil liberties will be less prone to terrorist attacks than their more authoritarian counterparts. This hypothesis is grounded in the assumption that the lack of civil liberties drives individuals to terrorism as the only available alternative for political advocacy. If this hypothesis is true, infringements on civil liberties imposed by counter-terrorism are not legitimate, and can in fact be counter-productive.

The choice of control variables for the model was driven by the literature on the causes of terrorism. Three groups of variables are incorporated in the model, each falling into the socioeconomic, political, and cultural categories of the sources of terrorism (Von Hippel 2002; Ozdogan 2006). To control for socioeconomic conditions, GDP per capita was included in the model (UN Statistics Division 2004). Corruption, as a proxy for crime, refers to the perception of the level of corruption in the country by business representatives and country analysts. The score for corruption ranges from 10 (highly clean) to 0 (highly corrupt) and is derived from the Transparency International Corruption Perception Indexes, 2004–2007.

In the political group of variables are included regime durability, government constraint, and openness of executive recruitment. The data for these variables was obtained from the Polity IV Project (Marshall & Jaggers 2005). Regime durability indicates the number of years a state has been in existence. Government constraint reflects the level of institutional limitations placed on the decision-making powers of chief executives. Openness of executive recruitment signifies the existence of venues for initiating peaceful change instead of resorting to terrorism and is considered open when citizens have an opportunity to attain an executive position without regulation. These variables control for the effect regime characteristics exert on the probability of terrorism. In addition, a variable of armed conflict (Gleditsch et al. 2007) was utilized to trace the potential correlation between terrorism and involvement of a state in an armed confrontation. This variable reflects if a state within given years was (1) or was not (0) involved in a conflict.

Finally, under the cultural category, I controlled for religion, ethnic composition, and the level of ethnic fractionalization. The variable of religion (CIA 2004b) indicates whether a country has one dominant religion (50–100% of the population) or incorporates multiple religions (the most numerous one comprising under 50% of the population). Ethnic composition (CIA 2004a) reflects the percentage of the population belonging to the dominant ethnic group. Finally, the level of ethnic fractionalization (Alesina et al. 2003) indicates how diverse the composition of the society is. These variables are considered important in predicting societal dissatisfaction and the desire to engage in violence, and were therefore employed in the model.

Thus, the model predicts the probability of terrorist attacks as follows:

$$\text{Terrorism} = \alpha + \beta_1\text{*Civil Liberties} + \beta_2\text{*GDP per capita} + \beta_3\text{*Corruption} + \beta_4\text{*Regime Durability} + \beta_5\text{*Government Constraint} + \beta_6\text{*Openness of Executive Recruitment} + \beta_7\text{*Armed Conflict} + \beta_8\text{*Religion} + \beta_9\text{*Ethnic Composition} + \beta_{10}\text{*Ethnic Fractionalization.}$$

The results of logistic regression analysis are presented in Table 1. As predicted, civil liberties exert an important influence on the probability of a terrorist attack in a state. At the significance level of 0.05, the variable of civil liberties is statistically significant and is negatively correlated with the probability of terrorism. This implies that with an increase in civil liberties a state faces a diminishing threat of terrorist attacks. This finding supports the hypothesis that higher levels of civil liberties reduce the probability of a terrorist attack. This leads to the conclusion that curtailment of freedoms produced by counter-terrorism is not justifiable in the light of these findings.

In addition, the variables of armed conflict, GDP per capita, and religion proved to be statistically significant. Thus, countries involved in armed conflicts are more likely to experience terrorist attacks. Wealthier states are more vulnerable to terrorism, which once again suggests that democracies are at a disadvantage, because richer states tend to be more democratic (Przeworski & Limongi 1997). States with one dominant religion are also more likely to experience terrorist attacks. These variables indicate potential sources of terrorism, such as armed conflicts, perceived relative wealth, and religious intolerance. These results point to potential policy areas that extend beyond counter-terrorism and law enforcement and need to be addressed in order to successfully fight the threat of terrorism.

The empirical analysis illustrates the significant relationship between civil liberties and terrorism. In this respect we have empirical evidence against imposing constraints on civil liberties in the name of security. This suggests that civil liberties should be guarded and preserved not only as an inherent democratic

Table 1 Logistic regression analysis predicting the probability of terrorist attacks

	Regression coefficient	Standard error	*z*-test	*P*-value
Civil liberties	**−1.0149***	0.3333	−3.04	0.002
GDP per capita	**0.0002***	0.0001	3.10	0.002
Corruption	−0.3708	0.2903	−1.28	0.201
Regime durability	−0.0121	0.0105	−1.15	0.250
Government constraint	0.3897	0.2387	1.63	0.103
Openness of executive recruitment	−0.0320	0.1732	−0.18	0.853
Armed conflict	**2.5167***	0.8173	3.08	0.002
Religion	**1.7244***	0.6608	2.61	0.009
Ethnic composition	0.0052	0.0146	0.36	0.721
Ethnic fractionalization	−0.0072	0.0131	−0.55	0.581
Constant	0.6907	1.9980	0.35	0.730

*Indicates significance at the 0.05 level (highlighted in bold); number of observations = 134; LR $\chi^2(10) = 46.23$; prob > $\chi^2 = 0.0000$; pseudo $R^2 = 0.2682$

value, but also as a means of reducing the probability of terrorist attacks. Because counter-terrorism, while largely ineffective in fighting the threat, has a negative impact on civil liberties, institutionalization of additional anti-terrorist measures and provisions is not justifiable in the name of security. Instead, the law enforcement model of addressing terrorism might offer a more legitimate approach for treating terrorism as a subcategory of crime under the existing law enforcement framework.

Discussion and Conclusions

The analysis presented in this chapter demonstrates the significance of civil rights and liberties in the efforts to fight terrorism. Thus, states with higher levels of freedoms will face a lower probability of a terrorist attack. This correlation suggests that successful responses to terrorism should be targeted at enhancing civil rights and liberties. As we have seen, counter-terrorism as an approach to combating the threat, places additional constraints on freedoms, thus infringing upon them instead of enhancing them. In addition, many anti-terrorist measures have been previously proven largely ineffective in eradicating terrorism. These observations, combined with the significance of civil liberties, might be indicative of the dangers that the counter-terrorism approach poses for liberal democracies. As a result, the law enforcement model, which does not impose additional restrictions on citizens, may be more appropriate for addressing the threat of terrorism.

This chapter outlines the complex nature of considerations behind the choice of counteraction to terrorism. In this respect, delineation between counter-terrorism and law enforcement offers some guidelines for policymakers in implementing anti-terrorist measures and provisions. Aside from the effectiveness and legitimacy concerns, the choice of response strategies is key for the success in the fight against terrorism. It is important to remember that institutionalized anti-terrorist measures and provisions are rather sticky, and, due to the mechanisms of path-dependence (Pierson 2004) are rarely revoked. Thus, once in place, these measures will have an enormous impact on the future evolution of anti-terrorism, and can further affect the nature of democracy in a state.

Additionally, the results of the present analysis point to the significance of such factors as religion, armed conflict and societal wealth for the outcome of terrorism. These findings require further investigation in policy areas beyond counter-terrorism and law enforcement. For instance, terrorism as an outcome of armed conflicts may be best addressed through conciliation (Sederberg 1995), and poverty reduction may discourage individuals from resorting to terrorism as a means of political advocacy. Finally, another venue for future research is the investigation of interests vested in different models of response to terrorism, which might further explain the current predominance of counter-terrorism and relative unpopularity of law enforcement.

References

Alesina, A., Devleeschauwer, A., Easterly, W., Kurlat S., & Wacziarg, R. (2003). Fractionalization. *Journal of Economic Growth* **8**(2), 155–194.

Antiterrorism and Effective Death Penalty Act (1996). U.S. Code.

Banks, C. (2004). Protecting (or destroying) freedom through law: The USA Patriot Act's constitutional implications. In: D.B. Cohen & J.W. Wells (Eds.), *American National Security and Civil Liberties in an Era of Terrorism* (pp. 29–70). New York: Palgrave MacMillan.

Bremmer, L.P. (1992). The West's counter-terrorist strategy. *Terror. Pol. Viol.* **4**(4), 255–262.

Briggs, R., Fieschi C., & Lownsbrough H. (2006). *Bringing It Home: Community-Based Approaches to Counter-Terrorism*. London: Demos.

Cauley, J., & Im, E.I. (1988). Intervention policy analysis of skyjackings and other terrorist incidents. *Am. Econ. Rev.* **78**(2), 27–31.

Central Intelligence Agency (2004a). *The CIA World Factbook: Ethnic Groups*. Washington, DC: CIA.

Central Intelligence Agency (2004b). *The CIA World Factbook: Religions*. Washington, DC: CIA.

Chalk, P. (1998). The response to terrorism as a threat to liberal democracy. *Aus. J. Pol. & His.* **44**(3), 373–388.

Charters, D.A. (1994). Conclusions: Security and liberty in balance – Countering terrorism in the democratic context. In: D.A. Charters (Ed.), *The Deadly Sin of Terrorism: Its Effect on Democracy and Civil Liberty in Six Countries* (pp. 211–227). Westport, CT: Greenwood.

Clarke, R.V., & Newman, G.R. (2007). Police and the prevention of terrorism. *Policing* **1**(1), 9–20.

Crelinsten, R.D. (1998). The discourse and practice of counter-terrorism in liberal democracies. *Aus. J. Pol. & His.* **44**(1), 389–413.

Crenshaw, M. (2000). The psychology of terrorism: An agenda for the 21st century. *Pol. Psych.* **21**(2), 405–420.

Enders, W., & Sandler, T. (1993). The effectiveness of antiterrorism policies: A vector–autoregression–intervention analysis. *Am. Pol. Sci. Rev.* **87**(4), 829–844.

Enders, W., & Sandler, T. (2002). Patterns of transnational terrorism, 1970–1999: Alternative time-series estimates. *Int. Stud. Quart.* **46**(2), 145–165.

Enders, W., & Sandler, T. (2006). *The Political Economy of Terrorism*. Cambridge: Cambridge University Press.

Faria, J.R. (2006). Terrorist innovations and anti-terrorist policies. *Terror. Pol. Viol.* **18**(1), 47–56.

Freedom House (2006). *Freedom in the World Country Ratings: 1972–2006*. New York: Freedom House.

Gleditsch, N.P., Wallensteen, P., Eriksson, M., Sollenberg, M., & Strand, H. (2007). *UCDP/PRIO Armed Conflict Dataset*. Version 4–2007, CDP/PRIO.

Henry, V.E. (2002). The need for a coordinated and strategic logical police approach to terrorism: A practitioner's perspective. *Police Pract. Res.* **3**(4), 319–336.

Hewitt, C. (1984). *The Effectiveness of Anti-Terrorist Policies*. Lanham, MD: University Press of America.

Innes, M. (2006). Policing uncertainty: Countering terror through community intelligence and democratic policing. *Ann. Amer. Acad. Pol. Soc. Sci.* **605**(1), 222–241.

Katzenstein, P.J. (1993). Coping with terrorism: Norms and internal security in Germany and Japan. In: J. Goldstein & R.O. Keohane (Eds.), *Ideas and Foreign Policy, Beliefs, Institutions, and Political Change* (pp. 265–295). Ithaca: Cornell University Press.

LeVine, V.T., & Salert, B.A. (1996). Does a coercive official response deter terrorism? The case of the PLO. *Terror. Pol. Viol.* **8**(1), 22–49.

Li, Q. (2005). Does democracy promote or reduce transnational terrorist incidents? *J. Conflict Res.* **49**(2), 278–297.

Liao, T.F. (1994). *Interpreting Probability Models: Logit, Probit, and Other Generalized Linear Models*. Thousand Oaks, CA: SAGE.

Lum, C., Kennedy, L.W., & Sherley, A.J. (2006). The effectiveness of counter-terrorism strategies: A Campbell systematic review. Retrieved from http://db.c2admin.org/doc-pdf/Lum_Terrorism_Review.pdf.

Marshall, M.G., & Jaggers, K. (2005). *Polity IV Project: Political Regime Characteristics and Transitions, 1800–2004*. Arlington, VA: Center for Global Policy.

Mickolus, E.F., Sandler, T., Murdock, J.M., & Flemming, P.A. (2004). *International Terrorism: Attributes of Terrorist Events, 1968–2003*. Dunn Loring, VA: Vinyard Software.

Miller, G.D. (2007). Confronting terrorisms: Group motivation and successful state policies. *Terror. Pol. Viol.* **17**(3), 331–350.

Murray, J. (2005). Policing terrorism: A threat to community policing or just a shift in priorities? *Police Pract. Res.* **6**(4), 347–361.

Nunn, S. (2003). Seeking tools for the war on terror: A critical assessment of emerging technologies in law enforcement. *Policing Int. J. Police Strat. Man.* **26**(3), 454–472.

Ozdogan, A. (2006). Where do terrorists come from? In: R.W. Orttung & A. Makarychev (Eds.), *National Counter-Terrorism Strategies*, Washington, DC: IOS Press, pp. 21–42.

Pierson, P. (2004). *Politics in Time*. Princeton, NJ: Princeton University Press.

Przeworski, A., & Limongi, F. (1997). Modernization: Theories and facts. *World Pol.* **49**(2), 155–183.

Putin, V. (2006a). On counterterrorist measures. *Presidential Decree, No. 116*. February 15, 2006. Moscow: Kremlin.

Putin, V. (2006b). On counteraction of terrorism, *Federal Law of the Russian Federation, No. 35-FZ*, March 6, 2006. Moscow: Kremlin.

Reinares, F. (1998). Democratic regimes, internal security politics, and the threat of terrorism. *Aus. J. Pol. & His.* **44**(3), 351–371.

Schmid, A.P. (1992). Terrorism and democracy. *Terror. Pol. Viol.* **4**(4), 14–25.

Sederberg, P.C. (1995). Conciliation as counter-terrorist strategy. *J. Peace Res.* **32**(3), 295–312.

Transparency International (2004). *Corruption Perceptions Index*. Retrieved from http://www.transparency.org/policy_research/surveys_indices/cpi/2004.

United Nations Statistics Division (2004). *GDP per capita, Current Prices, in U.S. Dollars*. Retrieved from http://unstats.un.org/unsd/snaama/dnlList.asp.

United States House of Representatives. Subcommittee on National Security, Emerging Threats, and International Relations of the Committee on Government Reform (2004). *Effective Strategies Against Terrorism*. 108th Cong., 2nd Sess., 3 February.

Uniting and Strengthening America by Providing Appropriate Tools Required to Intercept and Obstruct Terrorism Act of 2001 (USA PATRIOT Act). 2001. 107th Cong., 1st Sess., HR 3162 RDS.

Viscusi, W.K., & Zeckhauser, R.J. (2003). Sacrificing civil liberties to reduce terrorism risks. *J. Risk Uncertain.* **26**(2/3), 99–120.

Von Hippel, K. (2002). The roots of terrorism: Probing the myths. In: L. Freedman (Ed.), *Superterrorism: Policy Responses* (pp. 25–39). Malden, MA: Blackwell.

Yeltsin, B. (1998). *On the fight against terrorism. Federal Law of the Russian Federation, No. 130-FZ*, July 25, 1998. Moscow: Kremlin.

Zimmerman, D., & Wenger, A. (2007). Toward efficiency and legitimacy. In: D. Zimmerman & A. Wenger (Eds.), *How States Fight Terrorism: Policy Dynamics in the West* (pp. 203–229). Boulder, CO: Lynne Rienner.

Divided We Stand? American and European Perspectives in the Fight Against Transnational Terrorism[1]

M. Victoria Pérez-Ríos

> The United States and its allies will win the war only if they fight it in the right way – with the same sort of patience, strength, and resolve that helped win the Cold War and with policies designed to provide alternative hopes and dreams to potential enemies (Gordon 2007, November/December, pp. 59–60).

Introduction

In the immediate aftermath of 9/11, a common front against terrorism developed among the members of the United Nations (UN). Not only was the UN Security Council Resolution (UNSCR) 1373 on international terrorism unanimously approved on September 28, 2001 (U.S. Department of State 2001, December 19),[2] but the number of parties to the already existing 12 international legal instruments on counter-terrorism also rapidly increased (Counter-Terrorism Committee 2009, September 18).[3] Moreover, President George W. Bush (2001–2009) was able to rally a "coalition of the willing," including Spain and the United Kingdom, to fight the Taliban in Afghanistan and then to help in stabilizing Iraq after the official end to the war. However, adopting specific counter-terrorism measures remains controversial, in part, as a result of disagreement on the concept of terrorism.

Although defining terrorism is complicated for political and moral reasons, in this chapter it is defined as "the premeditated use or threat of use of violence by individuals or subnational groups to obtain a political or social objective through intimidation of a

[1]Preliminary research for this chapter started at the 2006 NEH Human Institute on "Human Rights in Conflict: Interdisciplinary Perspectives" (New York City, June 26–July 28). However, any views, findings, conclusions, or recommendations expressed in this publication do not necessarily reflect those of the National Endowment for the Humanities.

[2]UNSCR 1373 (2001) made international counter-terrorism legislation legally binding on all the members of the UN immediately after 9/11.

[3]Currently there are sixteen international instruments (13 Conventions) on terrorism and "some two-thirds of UN Member States have either ratified or acceded to at least 10" (Counter-Terrorism Committee, 2009, September 18).

M.V. Pérez-Ríos (✉)
Department of Political Science, John Jay College of Criminal Justice, New York, NY, USA
e-mail: mvictoriasp@hotmail.com

G. Andreopoulos et al. (eds.), *International Criminal Justice: Critical Perspectives and New Challenges*, DOI 10.1007/978-1-4419-1102-5_6,
© Springer Science+Business Media, LLC 2011

large audience beyond that of the immediate victims" (Enders 2006, June, p. 369). This definition excludes state terrorism, which could justify foreign military intervention.[4]

In addition, I focus on Islamist terrorism,[5] which is, first, transnational,[6] that is, it affects more than one state;[7] and, second, it consists of networks of independent cells, each with their own characteristics. For example, while the cells operating in the UK were homegrown, those in the United States and Spain were filled with outsiders. Due to the diversity in the composition of the different cells, this type of terrorism is resilient.[8]

As a consequence of the terrorist attacks of 9/11, security became the main concern of most states. Although no "pure" approach to counter-terrorism exists, it can be affirmed that while the government of the United States sponsored an exceptional approach, its European Union (EU) counterparts supported more firmly a criminal justice approach – even after Islamist terrorists attacked Spain in 2004 and the UK in 2005.[9]

The exceptional, or "war," approach refers to any counter-terrorism perspective that views suspected terrorists as enemies to be destroyed. Thus, the government is engaged in a "war" in which the protection of the individual rights – including due process – of "enemies" wanes or is severely constrained; but contrary to a conventional war, the government rejects the application of the Geneva Conventions or international humanitarian law. This approach characterizes the "war on terror" against al-Qaeda and the Taliban.[10] The rule of law, or criminal justice, approach treats alleged terrorists as ordinary criminals. Even though quantitative differences such as longer periods of detention may exist in the rule of law approach, counter-terrorism regulations have to respect core rights – including due process. Democratic regimes tend to prefer this last approach.[11]

---

[4]According to the doctrines of humanitarian intervention (HI) and, more recently, of the Responsibility to Protect (R2P) the use of force is legitimate when a State is accused of genocide or crimes against humanity (Wheeler 2000, and International Coalition for the Responsibility to Protect (n.d)).

[5]"[T]he enemy is not just 'terrorism,' some generic evil.... It is the threat posed by *Islamist* terrorism – especially the al-Qaeda network, its affiliates, and its ideology" (The 9/11 Commission, 2004, p. 362).

[6]Transnationalism is a question of degree because "[m]any terrorist organizations (such as the PLO, IRA, and ETA) have operated and trained across jurisdictions [in the past]" (Gross and Ní Aoláin, 2006, pp. 379–380).

[7]"[T]he perpetrators, victims, or audience are from two or more [States]" and/or "the attacks occurred in two or more States" (Sandler and Arce 2008, March 6, p. 9).

[8]Some argue that the lethality of these cells can be overstated, with negative effects for human rights protection (Matthew and Shambaugh, 2005, p. 617).

[9]The president of the United States, and the prime ministers of Spain and the UK met in the Azores where they agreed to a common front against terrorism in Iraq (BBC News 2003, March 16).

[10]International humanitarian law or the laws of war are not the focus here, but are mentioned when relevant.

[11]Prior to 9/11, the United States criminally prosecuted Islamist terrorists. For example, those accused of the February 26, 1993, bombing of the World Trade Center (The 9/11 Commission, 2004, p. 72). In the rule of law approach, the military is used sparingly and as a last resort.

The assessment of these two approaches – even one like this study, which must be preliminary due to the ongoing nature of the "war on terror" – has normative and policy implications for states: First, the assessment can help us to decide the type of society that we want – one that prioritizes civil/political and human rights, including security, or one in which security is the overriding right to which the rest are subservient. Second, it allows us to design a more effective counter-terrorism system. And third, it facilitates counter-terrorism cooperation among states by showing commonalities among different approaches.

I have introduced the following limitations into my analysis: First, I examine the relevant counter-terrorism policies adopted in three democracies – the United States, Spain, and the United Kingdom – in the aftermath of Islamist attacks in each country, with a primary focus on the Bush administration in the case of the United States.[12] Second, the specific measures examined refer mainly to due process and interrogation techniques. Due process is a key right because historically its violation has fostered widespread governmental abuses[13] and interrogation techniques affect the ban on torture, which is *jus cogens*, that is, it constrains all States, whether party or not to the 1984 Convention against Torture, to comply with it.[14] And third, in order to assess the mentioned measures, I consider their level of respect toward human rights and especially non-derogable rights.[15] Non-derogable human rights are relevant because no state can use an emergency situation, such as the "war on terror," to justify their violation.

In the rest of the chapter, I examine first, the United States as a model of the "war" approach;[16] second, Spain as a model of the criminal justice approach;[17] and

[12]After 9/11 and prior to the Madrid and London bombings, successful attacks included Indonesia, Morocco, and Turkey (Shuster 2005, July 7).

[13]For example, the military regimes in Argentina and Chile during the Cold War effectively curtailed *habeas corpus* and no judicial control favored the systematic practice of torture and disappearances.

[14]Convention Against Torture, Cruel, Inhuman and Degrading Treatment (CAT). In G.A. Res. 39/46, 39 UN GAOR, Supp. (No. 51), UN Doc. A/39/51, at 197 (1984). The Convention Against Torture was adopted on December 10, 1984, and entered into force on June 26, 1987. Spain (October 21, 1987), the UK (December 8, 1988) and the United States (October 21, 1994) are parties to it (see dates of ratification between parentheses) and to the monitoring of the Committee on Torture.

[15]Listed in Art. 4 (2) of the International Covenant on Civil and Political Rights (ICCPR). They include the right to life (Art. 6), the right to be free from torture (Art. 7 of the ICCPR), the right to be free from slavery and servitude (Art. 8), nonretroactivity of criminal law or *nullum crimen sine lege* (Art. 15), recognition as a person before the law everywhere (Art. 16), and freedom of thought, conscience, and religion (Art. 18). The ICCPR was adopted on December 16, 1966, and entered into force on March 23, 1976. For its complete text, see G.A. Res. 2200A (XXI), UN Doc. A/6316 (1966), 999 UNTS 171, reprinted in 6 ILM 368 (1967). Spain, the UK, and the United States are parties to the ICCPR. The dates of ratification of the three are as follows: Spain (April 27, 1977), the UK (May 20, 1976) and the United States (June 8, 1992). For wartimes, common Article 3 of the Geneva Conventions lists non-derogable rights. See footnote 41 below.For an in-depth analysis of states of emergency with a focus on terrorism, which is beyond the scope of this chapter, see Gross and Ní Aoláin (2006, Chap. 7).

[16]Hereinafter, "war" and "exceptional" are used as synonyms.

[17]Hereinafter, "criminal justice," "rule of law," and "law enforcement" are used as synonyms.

third, the UK as an example of the evolution from a "war" approach to one more grounded on criminal justice.

***Finally, I conclude that the two approaches are equally effective because no new attacks have succeeded (a counter-factual); that the "war" approach is more prone to human rights violations; and that respect for the rule of law fosters needed counter-terrorism cooperation at the international level.

A "War" Approach to Counter-Terrorism: The United States[18]

On September 11, 2001, 19 terrorists used American civilian planes to attack a civilian (World Trade Center) and a military (the Pentagon) target, causing more than 3,000 deaths (The 9/11 Commission 2004).[19] The high death toll and the terrorists' success in overcoming U.S. airspace security to attack symbols of American might – including the unfulfilled threat to the White House and the Capitol – signaled to the country its vulnerability and made security the top priority of the nation.[20]

The government's reaction was to announce a "war on terror" – of unlimited duration – which President Bush summed up in his September 20, 2001, address to the American people: "Our enemy is a radical network of terrorists, and every government that supports them. Our war on terror begins with al-Qaeda, but it does not end there. It will not end until every terrorist group of global reach has been found, stopped, and defeated" (Bush, 2001, p. 185).

Although, since 9/11 the United States has used the regular court system to criminally prosecute some alleged terrorists – as did Spain and the UK after they were the victims of Islamist terrorism[21] – an exceptional approach for the most part characterized

---

[18]Based largely on the 9/11 Commission Report, relevant domestic laws including the Patriot Act, significant Supreme Court decisions, and intergovernmental and nongovernmental organization reports.

[19]On the morning of 9/11 four teams of suicide terrorists (three teams of five and one of four) hijacked four American planes with transcontinental routes – American 11 and United 175 departing from Boston, American 77 departing from Washington, DC, and United 93 departing from Newark, NJ. The terrorists flew the first two planes into the World Trade Center in New York City causing close to 3,000 civilian deaths and numerous injuries (The 9/11 Commission, 2004, Chap. 1). The third plane was flown into the Pentagon in Arlington (VA) killing 189 individuals – 64 civilians on board and 125 people in the Pentagon, of which 55 were military personnel – and injuring over 100 (The 9/11 Commission, 2004, p. 314). United 93 did not reach its objective because the passengers forced the four terrorists to crash it in Shanksville, PA. A total of 33 passengers, 7 crew members and the 4 terrorists died (The 9/11 Commission, 2004, p.14).

[20]For example, the government closed our national airspace. "For the first time [in the nation's history] all nonemergency civilian aircraft in the United States were grounded" (The 9/11 Commission 2004, p. 326).

[21]In the United States, as a rule, convictions are based on charges of material support to terrorism (Zabel and Benjamin 2009, July, Preface).

the counter-terrorism efforts of the Bush administration.[22] This approach, coupled with an "imperial" view of the power of the presidency in emergencies,[23] produced laws and regulations of due process and interrogation techniques that were often contrary to constitutional and international law. These laws and regulations included the 2001 Patriot Act; the 2001 Military Order on "Detention, Treatment, and Trial of Certain Non-Citizens in the War Against Terrorism;" the 2006 Military Commissions Act; and the so-called "torture memos." Moreover, courts have exercised judicial review sparingly and slowly in this area because traditionally the U.S. judiciary has deferred war-related issues to the elected branches.

Limited Due Process

Limiting due process on a temporary basis in times of crisis is commonplace.[24] Usually, once the imminent threat against national security has ended, governments abandon the exceptional measures adopted and the courts start to exercise judicial review over alleged past abuses derived from these measures.[25] However, because the "war on terror" is assumed to be of unlimited duration, any restrictions to the right of alleged terrorists to judicial redress magnify the scope of the human rights violations derived from the "war" approach. Relevant restrictions to due process adopted in the United States as part of the "war on terror" and related constitutional jurisprudence include the following:

The U.S. Congress approved the USA Patriot Act in October 2001.[26] The Act's most controversial provisions (i.e., those that interfere with judicial scrutiny of

---

[22] The adoption of the ongoing war in Afghanistan was the least problematic of these measures because according to international law – the UN allows the use of force in self-defense (Art. 51 of the Charter of the UN) – the US had the right to strike back against the country that, at a minimum, harbored al-Qaeda. The "Enduring Freedom" operation against the Taliban started at the end of September 2001.

[23] An important supporter of this view is David S. Addington, Chief-of-Staff of the Vice-President (Dick Cheney) and responsible for "the New Paradigm, [a] strategy [that] rests on a reading of the Constitution that few legal scholars share – namely that the President, as Commander-in-Chief, has the authority to disregard virtually all previously known legal boundaries, if national security demands it" (Mayer 2006, July 3, p. 44).

[24] In the United States, past limitations to due process include President Abraham Lincoln's (1861–1865) suspension of the writ of *habeas corpus* to save the Union during the Civil War and President Franklyn D. Roosevelt's (1933–1945) forced internment of any person of Japanese ancestry living in the mainland during WW II.For a detailed history of military commissions in the United States, see Louis Fisher (2005).

[25] Pious briefly comments on crucial Supreme Court precedents. For example, *Ex Parte Milligan* and *Ex Parte Endo* which affirmed that although the elected branches can suspend *habeas corpus*, the judiciary has jurisdiction to hear cases involving such suspension (Pious, 2006, pp. 125–26).

[26] The acronym stands for "Uniting and Strengthening America by Providing Appropriate Tools Required to Intercept and Obstruct Terrorism" (2001, October 26). 115 STAT. 272, Public Law 107–156. Act signed into law by President George W. Bush on October 26, 2001 after it passed the House of Representatives (October 24) and the Senate (October 25). Hereinafter referred to as the Patriot Act.

governmental activity), include the unlimited detention of noncitizens and the creation of administrative commissions (Section 412) that affect the right to due process protected in the Fifth, Sixth, and Seventh Amendments to the U.S. Constitution.[27] Unlimited detention without charges also affects American citizens classified by the government as "unlawful enemy combatants" (Van Bergen and Valentine 2005–2006, pp. 449–508).[28]

The November 13, 2001, Military Order on Detention, Treatment, and Trial of Certain Non-Citizens in the War Against Terrorism (pp. 25–26)[29] usurps the power of the judiciary by extracting the individual from the normal judicial process through the creation of a parallel detention system that answers directly to the secretary of defense and, ultimately, to the president (pp. 27–28).[30] For example, until recently, the few detainees who had been classified as "enemy combatants" only had access to a Combatant Status Review Tribunal (CSRT) in Guantánamo Bay, Cuba – which is not an ordinary court.[31]

Because the U.S. Supreme Court in *Hamdam v. Rumsfeld* (2006) stated the administration's duty to establish tribunals with a minimum level of respect for due process, the U.S. Congress approved the 2006 Military Commissions Act (MCA).[32] However, this act "sanctions the determinations made by…CSRTs and it authorizes the President or Secretary of Defense to create undefined tribunals with power to classify individuals as 'unlawful enemy combatants.'… However, all substantive provisions of the Act which limit the rights of unlawful enemy combatants apply exclusively to non-citizens." (Center for Constitutional Rights n.d., p. 2). Because judicial control is lacking, the Military Commission Act continues to sanction due process violations.

Furthermore, the Bush administration, with the help of its allies, ran secret detention centers, or "black holes" (Council of Europe 2007, June 7, paras. 7 & 8), and practiced extraordinary renditions or illegally sent suspected terrorists to countries

[27] Justified in "Memorandum for General Counsel William J. Haynes, II, U.S. DoD" (Philbin and Yoo, 2001, December 28, p. 29). The Patriot Act also interferes with the right to privacy of the Fourth Amendment to the U.S. Constitution. In addition, it broadens the definition of terrorism to include domestic terrorism (ACLU 2002, December 6).

[28] For example, Yaser Esam Hamdi, José Padilla, and Ali Saleh Kahlah al-Marri are all American citizens.

[29] 3 C.F.R. 918 (2001 comp.); 66 Fed. Reg. 57833 (Nov. 16, 2001). This Order establishes military tribunals (Section I.e) without the protection of "the principles of law and the rules of evidence generally recognized in the trial of criminal cases in the United States district courts" (Section I.f).

[30] See: Sec. IV.c.(8) and Sec. VII.a.(2) of the Military Order on "Detention, Treatment, and Trial of Certain Non-Citizens in the War Against Terrorism.

[31] The Supreme Court upheld the process of review established in the Detainee Treatment Act of 2005 (2005, December 30). Tit. X, 119 Stat. 2739 (Center for Constitutional Rights 2007, April).

[32] MCA (2006, October 17). Pub. L. No. 109–336, 120 Stat. 2600 (codified in scattered sections of 10 and 18 U.S.C.). For a brief critique of the MCA, see Center for Constitutional Rights (n.d.).

where it was known that the authorities torture detainees routinely.[33] Spain and the UK aided the United States with these renditions.

Limitations to due process have been regularly contested in U.S. courts, but the courts have generally shown deference to the executive branch, except in the most serious departures from the rule of law. For example, the Supreme Court has not annulled the 2006 Military Commissions Act; it has not ordered the closing of Bagram and Guantánamo, where individuals continue to be detained without charges; and it lacks a uniform case law on how to treat those detained as a result of the "war on terror," which creates insecurity and affects the principle of equal protection under the law of the Fourteenth Amendment.

However, the Supreme Court has unequivocally affirmed the right to *habeas corpus* of both citizen (*Hamdi v. Rumsfeld*)[34] and noncitizen (*Boumediene v. Bush*)[35] "enemy combatants." Second, it has stated that the principle of judicial control extends to any detention (*Rasul* v. *Bush*)."[36] And third, it has ruled that the Geneva Conventions – which prescribe "regularly constituted courts" without defining them – apply in the United States. Thus, military commissions must comply with minimum international standards (*Hamdam v. Rumsfeld*).[37]

Extreme Interrogation Techniques[38]

Historically, authorities have legally used torture and cruel, inhuman, or degrading treatment to extract confessions, among other goals (Peters, 1996). Although as early as 1791, the Eighth Amendment banned "cruel and unusual punishment," the ban on

[33] A former CIA agent, Robert Baer, explained: "If you want them to be tortured, you send them to Syria. If you want someone to disappear…you send them to Egypt (Human Rights Watch 2006, November, p. 33). See also The Committee on International Rights (2005, p. 13). In addition, "President Bush decided on 6 September 2006 to reveal the existence of the covert programme implemented by the CIA to arrest, detain, and interrogate overseas high-value terrorist suspects" (Council of Europe 2007, June 7, paras. 22 & 25). Art. 3 of the 1984 CAT forbids extraordinary renditions or réfoulement.

[34] *Hamdi v. Rumsfeld* 542 U.S. 507 (2004), decided June 28. Plurality decision with three dissents. In *Rumsfeld v. Padilla* 124 S. Ct. 2711; 159 L. Ed. 2d 2729 (2004), June 28, the Supreme Court (by 5 to 4) rejected the ruling of the Court of Appeals – *Padilla v. Rumsfeld*, 352 F.3d 695 (2003, December 18) – based on a procedural issue, i.e., use of the wrong court. Afterwards, "[o]n November 22, 2005, the Bush administration switched its legal strategy of dealing with citizen detainees. It indicted José Padilla" (Pious 2006, p. 141).

[35] *Boumediene v. Bush* 128 S. Ct. 2229 (2008), decided 5–4 on June 12, 2008. Litigation in U.S. federal courts is allowed to those detained at Guantánamo.

[36] *Rasul v. Bush* 542 U.S. 466 (2004). Decision of 6–3 on 28 June 2004. As a response to this ruling, the Bush Administration created the Combatant Status Review Tribunal (CSRT) to determine the legality of individual detentions in Guantánamo.

[37] *Hamdam v. Rumsfeld* 548 U.S. 557 (2006). Decision of 5–3 on June 29, 2006. The case refers to a non-citizen in custody in Guantánamo since 2002. For Justice Alito (dissenting opinion) the commissions are "regularly constituted courts."The Court also declared that it retains its judicial power and that "Guantánamo Bay is neither enemy-occupied territory nor under martial law."

[38] For a comprehensive collection of U.S. torture-related documents from 2001 to 2004, see Greenberg and Dratel (2005) and for updated information, see ACLU (2009, August 24).

torture and cruel, inhuman, or degrading treatment at the international level only came later on. The 1948 Universal Declaration of Human Rights (UDHR) and the legally binding International Covenant on Civil and Political Rights (ICCPR) forbid torture in general[39] and the 1949 Geneva Conventions forbid torture for wartimes – including in internal conflict.[40] The 1984 Convention Against Torture (CAT) provides a more detailed regulation of the ban.[41]

The United States is a party to the CAT, but because international law is not self-executing in this country, the convention is implemented through Sections 2340 and 2340A of Title 18 of the U.S. Code that ban torture. In addition, when the United States ratified the CAT, it reserved the right to interpret cruel, inhuman, and degrading treatment according to the parameters of the Eighth Amendment to its Constitution. Nevertheless, even if domestic regulation were repealed, the United States is compelled to abide by the international proscription of torture because of its *jus cogens* status, that is, laws that all States have to comply with internationally. For these reasons, the "torture memos" produced during the Bush administration to justify the use of torture by civil servants violate constitutional, federal, and international laws.[42]

In practice, torture and cruel, inhuman, and degrading treatment have been relatively widespread and systematic after 9/11 in occupied Afghanistan (e.g., Bagram) and Iraq (e.g., Abu Ghraib); in Guantánamo; and as part of the CIA's "high-value detainee" program.[43] Nevertheless, this chapter analyzes regulations conducive to an increase in the practice of torture, not actual instances of torture and cruel, inhuman, or degrading treatment.

---

[39] Art. 5 of the UDHR and Art. 7 of the ICCPR.

[40] See Third Geneva Convention, Relative to the Treatment of Prisoners of War, Aug. 12, 1949 [1955] 6 U.S.T. 3316, 3320, T.I.A, S. No. 3364. Common Article 3, bans "mutilation, cruel treatment and torture" (a) and "outrages upon personal dignity, in particular humiliating and degrading treatment" (c).

[41] Art. 1(1) of the CAT defines "torture" as "any act by which severe pain or suffering, whether physical or mental, is intentionally inflicted on a person for such purposes as obtaining from him or a third person information or a confession, punishing him for an act he or a third person has committed or is suspected of having committed, or intimidating or coercing him or a third person, or for any reason based on discrimination of any kind, when such pain or suffering is inflicted by or at the instigation of or with the consent or acquiescence of a public official or other person acting in an official capacity. It does not include pain or suffering arising only from, inherent in or incidental to lawful sanctions." Art 2 (1) imposes the duty on "[e]ach state party…to take effective [measures]…to prevent acts of torture in any territory under its jurisdiction." Art. 2 (2) bans any derogation of this prohibition. And Art. 2 (3) denies the validity of following orders to eliminate individual responsibility for torture.

[42] The government has to comply with these laws according to the supremacy clause of Art.VI of the Constitution. J. E. Alvarez (2006) summarizes the main international rules violated.

[43] "He handed us a piece of paper called an IROE (Interrogation Rules of Engagement). It listed the things that the Pentagon said were acceptable to use during interrogations, but it was also sort of an open-ended document – it encouraged the interrogator to be creative" (Conroy 2007, March 2, p. 14). The International Committee of the Red Cross was in Iraq between March and November 2003 (ICRC 2004, February). In a later report, "the ICRC clearly considers that the allegations of the fourteen include descriptions of treatment and interrogations techniques – singly or in combination – that amounted to torture and/or cruel, inhuman or degrading treatment" (February 2007, p. 5).

Although the Bush administration provided in its rules and regulations for the humane treatment of detainees, these provisions were insufficient to curtail the practice of torture fostered by unlimited detention without judicial supervision and by the approval of regulations based on the modifications introduced into the international and federal regulations on torture by the so-called "torture memos."[44] For example, the November 2001 Military Order on "Detention, Treatment, and Trial of Certain Non-Citizens in the War Against Terrorism" imposes the duty of treating the detainees "humanely" (Section III.b) and to provide them with "adequate food, drinking water, shelter, clothing, and medical treatment" (Section III.c) (Greenberg and Dratel, 2005, pp. 25–28).[45] This duty is reiterated in a February 7, 2002, presidential memo on the inapplicability of the Geneva Conventions to al-Qaeda and Taliban detainees. However, this duty to treat the detainees "humanely" concerns the Armed Forces and not other institutions such as the CIA; and second, it is limited "to the extent appropriate and consistent with military necessity, in a manner consistent with the principles of Geneva."[46]

One of the "torture memos," from Assistant Attorney General Jay S. Bybee to Alberto R. Gonzales, Counsel to the President, restricted the meaning of torture to the extent

> that for an act to constitute torture as defined in Section 2340 [of Title 18 of the U.S. Code], it must inflict pain that is difficult to endure…must be equivalent in intensity to the pain accompanying serious physical injury, such as organ failure, impairment of body function, or even death. For purely mental pain or suffering to amount to torture under Section 2340, it must result in significant psychological harm of significant duration, e.g., lasting for months or even years…. We conclude that the statute…prohibit[s] only extreme acts. (p. 172)

Moreover, several memos approved the specific interrogation techniques that constituted the alleged torture – including the infamous waterboarding (Greenberg and Dratel, 2005, pp. 227–28).[47] To adopt the more dire techniques (all of category III) it is necessary to "submit […] a request through the Director, JIG [Joint Interrogation Group], for approval by the Commanding General with appropriate legal review and information to Commander, USSOUTHCOM" (Phifer 2002, October 11, p. 228). However, no authorization of any kind can excuse this criminal behavior (Art. 2 (3) of the CAT. See note 42). Because there is widespread agreement at home and abroad that some of the techniques mentioned are torture, the

---

[44]The memos positioned the president above the law. For example, Attorney General Alberto Gonzales stated in early 2005: "I guess I would have to say that hypothetically that authority [of the President to violate the ban on torture] may exist" (Lichtblau 2005, January 7).

[45]This definition is in violation of Art. 1 of the CAT. See note 42.

[46]G.W. Bush. "Memorandum on Humane Treatment of al-Qaeda and Taliban Detainees" (p. 135). The Director of Central Intelligence and the Chairman of the Joint Chief of Staff were among the addressees of this memo.

[47]The techniques are classified into three categories of increased duress, including, for example, "[s]tress positions (like standing) for a maximum of four hours" (Category II, (1)); "isolation…up to 30 days [renewable]" (Category II (3)); "deprivation of light and auditory stimuli" (Category II, (5)); "[u]se of a wet towel and dripping water to induce the misperception of suffocation" (Category III (3)) [waterboarding] (Phifer, 2002, October 11).

reminder that Secretary of Defense Donald Rumsfeld voiced to the Commander of USSOUTHCOM that "[i]n all interrogations, you should continue the humane treatment of detainees, regardless of the type of interrogation technique employed" (2003, January 15, p. 239) can be qualified as lip service to preventing the practice of torture.

Disregarding the mentioned rules and regulations conducive to the violation of the ban on torture and the evidence of actual torture, the 2005 *Second Periodic Report of the United States of America to the Committee Against Torture* affirmed the compliance of the United States with the Convention Against Torture (2005, May 6). However, by December of that year, the president was reticent to sign a bill that explicitly banned the use of cruel, inhuman, and degrading treatment.[48]

A Criminal Justice Approach to Counter-Terrorism: Western Europe – Spain and the UK[49]

The EU in general favors a criminal justice approach. The 2005 European Union Counter-Terrorism Strategy – adopted after the attacks in Madrid (March 2004) and London (July 2005), and still in effect – emphasizes the need to "bring [the terrorists] to justice, while continuing to respect human rights and international law" (Council of the European Union 2005, December 1). Nevertheless, because member states retain most of their sovereignty in this area, it is relevant to examine the policies of individual EU members.

Among the 27 EU countries, I have chosen Spain and the UK for three main reasons. First, they were allies of the United States in the war in Iraq – Spain until 2004 – and both were the targets of Islamist terrorism themselves after 9/11, due in part to their participation in this war. Second, they are among the six EU countries that had counter-terrorism legislation previous to 9/11, which is the result of their history of homegrown terrorism – neutralized in the UK and controlled to a great extent in Spain.[50] And third, the two countries have rejected questionable pre-9/11 counter-terrorism practices – the UK against the IRA (Irish Republican Army)[51] and

---

[48] He finally signed the bill with an amendment that "prohibit[s] the 'cruel, inhuman, or degrading' treatment of any detainee in U.S. custody anywhere in the world." (White 2005, December 16).

[49] For a brief description of the relevant counter-terrorism mechanisms created by the Council of Europe and the EU after 9/11, see Thieux (2004).

[50] In England through the Good Friday Agreement of April 10, 1998. ETA has been operationally weak since at least the late 1990s. See "Speech of Miguel Linán Macías, Representative from the Spanish Ministry of Defense, Before a NATO Seminar on Terrorism," in Warsaw, Poland on February 22, 2002 (pp. 118, 122).

[51] Questionable practices included "bruising, contusions, hyper-extension and hyper-flexion of joints, hair-pulling, jabbing, rupture of the ear drums and increased mental agitation" (Borders 1979, March 17, p. A3; O'Boyle, 1977 October, pp. 674–706).

Spain against ETA (Euskadi Ta Askatasuna).[52] They differ because until recently the UK supported more firmly a "war" approach to counter-terrorism.[53]

Spain:[54] A Criminal Justice Approach

Terrorists used backpacks filled with explosives activated through cellphones against four commuter trains in Madrid on March 11, 2004 (referred to as 11-M in Spanish texts and as 3/11 in English texts). This attack left 191 dead and 1,856 injured, from different nationalities, and was a vivid sign that attacks similar to those of 9/11 could happen in Europe (Bernstein 2004, March 15, A13).[55] Even though the conservative Spanish Prime Minister, José María Aznar (1996–2004), mistakenly linked the bombings to the home-grown ETA, the Spanish law enforcement community quickly changed its target to Islamist cells.[56] Less than a month after the bombings, on April 3, 2004, the Spanish police surrounded alleged terrorists linked to 3/11 in an apartment building located in Leganés (Madrid), where the terrorists committed suicide. The blast killed 1 police officer and wounded 11 others too.

Although in May 2004 the Spanish government created the National Center of Counter-Terrorism Coordination to bring together the efforts of different law enforcement agencies (Archick et al., 2006, July 24, p. 35),[57] the overall Spanish counter-terrorism strategy has differed from that of the United States. Prime Minister Aznar's support for the "war on terror" was quickly substituted by the rule of law approach after the election of the current Socialist Prime Minister, José Luis Rodríguez Zapatero (2004–present).[58] Thus, alleged

---

[52] "[B]etween 1983 and 1987, the Antiterrorist Liberation Groups (GAL) which were death squads financed by secret funds of the Interior Ministry, killed 28 people, a number of whom later turned out to be unconnected to ETA" (Human Rights Watch 2005, January 27, p. 14). Central figures of the GAL were prosecuted and sentenced to prison terms (Gordillo 2003, December 6).

[53] After the 2005 terrorist attacks the "war" paradigm lost its full strength in the UK (Transnational Terrorism, Security, and the Rule of Law 2008, November 12, pp. 6, 37–38).

[54] Important sources for this subsection are the "Report of the Commission on the 3/11" as reproduced in Comisión de Investigación del 11-M, "Dictamen de conclusiones y recomendaciones" (June 8, 2005); decisions of Spanish courts; and country reports from the U.S. Department of State, IGOs, and NGOs.

[55] The 3/11 terrorist attacks occurred only 3 days before the Spanish national elections, but I focus on Spanish counter-terrorism strategy. The debate continues on the impact of the bombings on the Spanish electorate (Lago and Montero 2006, July, pp. 13–36).

[56] Some believe that Prime Minister Aznar intentionally misled the country to avoid the electoral defeat of his party in the upcoming elections (Rodríguez 2005, June 23).

[57] Or *Centro Nacional de Coordinación Antiterrorista* (CNCA) in Spanish. It followed the example of the U.S. Department of Homeland Security.

[58] Zapatero's perspective is in Archick et al. (2006, July 24, p. 32). Aznar's perpective is in Gaynor (2004, March 12).

terrorists[59] are tried in Spanish regular courts, using regular criminal procedure.[60] Spanish criminal procedure is divided into an investigative and an oral phase. In the first phase the investigative judge authorizes the police to gather evidence and to secure the person and belongings of the alleged criminals, and decides whether there is enough evidence to start the next phase. In the second phase evidence of charge and discharge is heard and a verdict is handed down.

On November 4, 2006, investigative Judge Juan del Olmo indicted formally a third of the 116 individuals suspected of having ties to 3/11 (Mercado 2006, April 11). The oral phase started on February, 15, 2007 in the *Audiencia Nacional* or National Court (Yoldi 2006, November 1) and ended with a guilty verdict for 21 of the accused on October 31, 2007 (Rodríguez 2007, November 2). Three accused received the steepest punishment (Audiencia Nacional 2007, October 31), confirmed in appeals: José Emilio Suárez Trashorras was condemned to 25 years in prison for each of the 192 homicides (191 in the trains and one in an apartment building in Leganés) and two abortions; 15 years of prison for each of the 1,856 attempted homicides of those injured in 3/11; and 10 years for the destruction of each of the four trains and for one apartment building. In addition, Jamal Zougam and Othaman El Gnaoui were punished, each, with 12 years in prison for belonging to a terrorist group; 30 years in prison for each of the 191 homicides and two abortions; 20 years in prison for each of the 1,856 attempted homicides; and 15 years for each destroyed train (Tribunal Supremo 2008, July 17, *Antecedentes* [Facts], *Segundo*, 1–3 & *Fallo* [Verdict].2).[61]

The Spanish National Court's decision was appealed using a *recurso de casación* before the criminal section of the Tribunal Supremo, or Spanish Supreme Court, for nonconstitutional issues.[62] On July 17, 2008, the five magistrates of the criminal section of the Tribunal Supremo decided on appeals to acquit Basel Ghalyoum, Mouhannad Almallah Dabas, Abdelilah el Fadoual El Akil, and Raúl González Pérez of all charges;[63] to impose a more severe punishment on several of

---

[59]The definition of a terrorist in Art. 571 of the November 23, 1995, Spanish Penal Code (modified in 2003) is specific and includes an objective element, either destruction or arson apart from "the goal of subverting the constitutional order or seriously alter the public peace" [my translation from Spanish]. The punishment is of "15 to 20 years of deprivation of freedom in addition to the punishment reserved to [any physical or material harm caused]." Nobody can serve more than 40 years in prison in one conviction (Art 76 (1)c).For the Code's text in Spanish, see: Ley Orgánica 10/1995, de 23 Noviembre, del Código Penal, BOE núm. 281, de 24 de noviembre; corrección de errores en BOE núm. 54, de 2 de marzo de 1996. The modifications can be checked in BOE no. 283 (26 November 2003), no. 65 (16 March 2004), no. 80 (2 April 2004) and no. 309 (26 December 2003). The BOE is the *Spanish Official Gazette*, where laws have to be published to have legal effects.

[60]According to Cándido Conde-Pumpido Tourón, the *Fiscal General del Estado* or Spain's chief prosecutor, those accused of the 3/11 'were imprisoned by 'an ordinary court with professional judges, without using any exceptions [or] shortcuts or making any legal changes' [my translation from Spanish] (Conde-Pumpido afirma 2008, May 29).

[61]Mitigating circumstances were applied to José Emilio Suárez Trashorras due to his mental condition. No mitigation circumstances were applied to either one of the others.

[62]The office of the prosecutor, the defendants and associations of citizens appealed the verdict.

[63]Rabei Osman el Sayed, known as The Egyptian, was acquitted in the *Audiencia Nacional* due mainly to double jeopardy (U.S. Department of State 2009, April, p. 98).

the accused; and to improve the rights of some of the victims of 3/11 (Tribunal Supremo 2008, July 17, 2nd Sentencia, *fundamento de derecho único & fallo* [verdict]).[64]

Notwithstanding these successful prosecutions, Spain has been criticized for allegedly violating the right to due process and the prohibition against torture. Nevertheless, because the Spanish Constitution (1978, Art. 15) and its laws forbid torture and cruel, inhuman, and degrading treatment, I focus on the crux of the allegations of due process violations, that is, the practice – legal in Spain – of incommunicado pretrial detention of up to 13 days since November 2003 (Human Rights Watch 2005, January 27).

Incommunicado detention is used to secure evidence and the presence of suspects to stand trial. Its usefulness is based on years of experience countering the terrorism of ETA (Transnational Terrorism, Security, and the Rule of Law 2008, October 27). Notwithstanding Human Rights Watch's criticism of incommunicado detention for "giv[ing] rise to a greater risk of ill-treatment in detention," important sections of a Human Rights Watch report on incommunicado detention in Spain (2005, January 27) have been disqualified. According to the Spanish government, "[HRW] confuse[d] incommunicado detention with prison, [and did] not mention that it is decided by a judge" (Spanish Ministry of Justice 2005, February 14). The position of the Spanish government is reinforced in the 2007 U.S. Human Rights Country Report on Spain, which explains that incommunicado detention is practiced under judicial supervision and respects legal representation.

In addition, the Spanish Ombudsman's Report to the Human Rights Council in 2009 disagreed on the need of eliminating incommunicado detention – demanded in the report of the UN Special Rapporteur Martin Scheinin (UN General Assembly 2008, December 16) – because according to the Spanish Ombudsman this measure is not per se conducive to torture (UN General Assembly 2009, February 13).

United Kingdom: War Analogy Abandoned[65]

Suicide bombers attacked trains and buses in London on July 7, 2005. The attack left 56 dead individuals, including the 4 suicide bombers; more than 700 injured; and a wake-up call for a society that had adopted a policy of tolerance toward Muslim communities (Sciolino and Van Natta 2005, July 10, pp. 1, 9). Because the bombers were homegrown – a difference from 9/11 and, for the most part, from 3/11 – the government knew it had to adopt new policies toward minorities (Department for Communities 2007, April, p. 4, para. 6). And similarly to the United States and Spain,

---

[64] For example, Hamid Ahmidan was sentenced to 12 years in prison for belonging to a terrorist organization and Kenneth Odey Agi was recognized as a victim with a right to compensation and Dumitri Amariei was awarded a higher amount of compensation (Tribunal Supremo, 2008, July 17, Verdict).

[65] Based on decisions of the courts and reports from IGOs and NGOs.

the UK established a new organ to foster interagency coordination in the area of counter-terrorism (Archick et al., 2006, July 21, p. 41).[66]

British Prime Minister Tony Blair's (1997–2007) rhetoric was identical to that of President Bush, that is, according to both of them, the new threats required new measures.[67] This rhetoric can and in fact did foster quickly the violation of rights as demonstrated by the uncharacteristically violent action of the London Metropolitan Police on July 22, 2005, against Charles de Menezes, a Brazilian electrician, who was shot seven times in the head after being immobilized on the floor (BBC News 2006, February 1).[68] However, coinciding with the end of President Bush's term in the White House (January 2009), the British government publicly abandoned its war rhetoric.[69]

Notwithstanding the prevalence of the war rhetoric, law enforcement measures have accompanied it. Moreover, courts have played a more significant role in upholding human rights than in the United States (Archick et al., 2006, July 24, pp. 38–41). In the UK, the Crown courts (Her Majesty's Courts System 2009, April 2), constituted by a Judge and a 12-person jury, hear cases involving terrorism after the Crown Prosecution Service (CPS) "decides whether criminal proceedings, which have been started by the police, should" reach the courts (Her Majesty's Courts System 2006, January 25). Appeals are heard in the Criminal Division of the Court of Appeal (Her Majesty's Courts System 2007, June 4).

Relevant prosecutions include the trial of those accused of 7/7, of the failed attacks of July 21, 2005, and of the frustrated plot to blast several airplanes en route to the United States in August 2006. On July 9, 2008, "four of the would-be suicide bombers [of July 21, 2005] were found guilty of conspiracy to commit murder and received life sentences. One defendant was acquitted" (U.S. Department of State 2008, April 30, p. 35). On April 28, 2009, two of the accused perpetrators of 7/7 were found guilty of "participating in a terrorist training camp" (Malingre 2009, May 2), but three of the accused were acquitted of the actual terrorist attack.

The trial involving the 2006 frustrated airplane plot has been especially complicated because of the acquittal of all the accused due to lack of agreement among the members of the jury (BBC News 2008, September 8). The prosecutor's office sought a retrial (Allen 2009, September 7) – at a cost of £10 million based on

---

[66]The failed terrorist attack of July 21, 2005, reinforced the need for change.

[67]On August 5, 2005, Prime Minister Tony Blair affirmed: "The rules of the game are changing" (2005, August 5). Moreover, Mr. John Reid, Interior Minister in 2006 emphasized that "we may have to modify some of our freedoms in the short term in order to prevent their misuse and abuse" (BBC News 2006, August 9).

[68]Those responsible for this excess remain unpunished. A new review by the Independent Police Complaints Commission (IPCC) concluded in October that is "standing by their original decision not to recommend disciplining the officers" (BBC News 2009, October 2).

[69]Laborist Foreign Secretary David Miliband affirmed: "the idea had unified disparate 'terrorist groups' against the West. He said the right response to the threat was to champion law and human rights – not to subordinate it" (BBC News 2009, January 15). The current British Prime Minister, the Laborist Gordon Brown (2007–present), on the eve of the approval of a new counter-terrorism strategy in March 2009 stated his absolute stance against torture (2009, March 22).

"a count…of conspir[ing] to detonate improvised explosive devices on transatlantic passenger aircraft" (Dodd 2008, September 11). The retrial took place from February to September of 2009. Finally, Abdulla Ahmed Ali (the leader), Assad Sarwar, and Tanvir Hussain were declared guilty "of conspiring to murder crew and passengers on transatlantic flights" (Dodd 2009, September 7) and convicted to prison terms of a minimum of 40, 36, and 32 years, respectively (BBC News 2009, September 14). However, another trial is possible.

Moreover, British courts have actively enforced the rule of law against alleged governmental excesses. In December 2004, "the law lords [the UK's highest court] ruled by 8–1 that the detention without trial of foreign nationals in Belmarsh and Woodhill prisons and the Broadmoor high security hospital breached human rights laws" (Dyer 2005, June 11). And in February 2008, the Court of Appeal found that the process of extradition to the United States of Lofti Raissi "amounted to an abuse of process" (Amnesty International 2008, February 20) in the absence of any terrorist charges against him. But the British High Court also gave legitimacy to a detention without charges of more than 14 days, approved by a law of 2006 (Cowell 2006, August 23).

Although – like the United States and Spain – the UK has had effective prosecutions, the government of the UK has been criticized for, first, violating due process by adopting a 28-day pretrial detention without charges in cases of terrorism[70] and by using control orders against individuals suspected of terrorist activities whose trial or extradition might compromise national security.[71] And second, for violating the ban on torture through the authorization of *réfoulement* based on diplomatic assurances that no torture was going to be used (Human Rights Watch 2006, July 1).[72] Nevertheless, the UK's report to the April 10, 2008, meeting of the Working Group on Universal Periodic Review (UPR) before the UN Human Rights Council explained that any counter-terrorism measure adopted balanced the right to security with respect for human rights.[73]

---

[70] The government tried to stretch this limit to 42 days (Sunderland 2008, April 22), but it gave up on the 42 days in October 2008 (Government abandons 42-day detention plan 2008, October 13).

[71] The 2005 Prevention of Terrorism Act allowed the home secretary to issue control orders to limit a person's freedom. Control orders are problematic from a human rights perspective because of their unlimited duration (issued for periods of 12 renewable months) and limited judicial oversight. Currently 17 individuals – including 8 foreigners – are under control orders (Travis 2009, May 21).

[72] It is contrary to the jurisprudence of the ECtHR. See *Soering v. United Kingdom*, Judgment of July 7, 1989. Alleged torture by British troops in Iraq is beyond the scope of this chapter. The broad definition of terrorism of the 2006 Terrorism Act, which includes encouragement of terrorism, exacerbates the negative effects of these violations.

[73] "[I]ts plans to extend pretrial detention, the use of control orders and the policy of deportation of terrorist suspects, [are based on]…its position…that terrorism undermines fundamental human rights…. *At present, all detention beyond 48 hours must be authorized by a judge and the person concerned can…be legally represented. Continued detention is agreed only if the detention is still judged to be necessary* and the investigation is being carried out diligently and expeditiously" [emphasis added] (UN General Assembly 2008, May 23, para. 8).

Concluding Remarks

Taking into account the counter-terrorism approaches of the three countries basically remain the same today as discussed in this chapter (despite a new American president) – i.e., the "war" approach in the United States,[74] the criminal justice approach in Spain, and a mixture of the two with a tendency toward the criminal justice approach in the UK – it is possible to reach the following conclusions:

First, in view of the fact that no al-Qaeda or al-Qaeda-inspired attack has succeeded in the United States after 9/11, in Spain after 3/11, or in the UK after 7/11 (all counter-factuals), it can be stated that the counter-terrorism approaches of the three states are effective in guaranteeing the security of the people under their respective jurisdictions. Therefore, the statement that the "war" approach is more effective than the rule of law approach is not based on available data. From the perspective of their effectiveness, neither approach is superior. Nevertheless, the purpose of this chapter was to assess which of the two approaches is better from an international human rights law perspective.

Second, prima facie international human rights law does not reject either one of the two approaches mentioned in the article. The international human rights regime allows states to respond to terrorist attacks with a variety of measures.[75] Moreover, in order to secure the lives, freedoms, and property of the individuals under their respective jurisdictions, states can limit non-derogable rights if an emergency is "threaten[ing] the life of the nation and…is officially proclaimed."[76] After this type of emergency has passed, the State has the duty to revoke any extraordinary counter-terrorism measures.[77] However, unlimited detentions, control orders, and suspensions of non-derogable rights are unacceptable measures.[78] Although the three case studies show violations of human rights in their regulations, the United States with its "war" approach is the least respectful of human rights of the three cases examined. The UK is similarly disrespectful with its control orders of unlimited duration. In addition, judicial control in the area of counter-terrorism has been more present

[74]Although "[i]n his May 21, 2009 speech at the National Archives, President Obama indicated that the administration may suggest a more formalized approach to the detention of dangerous individuals who cannot be prosecuted but who 'in effect, remain at war with the United States;'" de facto, the "war" approach continues to dominate (Obama 2009, May 21). However, it may change because John Brennan, the White House's Counter-terrorism Chief disagrees not only with the terminology ("war") but also with its tactics (focus on the use of the military, torture techniques and unlimited detention) (Kelly 2009, August 6).

[75]See Art. 29.2 and 30 of the Universal Declaration of Human Rights (UDHR) adopted December 10, 1948, G.A. Res. 217A (III), UN Doc. A/810, at 71 (1948).

[76]Art. 4 (1) of the ICCPR. In addition, the limitations have to respect other treaty obligations and the principle of nondiscrimination.

[77]According to the Office of the High Commissioner for Human Rights (OHCHR), "[t]he purpose of security measures is, fundamentally, to protect freedom and human rights" (Office of the High Commissioner 2002, September 23).

[78]Even when confronted with national security interests.

in Spain and the UK than in the United States and the scope of the violations of human rights has been more limited in Spain and the UK than in this country.

Third, considering that there is widespread agreement about the need to increase inter-state cooperation to counter Islamist terrorism, and considering that it is also agreed that the measures adopted as part of the "War" Approach to Counter-Terrorism: The United States: Limited Due Process – have been detrimental to cooperation between the United States and its European allies,[79] the rule of law approach can be considered more effective in this area than the "war" approach. Not only has the "war" approach de-legitimized the United States as a state on the forefront of human rights protection, but it has also compelled the allies of the United States in the "war on terror" to violate international law. Complicity in the extraordinary rendition program is one of the most significant examples of illegal and illegitimate cooperation efforts (Grey, 2006, Appendices B & C) which have endangered transatlantic counter-terrorism efforts. Overcoming this delegitimization will solidify a common United States–European Union front against transnational terrorism.

References

Allen, N. (2009, September 7). Prosecutors pursued retrial to justify liquids ban. The Telegraph. Retrieved from http://www.telegraph.co.uk/news/uknews/terrorism-in-the-uk/6152046/WITH-LEGAL-Prosecutors-pursu.

Alvarez, J. E.(2006). Torturing the Law. Case Western Reserve Journal of International Law 37 (2/3), 175–223.

American Civil Liberties Union (ACLU). (2002, December 6). How the PATRIOT Act redefines "domestic terrorism." Retrieved from http://www.aclu.org/national-security/how-usa-patriot-act-redefines-domestic-terrorism.

American Civil Liberties Union (ACLU). (2009, August 24). Department of Justice Office of Legal Counsel. Letters and memos to CIA regarding detention and interrogation policies (documents responsive to 2004 torture FOIA). Retrieved from http://www.aclu.org/safefree/torture/40834res20090824.html.

Amnesty International. (2008, February 20). Court win for man wrongly accused of terrorism. Retrieved from http://www.amnesty.org/en/news-and-updates/good-news/court-win-for-man-wrongly-accused-terroris.

Archick, K., Ek, C., Gallis, P., Miko, F. T., & Woehrel, S. (2006, July 24). European approaches to homeland security and counterterrorism. In *Congressional research service report for Congress*. Retrieved from http://www.fas.org/sgp/crs/homesec/RL33573.pdf.

Audiencia Nacional (Sala de lo Penal, Seccion segunda). (2007, October 31). Sentencia 65/2007. Retrieved from http://www.asociacion11m.org/sumario_20_04_sentencia_an.php.

BBC News. (2003, March 16). Azores summit statement. Retrieved from http://news.bbc.co.uk/2/hi/middle_east/2855567.stm.

[79]"The U.S. policy on treating detainees is undermining the war on terrorism by tarnishing America's reputation as a moral leader, says a report released Monday by former members of the bipartisan commission that investigated the 9/11 terrorist attacks" (Slavin 2005, November 15).

BBC News. (2006, February 1). Leak disputes Menezes death story. Retrieved from http://news.bbc.co.uk/1/hi/uk/4157892.stm.
BBC News. (2006, August 9). Terror "may force freedom curbs." Retrieved from http://news.bbc.co.uk/2/hi/uk_news/politics/5257518.stm.
BBC News. (2008, September 8). Three guilty of bomb conspiracy. Retrieved from http://newsvote.bbc.co.uk/mpapps/pagetools/print/news.bbc.co.uk/2/hi/uk_news/i7528483.stm.
BBC News. (2009, January 15). Miliband regrets "war on terror." Retrieved from http://newsvote.bbc.co.uk/mpapps/pagetools/print/news.bbc.co.uk/2/hi/uk_news/politics/7829946.stm?ad.
BBC News. (2009, September 14). Airline plot trio get life terms. Retrieved from http://news.bbc.co.uk/2/hi/uk_news/8254156.stm.
BBC News. (2009, October 2.) IPCC sticks to Menezes decision. Retrieved from http://news.bbc.co.uk/go/pr/fr/-/2/hi/uk_news/2826789.stm.
Bernstein, R. (2004, March 15). A shocking confrontation with terror on home turf. New York Times, p. A13.
Blair, T. (2005, August 5). Full text of Blair's statement on extremism. Retrieved from http://www.timesonline.co.uk/tol/news/uk/article551991.ece.
Borders, W. (1979, March 17). Torture of Ulster prisoners indicated in British report. *New York Times*, p. A3.
Boumediene v. Bush, *128 S. Ct. 2229* (2008, June 12).
Brown, G. (2009, March 22). We are about to take the war against terror to a new level. *Guardian.co.uk: The Observer.* Retrieved from http://www.guardian.co.uk/commentisfree/2009/mar/22/gordon-brown-terrorism.
Bush, G. W. (2001, September 20). Address to a joint session of Congress and the American people. In J. F. Hoge & G. Rose (Eds.), (2005), *Understanding the war on terror* (p. 185). New York: Foreign Affairs.
Bush, G. W. (2002, February 7). Memorandum on humane treatment of al Qaeda and Taliban detainees. In K. J. Greenberg, & Dratel, J. L. (Eds.), (2005), *The torture papers: The road to Abu Ghraib* (pp. 134–135). New York: Cambridge University Press.
Bybee, J. S. (2002, August 1). Memorandum to Alberto R. Gonzales, Counsel to the President, on Standards of Conduct for Interrogation under 18 U.S.C. §§ 2340-2340A (Washington D.C.). In K. J. Greenberg, & J. L. Dratel, (Eds.), (2005), *The torture papers: The road to Abu Ghraib* (pp. 172–217). New York: Cambridge University Press.
Center for Constitutional Rights. (n.d.). Military Commissions Act of 2006: A summary of the law. Retrieved from http://ccrjustice.org/files/report_MCA.pdf.
Center for Constitutional Rights. (2007, April). Supreme Court denies immediate review of Guantanamo cases. Retrieved from http://ccrjustice.org/newsroom/press-releases/supreme-court-denies-immediate-review-guantanamo-cases.
Comisión de Investigación del 11-M (2005, June 8). Dictamen de conclusiones y recomendaciones. Retrieved from http://www.elpais.com/elpaismedia/ultimahora/media/200506/09/espana/20050609elpepunac_4_P_PDF.pdf.
The Committee on International Rights. (2005). Torture by proxy: International and domestic law applicable to "extraordinary renditions." The Record of the Association of the Bar of the City of New York 60 (1), 13–196.
Conde-Pumpido afirma en Panamá que la lucha contra el terrorismo no puede ser planteada en términos bélicos. (2008, May 29). Madrid: Europa Press. Retrieved from http://www.lukor.com/not-esp/terrorismo/portada/08052938.htm.
Conroy, J. (2007, March 2). Confessions of a torturer: An army interrogator's story. Chicago Reader, Section 1, 1 & 14–8.).
Convention against Torture, Cruel, Inhuman and Degrading Treatment, G.A. Res. 39/46, 39 UN GAOR, Supp. (No. 51), UN Doc. A/39/51, at 197 (1984). [The CAT was adopted on 10 December 1984 and entered into force on 26 June 1987].
Council of the European Union, Justice and Home Affairs Council. (2005, December 1). The European Union counter-terrorism strategy. Retrieved from http://www.consilium.europa.eu/uedocs/cms_Data/docs/pressdata/en/jha/87257.pdf.

Council of Europe, Parliamentary Assembly, Committee on Legal Affairs and Human Rights. (2007, June 7). Secret detentions and illegal transfers of detainees involving Council of Europe member states: Second report: Explanatory memorandum [Rapporteur: Mr Dick Marty, Switzerland, ALDE]. Retrieved from http://assembly.coe.int/committeeDocs/2007/Emarty_20070608_noEmbargo.pdf.

Counter-Terrorism Committee. (2009, September 18) International laws. Retrieved from http://www.un.org/sc/ctc/laws.html.

Cowell, A. (2006, August 24). Court permits British investigators to hold 10 terror suspects longer. New York Times. Retrieved from http://www.nytimes.com/2006/08/24/world/europe/24britain.html?_r=1.

Department for Communities and Local Government. (2007, April). Preventing violent extremism: Winning hearts and minds. London: Crown. Retrieved from http://www.communities.gov.uk/documents/communities/pdf/320752.pdf.

Detainee Treatment Act (DTA), Tit. X, 119 Stat. 2739 (2005, December 30).

Dodd, V. (2008, September 11). CPS applies for retrial over plane "bomb plot." Guardian.co.uk. Retrieved from http://www.guardian.co.uk/uk/2008/sep/11/4.

Dodd, V. (2009, September 7). Three guilty of transatlantic bomb plot. Guardian.co.uk. Retrieved from http://www.guardian.co.uk/uk/2009/sep/07/plan-bomb-plot-trialo-verdicts/print.

Dyer, C. (2005, June 11). Britain accused of creating terror fears. Guardian Unlimited. Retrieved from http://www.guardian.co.uk/uk_newsstory/0,3604,1504231,00.html.

Enders, W. (2006, June). Distribution of transnational terrorism among countries by income class and geography after 9/11. International Studies Quarterly 50 (2), 367–393.

Fisher, L. (2005). Military tribunals and presidential power. Lawrence, KS: University of Kansas Press.

Gaynor, T. (2004, March 12). Aznar put war on terror at the heart of his government. The Independent. Retrieved from http://www.independent.co.uk/news/world/europe/aznar-put-war-on-terror-at-the-heart-of-his-government-566053.html.

Government abandons 42-day detention plan. (2008, October 13). The Independent. Retrieved from http://www.independent.co.uk/news/uk/politics/government-abandons-42day-detention-plan-960075.html.

Gordillo, I. (2003, December 6). La justicia pudo con los GAL. El Mundo no. 5113. Retrieved from http://www.elmundo.es/papel/2003/12/06/docume/1537134.html.

Gordon, P. H. (2007, November/December). Can the war on terror be won? How to fight the right war. Foreign Affairs 86 (6), 53–66.

Greenberg, K. J. & Dratel, J. L. (Eds.). (2005). The torture papers: The road to Abu Ghraib. New York: Cambridge University Press.

Grey, S. (2006). Ghost plane: The true story of the CIA rendition and torture program. New York: St. Martin's Griffin.

Gross, O. & Ní Aoláin, F. (2006). Law in times of crisis: Emergency powers in theory and practice. Cambridge: Cambridge University Press.

Hamdam v. Rumsfeld, 548 U.S. (2006, June 29).

Hamdi v. Rumsfeld, 542 U.S. 507 (2004, June 28).

Her Majesty's Courts System (2006, 25 January). The Crown Prosecution System. Retrieved from http://www.hmcourts-service.gov.uk/infoabout/cps/index.htm.

Her Majesty's Courts System (2007, June 4). Court of Appeal. Retrieved from http://www.hmcourts-service.gov.uk/cms/courtofappeal.htm.

Her Majesty's Courts System (2009, April 2). The Crown Court. Retrieved from http://www.hmcourts-service.gov.uk/infoabout/crown/index.htm.

Human Rights Watch. (2005, January 27). Spain: Counterterrorism measures infringe basic rights: Leadership in confronting terrorism requires better rights protection for suspects. Retrieved from http://hrw.org/english/docs/2005/01/27/spain10066.htm.

Human Rights Watch. (2006, July 1). United Kingdom: Parliamentary committee denounces British torture practices. Retrieved from http://www.hrw.org/en/news/2006/07/01/united-kingdom-parliamentary-committe-denounces-british-t.

Human Rights Watch. (2006, November). Dangerous ambivalence: UK policy on torture since 9/11. Retrieved from http://www.hrw.org/en/reports/2006/11/02/dangerous-ambivalence.
International Coalition for the Responsibility to Protect (n.d). An introduction to the Responsibility to Protect. Retrieved from http://www.responsibilitytoprotect.org/index.php/about-rtop.
International Committee of the Red Cross (ICRC). (2004, February). Report on the treatment by the coalition forces of prisoners of war and other protected persons by the Geneva Conventions in Iraq during arrest, internment and interrogation. Retrieved from http://www.derechos.org/nizkor/us/doc/icrc-prisoner-report-feb-2004.pdf.
International Committee of the Red Cross (ICRC). (2007, February). Report on the treatment of fourteen "high value detainees" in CIA custody. Retrieved from http://www.nybooks.com/icrc-report.pdf.
International Covenant on Civil and Political Rights, G.A. Res. 2200A (XXI), UN Doc. A/6316 (1966), 999 UNTS 171, reprinted in 6 ILM 368 (1967).
Kelly, M. L. (2009, August 6). Obama aide seeks new war-on-terrorism approach. NPR.org. Retrieved from http://www.npr.org/templates/story/story.php?storyId=111629560.
Lago, I. & Montero, J. R. (2006, July). The 2004 election in Spain: Terrorism, accountability, and voting. Taiwan Journal of Democracy 2 (1), 13–36.
Lichtblau, E. (2005, January 7). Gonzales speaks against torture during hearing. New York Times. Retrieved from http://www.nytimes.com/2005/01/07/politics/07gonzales.html.
Macías, M.L, (2002, February 22). Speech before a NATO Seminar on Terrorism (Warsaw, Poland). In D. A. Miller, (Ed.), (2003), *Terrorism* [Great Speeches in History Series] (pp. 118, 122). San Diego, CA: Greenhaven.
Malingre, V. (2009, May 2). Pas de process pour les attentats de 2005 à Londres. LeMonde.fr Retrieved from http://www.lemonde.fr/cgi-bin/ACHATS/acheter.cgil?Offre=ARCHIVES&type_item=ART-ARCH_30J&.
Matthew, R. & Shambaugh, G. (2005). The limits of terrorism: A network perspective. International Studies Review 7 (4), 617–62.
Mayer, J. (2006, July 3). Letter from Washington: The hidden power: The legal mind behind the White House's war on terror. The New Yorker 82 (20), 44–55. Retrieved from http://www.lexisnexis.com/us/lnacademic/search/homesubmitForm.do.
Mercado, F. (2006, April 11). La audiencia nacional juzgará a 29 personas por los atentados del 11-M. Madrid: *ElPais.com*. Retrieved from http://www.elpais.com/articulo/espana/Audiencia/Nacional/juzgara/29/personas/atentados/11-M/elpporesp/20060411elpepunac_3/Tes.
Military Commissions Act, Pub. L. No. 109-336, 120 Stat. 2600-2637 (codified in scattered sections of 10 and 18 U.S.C.), (2006, October 17).
Military Order on Detention, Treatment, and Trial of Certain Non-Citizens in the War against Terrorism (2001, November 16). 3 C.F.R. 918 (2001comp.); 66 Fed. Reg. 57,833. In K. J. Greenberg, & J. L. Dratel, (Eds.), (2005), *The torture papers: The road to Abu Ghraib* (pp. 25-28). New York: Cambridge University Press.
Miller, D. A. (Ed.). (2003). *Terrorism* [Great Speeches in History series]. San Diego, CA: Greenhaven.
Nota del Ministerio de Justicia de España al informe ¿Sentando ejemplo? Medidas antiterroristas en España presentado por Human Rights Watch. Retrieved from http://hrw.org/spanish/docs/2005/02/15/spain10360_txt.htm.
The 9/11 Commission. (2004). The 9/11 commission report including executive summary: Final report of the national commission on terrorist attacks upon the United States. Baton Rouge, LA: Claitor.
Obama, B. (2009, May 21). Remarks by the President on National Security. Retrieved from http://www.whitehouse.gov/the_press_office/Remarks-by-the-President-On-National-Security-5-21-09/.
O'Boyle, M. (1977, October). Torture and emergency powers under the European Convention on Human Rights: Ireland v. the United Kingdom. American Journal of International Law 71 (4), 674–706.

Office of the High Commissioner for Human Rights. (2002, September 23.). Note to the chair of the counter-terrorism committee: A human rights perspective on counter-terrorist measures. Retrieved from http://www.un.org/en/sc/ctc/docs/rights/2002_09_23_ctcchair_note.pdf.

Padilla v. Rumsfeld, 352 F.3d 695 (2003, December 18).

Patriot Act, 115 STAT. 272-402, Public Law 107-56 (2001, October 26).

Peters, E. (1996). Torture (Expanded ed.). Philadelphia, PA: University of Pennsylvania Press.

Phifer, J. (2002, October 11). Memorandum for Commander, Joint Task Force 170 on Request for Approval of Counter-Resistance Strategies. In K. J. Greenberg & J. L. Dratel, (Eds.), (2005), *The torture papers: The road to Abu Ghraib* (pp. 227–228). New York: Cambridge University Press.

Philbin, P. F. & Yoo, J. C. (2001, December 28). Memorandum for General Counsel William J. Haynes, II, U.S. DoD. In K. J. Greenberg & J. L. Dratel, (Eds.), (2005), *The torture papers: The road to Abu Ghraib* (pp. 29–37). New York: Cambridge University Press.

Pious, R. (2006). The war on terrorism and the rule of law. Los Angeles, CA: Roxbury.

Rasul v. Bush, 542 U.S. 466, 321 F.3d 1134, reversed and remanded (2004, June 28).

Rodríguez, J. A. (2005, June 23). El congreso concluye que el gobierno de Aznar "manipuló y tergiversó" tras el 11-M. *ElPaís.com.* Retrieved from http://www.elpais.com/articulo/espana/Congreso/concluye/Gobierno/Aznar/manipulo/tergiverso/11-M/elpporesp/20050623elpepinac_11/Tes.

Rodríguez, J. A. (2007, November 2). Diez condenados por el 11-M inician una huelga de hambre. Madrid: *ElPais.com.* Retrieved from http://www.elpais.com/articulo/espana/condenados/11-M/huelga/hambre/elpepuesp/20071102el.

Rumsfeld, D. (2003, January 15). Memorandum for Commander USSOUTHCOM on counter-resistence techniques. (15 January 2003). In K. J. Greenberg & J. L. Dratel, (Eds.), (2005), *The torture papers: The road to Abu Ghraib* (p. 239). New York: Cambridge University Press.

Rumsfeld v. Padilla, 124 S. Ct. 2711, 2729 (2004, June 28).

Sandler, T. & Arce, D. G. (2008, March 6). Transnational terrorism [Challenge Paper]. Copenhagen Consensus Center. Retrieved from http://www.copenhagenconsensus.com/Files/Filer/CC08/Papers/Papers%2021 0208/CC0809_TERRORISM_060308.pdf.

Sciolino, E. & Van Natta, Jr., D. (2005, July 10). For a decade, London thrived as a busy crossroads of terror: In London, terrorists found a home for a decade and people to carry out threats. New York Times, pp. 1, 9.

Second periodic report of the United States of America to the Committee Against Torture. (2005, May 6). University of Minnesota Human Rights Library. Retrieved from http://www1.umn.edu/humanrts/cat/us-statereport2005.html.

Shuster, M. (2005, July 7). How al Qaeda has evolved since Sept. 11. *NPR.org.* Retrieved from http://www.npr.org/templates/story/story.php?storyId=4734552.

Slavin, B. (2005, November 15). Abuse of detainees undercuts U.S authority, 9/11 panel says. USA Today, 8A. Retrieved from http://www.lexisnexis.com/us/lnacademic/results/docview/docview.do?docLinkInd=true&risb=21_T8792529928&format=GNBFI&sort=BOOLEAN&startDocNo=1&resultsUrlKey=29_T8792529932&cisb=22_T8792529931&treeMax=true&treeWidth=0&csi=8213&docNo=2.

Soering v. United Kingdom, 11 Eur. Ct. H.R. (ser. A, no. 161) (1989, July 7).

Spanish Constitution of 1978, BOE núm. 311.1 de 29 de diciembre.

Spanish Ministry of Justice. (2005, February 14). Nota del Ministerio de Justicia de España al Informe ¿Sentando ejemplo? Medidas antiterroristas en España presentado por Human R. Retrieved from http://www.hrw.org/es/news/2005/02/14/nota-del-ministerio-de-justicia-de-espa-al-informe-sentando-ejemplo-medidas-antiterr.

Spanish Penal Code. Ley Orgánica 10/1995, de 23 Noviembre, del Código Penal, BOE núm. 281, de 24 de noviembre; corrección de errores en BOE núm. 54, de 2 de marzo de 1996. The modifications can be checked in BOE no. 283 (26 November 2003), no. 65 (16 March 2004), no. 80 (2 April 2004) and no. 309 (26 December 2003).

Sunderland, J. (2008, April 22). Algeria criticizes UK's human rights record. Open Democracy: Our Kingdom. Retrieved from http://www.hrw.org/legacy/English/docs/2008/0423/uk18621.htm.

Thieux, L. (2004). European security and global terrorism: The strategic aftermath of the Madrid bombings. Perspectives 22, 59–74.

Third Geneva Convention, Relative to the Treatment of Prisoners of War, 6 U.S.T. 3316, 3320, T.I.A,.S. No. 3364. Aug. 12, 1949, [1955].

Transnational Terrorism, Security, and the Rule of Law. (2008, October 27). Case study: Spain: The Ethical Justness of Counter-Terrorism Measures. Work Package 6, Deliverable 12 b, compiled and submitted by FRIDE. Retrieved from http://www.transnationalterrorism.eu/tekst/publications/Spain%20case%20study%20(WP%206%20Del%2012b).pdf.

Transnational Terrorism, Security, and the Rule of Law. (2008, November 12). Transnational terrorism: Theoretical approaches and policy discourse. Work Package 2, Deliverable 3. Retrieved from http://www.transnationalterrorism.eu/tekst/publications/WP2%20Del%203.pdf.

Travis, A. (2009, May 21). Home Office rejects control order time limit. Guardian.co.uk Retrieved from http://www.guardian.co.uk/politics/2009/may/21/terrorism-ocontrol-orders-time-limit.

Tribunal Supremo (sala de lo penal). (2008, July 17). Sentencia no. 503/2008, *Recurso de Casación* no. 10012/2008 P (includes Segunda Sentencia). Retrieved from http://supremo.vlex.es/vid/delito-terrorismo-ta-43498442#freetrial.

UN General Assembly, Human Rights Council. (2008, May 23). Universal periodic review: Report of the working group on the universal periodic review; United Kingdom of Great Britain and Northern Ireland. A/HRC/8/25. Retrieved from http://lib.ohchr.org/HRBodies/UPR/Documents/Session1/GB/A_HRC_8_25_United_Kingdom_E.pdf.

UN General Assembly, Human Rights Council. (2008, December 16). Promotion and protection of all human rights, civil, political, economic, social and cultural rights, including the right to development: Report of the special rapporteur on the promotion and protection of human rights and fundamental freedoms while countering terrorism, Addendum to Spain [Rapporteur Martin Scheinin]. A/HRC/10/3/Add.2 Retrieved from http://www.unhcr.org/refworld/type.MISSION...498c24562.0.html.

UN General Assembly, Human Rights Council. (2009, February 13). Information presented by the National Human Rights Commission of Spain. A/HRC/10/NI/2. Retrieved from http://daccess-dds-ny.un.org/doc/UNDOC/GEN/G09/109/05/PDF/G0910905.pdf?OpenElement.

The Universal Declaration of Human Rights (UDHR), G.A. Res. 217A (III), UN Doc. A/810, at 71 (1948).

U. S. Department of State. (2001, December 19). U.S. Report to the UN counter-terrorism committee. Retrieved from http://www.state.gov/p/io/rls/rpt/2001/6917.htm.

U.S. Department of State. (2005, May 6). Second Periodic Report of the United States of America to the Committee Against Torture. Retrieved from http://www.state.gov/g/drl/rls/45738.htm.

U. S. Department of State, Bureau of Democracy, Human Rights, and Labor. (2008, March 11). Spain: Country reports on human rights practices 2007. Retrieved from http://www.state.gov/g/drl/rls/hrrpt/2007/100586.htm.

U. S. Department of State, Office of the Coordinator for Counterterrorism. (2008, April 30). Country reports on terrorism 2007. Retrieved from http://www.state.gov/documents/organization/105904.pdf.

U. S. Department of State, Office of the Coordinator for Counterterrorism. (2009, April 30). Country reports on terrorism 2008. Retrieved from http://www.state.gov/s/ct/rls/crt/2008/122410.htm.

Van Bergen, J. & Valentine, D. (2005–2006). The dangerous world of indefinite detentions: Vietnam to Abu Ghraib. Case Western Reserve Journal of International Law 37, 449–508.

Wheeler, J. (2000). Saving strangers: Humanitarian intervention in international society. New York: Oxford University Press.

White, J. (2005, December 16). President relents, backs torture ban: McCain proposal had veto-proof support. Washington Post. Retrieved from http://www.washingtonpost.com/wp-dyn/content/article/2005/12/15/AR2005121502241.html.

Yoldi, J. (2006, November 1). La audiencia cierra la investigación del 11-M y da "luz verde" al juicio. Madrid: *ElPais.com*. Retrieved from http://www.elpais.com/articulo/espana/Audiencia/cierra/investigacion/11-M/da/luz/verde/juicio/elpepiesp/20061101elpepinac_6/Tes.

Zabel, R. B. & Benjamin, Jr., J. J. (2009, July). In pursuit of justice: Prosecuting terrorism cases in the federal courts: 2009 update and recent developments. Human Rights First. Retrieved from http://www.humanrightsfirst.org/pdf/090723-LS-in-pursuit-justice-09-update.pdf.

United Nations Counterterrorist Strategies and Human Rights

George Andreopoulos

The terrorist attacks of September 11, 2001, elicited a variety of responses from states, international organizations, and regional actors. Very early on, and with the certainty of a U.S. response in mind, there was a lot of discussion concerning the role of the United Nations (UN) in the emerging global antiterrorist campaign. Some analysts felt that irrespective of the nature of the appropriate response (i.e., whether the emphasis would be on law enforcement initiatives or military action), this was a campaign for which the UN was, by its very nature, mandate, and modus operandi, not "well equipped to be involved in."[1]

Yet, there were several arguments that could be made in favor of the UN's involvement:

- First, the issue of terrorism was on the international agenda well before 9/11. The main (but not exclusive) indication of this engagement is the adoption of 12 international conventions dealing with terrorism between 1963 and 1999. These conventions were developed under the auspices of the United Nations and its specialized agencies and the International Atomic Energy Agency (IAEA).
- Second, the responses to this threat cover a wide range of policies and "go well beyond conventional policing and intelligence work" (Smith 2007, December 13). In addition to strengthening legislation and boosting border security, there has been "a need to identify new strategies that sometimes involve a much wider range of agencies and even nongovernmental players in the community to address some of the technical challenges involved, as well as the social and cultural dimensions of the phenomenon" (Smith 2007, December 13);
- Third, among the main purposes of the organization are the maintenance of international peace and security and the promotion of human rights. International

[1]See Mike Smith, *The Role of the United Nations in Counter-Terrorism*, keynote address at the Policing Across Borders Workshop, John Jay College of Criminal Justice, City University of New York, December 13, 2007. Mike Smith is the Executive Director of the United Nations Counter-Terrorism Executive Directorate (CTED). Needless to say, Smith was critical of this view.

G. Andreopoulos (✉)
Department of Political Science, John Jay College of Criminal Justice and the Graduate Center, CUNY, New York, NY, USA
e-mail: chrights@jjay.cuny.edu

G. Andreopoulos et al. (eds.), *International Criminal Justice: Critical Perspectives and New Challenges*, DOI 10.1007/978-1-4419-1102-5_7,
© Springer Science+Business Media, LLC 2011

terrorism constitutes both a threat to international peace and security and a gross violation of human rights. No matter what other designation one wants to give to the 9/11 attacks, they constitute, first and foremost, a crime against humanity.
- Last, but not least, and related to the previous point, the UN, being the key institution in the development of the international human rights framework, has a responsibility to ensure that counterterrorist measures are consistent with the said framework.

It is not possible in one chapter to cover all aspects of the UN's involvement in counterterrorist initiatives. Instead, we will examine the work of one particular organ of the UN, the United Nations Security Council (hereinafter UNSC) and analyze and assess some of the policies undertaken under its auspices, policies that are marked by a serious human rights deficit. It is the argument of this discussion that this deficit needs to be urgently addressed because the main contribution that the organization can make during this critical period is to ensure that policies adopted as part and parcel of the counter-terrorist agenda do adhere to international rules and standards.

The UNSC in Action

There are several ways of looking at the UNSC and its role in counter-terrorist activities. One way is to use the conceptual lens of realism/neorealism. In this context, the UNSC is viewed as the organ whose actions are being shaped by the interests and agendas of the most powerful members of the international community and, in particular, of the United States. Such a reading would be consistent with the image of the UNSC as an organ that embodies par excellence the power asymmetries in the international system (permanent vs. nonpermanent members, with the former having veto power). Viewed through this lens, an argument can be made that whatever measures are adopted under the collective processes of international law would be consistent with, for example, the strategic priorities of the most powerful target state. Any appeals to norms and rules would be purely epiphenomenal; its main purpose would be to justify the adoption and implementation of measures relating to the said priorities.

Another way of looking at the UNSC is through the lens of liberal institutionalism. In this context, norms and rules can have an impact on state behavior, primarily because they can alter incentives for all entities involved (not only states, but organizations, interest groups, etc.) and can sustain the prospects for long-term beneficial cooperation (Keohane 1997, Spring).[2] According to this framework, the policies adopted under the said collective processes would reflect both state interests and a desire to enhance the prospects of long-term cooperation by, for example, linking the

---

[2]Keohane discusses both realism/neorealism and institutionalism under what he calls the "instrumentalist optic" (p. 490).

issue of terrorism with other issues of concern to the states involved (other internal security issues not necessarily linked to terrorism). Norms and rules would become relevant if they could effectuate such linkages; one way would be to identify different manifestations of internal violence as human rights violations.

Finally, one can draw on normative-based lenses to try to explain the UNSC role. At the risk of some overgeneralization,[3] a more normative approach would see UNSC involvement in counter-terrorism as an integral part of the UNSC's expanding post-Cold War agenda and its increasing sensitivity to nonmilitary threats to human welfare (Andreopoulos 2008).[4] This would also be consistent with the aforementioned point concerning the main purposes of the United Nations system and the concomitant obligation of the UNSC "to act in accordance with the Purposes and Principles of the United Nations."[5]

No single lens can fully explain UNSC action since the adoption of UNSC Resolution 1368. However, as the discussion below hopes to demonstrate, the realist/neorealist lens is more relevant during the earlier phase of the development of the UN's counter-terrorist agenda, while normative considerations (I would include some variants of institutionalism here) become more pronounced later on. It was not until January 2003, with the adoption of UNSC Resolution 1456, that states were called upon to respect human rights while countering terrorism.

Before addressing specific UNSC activities, it is important to note that an examination of UNSC counter-terrorist initiatives constitutes a useful antidote to certain simplistic assertions about the progressive marginalization/impotence of the UNSC. Such assertions are primarily drawn from the by-passing of the UNSC in the decision to use force against Iraq. However, the "war on terror" has sustained the viability of a contrasting image: that of an engaged UNSC, in line with its activist image of the previous decade. In this case, humanitarian activism has taken a back seat to counter-terrorist activism (Andreopoulos 2008).

Our discussion will focus primarily on the activities of two UNSC committees: the Counter-Terrorism Committee (CTC) and the 1267 Sanctions Committee. On the basis of the record of these two committees, this chapter will offer some preliminary conclusions and will identify some key challenges in the ongoing effort to ensure that, in implementing its counterterrorist agenda, the UNSC takes serious account of the relevant human rights issues.

---

[3]It is important to stress this point because several approaches can be included under this rubric; some of them are purely normative, others combine elements of normative and rationalist approaches. It is beyond the scope of this chapter to address this issue.

[4]I address aspects of the UNSC's expanding agenda in "The Challenges and Perils of Normative Overstretch" in Cronin and Hurd (2008).

[5]Article 24 of the United Nations Charter.

Legitimizing Deficient Legislation and Questionable Practices

The CTC was established on the basis of UNSC Resolution 1373. It monitors the implementation of Resolution 1373 by all states; the resolution "requested countries to implement a number of measures intended to enhance their legal and institutional ability to counter terrorist activities at home, in their regions and around the world."[6] Resolution 1373 is a rather unusual document, because it is the first Chapter VII-based resolution that applies to all the members of the UN system (Human Rights Watch 2004, August 10). It constitutes a telling example of UNSC's legislative activism:[7] the imposition of binding orders on all states regarding counter-terrorism, unconstrained by treaty and customary law obligations (Alvarez 2003, p. 874), as exemplified by the à la carte treatment of the Convention for the Suppression of the Financing of Terrorism. The resolution included the treaty's enforcement provisions that suited the counterterrorist agenda, and omitted key constraining provisions such as those relating to the rights of persons accused of terrorism-related offenses, and to the requisites of international human rights law (Alvarez 2003, p. 875).[8] In fact, the only reference to human rights in Resolution 1373 can be found in paragraph 3(f), which calls upon states to "take appropriate measures in conformity with the relevant provisions of national and international law, including international standards of human rights, before granting refugee status for the purpose of ensuring that the asylum-seeker has not planned, facilitated or participated in the commission of terrorist acts."

The CTC has asked all states to report to the committee on measures taken or planned to implement Resolution 1373. This task has provided an opening to many member states to use the 1373 process in order to engage in practices that violate fundamental tenets, as well as basic procedural guarantees, of human rights law and criminal law. The submission of actual or proposed legislation by member states to the CTC, as well as certain practices in the administration of justice, are reflective of the challenges posed by the lack of comprehensive human rights–sensitive control mechanisms in the 1373 process.

Concerning legislation, a key principle in the adoption of legislation is its compliance with the principle of legality. This principle, which requires precision in legislation and prohibits the adoption of ex post facto laws, is a non-derogable right in international human rights law, as per Article 4(2) of the International Covenant on Civil and Political Rights.[9]

---

[6]The discussion of UNSC Resolution 1373 draws on Andreopoulos (2005), "The Impact of the War on Terror on the Accountability of Armed Groups."

[7]There is no consensus in the literature as to the features that UNSC resolutions must have to qualify as legislative acts. For some scholars, resolutions that have determined the applicability of certain international legal instruments in particular situations, or have imposed economic sanctions qualify as legislative acts, while for others it is the general and abstract character of the obligations imposed that characterizes international legislation. For a general discussion, see Koskenniemi (1995) and Talmon (2005).

[8]Article 17 of the Convention includes a specific reference to international human rights law; http://untreaty.un.org/English/Terrorism/Conv12.pdf.

[9]Available at: http://www2.ohchr.org/english/law/ccpr.htm.

There are at least two factors that have facilitated member states' abuse of the said process. First, the CTC consistently refused over a long period of time to address in any serious manner the human rights implications of the campaign against terrorism. The tone was set early on with Sir Jeremy Greenstock's statement that the mandate of the CTC did not include the monitoring of the human rights performance of member states.[10]

The second flowed from the first: as a result of this attitude, there was a manifest lack of interest on the part of the CTC to scrutinize member states' records on human rights or to subject to legal scrutiny member states' laws and regulations with vague phrasing that invariably violated basic criminal law principles, in particular the principle of specificity.

For example, Egypt's definition of terrorism contained in Act No. 97 of 1992 included, among other things, "any use of force or violence or any threat or intimidation to which the perpetrator resorts in order to....*prevent* or impede the public authorities in the performance of their work." In fact, when the Human Rights Committee (HRC), the monitoring body that oversees implementation of each country's obligations under the International Covenant on Civil and Political Rights (ICCPR), examined Egypt's periodic report in November 2002, it expressed alarm at "the very broad and general definition of terrorism given in Act No. 97" (Human Rights Watch 2004, August 10, p. 8). No such concern was apparently raised by the CTC when it reviewed Egypt's initial report, submitted in December 2001, which contained the very same definition (Human Rights Watch 2004, August 10, pp. 8–9).

In a similar vein, the CTC expressed no misgivings about the pending legislation related to terrorism, when it reviewed the initial report submitted by the Philippines (Philippine Action and Initiatives Against Domestic and International Terrorism 2001, December 27). This attitude was in sharp contrast to the reaction of the HRC when it reviewed the country's consolidated second and third periodic reports. In its concluding observations, the HRC noted inter alia that, "While the Committee is mindful of the security requirements associated with efforts to combat terrorism, it is concerned by the exceedingly broad scope of the proposed legislation, as acknowledged by the delegation. The draft legislation includes a broad and vague definition of acts of terrorism which could have a negative impact on the rights guaranteed by the Covenant." And it concluded: "The State party should ensure that legislation adopted and measures taken to combat terrorism are consistent with the provisions of the Covenant" (ICCPR, United Nations 2003, January 12).

The most recent global survey on the implementation of UNSCR 1373, prepared by the CTC, confirms that problems in this area persist In particular, the survey

---

[10]Sir Jeremy Greenstock (United Nations Security Council 2002, January 18, p. 5) stated that "Monitoring performance against other international conventions, including human rights law, is outside the scope of the Counter-Terrorism Committee's mandate." He then went on to note: "But we will remain aware of the interaction with human rights concerns, and we will keep ourselves briefed as appropriate." See also Human Rights Watch (2004. August 10, p. 6). Sir Jeremy Greenstock was the first chairman of the CTC.

noted that "one issue of continuing concern is the definition of terrorist offences and related concepts (such as support and assistance) contained in criminal legislation in some states…definitions in some States remain vague or overbroad. This can lead to misuse and may also raise obstacles to international cooperation" (UNCTC 13 November 2009).

Concerning the administration of justice, an equally troubling picture emerges. While bringing those suspected of terrorist-related offenses to justice is a fundamental objective of UNSCR 1373 (2001, September 28, para. 2(e)) this goal has to be addressed within a framework that reflects adherence to internationally recognized rules and standards. Some of the critical issues involved here include provisions for investigative detention, access to counsel, the use of military or other special tribunals for terrorism-related cases, and the existence of "independent judicial oversight at all stages of terrorist investigations and prosecutions" (Flynn). A related issue is whether the country in question has declared a state of emergency. In such a case, it is important to ensure that (1) non-derogable rights are respected; (2) that adopted measures derogating from human rights obligations adhere to the principles of necessity and proportionality and are non-discriminatory; and (3) that derogations from certain rights do not undermine adherence to non-derogable rights.

The last point is particularly important because the record of states of exception has shown that noncompliance with derogable rights (e.g., minimum fair trial guarantees as per Article 14 of the ICCPR) often lead to violations of non-derogable rights (e.g., right to life). The relation between derogable and non-derogable rights was highlighted in General Comment 29 issued by the HRC:

> It is inherent in the protection of rights explicitly recognized as non-derogable in article 4, paragraph 2, that they must be secured by procedural guarantees, including often, judicial guarantees. The provisions of the Covenant relating to procedural safeguards may never be made subject to measures that would circumvent the protection of non-derogable rights. Article 4 may not be resorted to in a way that would result in derogation from non-derogable rights. Thus, for example, as article 6 of the Covenant is non-derogable in its entirety, any trial leading to the imposition of the death penalty during a state of emergency must conform to the provisions of the Covenant, including all the requirements of articles 14 and 15.

In this context, the CTC did not express any concern about Colombia's draft legislative act No. 10 of 2002 which sought to amend key provisions dealing with the administration of justice. On the contrary, the HRC registered its serious concern with the said act, while reviewing the country's fifth periodic report:

> The State party should take into consideration the fact that some of the provisions of this draft act would be in clear contradiction with provisions of the Covenant, in particular articles 2, 4 and 14. If it were to be adopted, such fundamental remedies as *amparo* proceedings could be jeopardized. (UNHRC, 26 May 2004, Colombia)

Likewise, the CTC did not raise issues relating to the administration of justice when reviewing Tajikistan's third periodic report submitted under the 1373 process. In particular, the conditions of detention and trial procedures for members of groups that had "engaged in particularly serious State crimes" (Republic of Tajikistan, 22 December 2004) did not seem to register with the committee. On the other hand, a few months later the HRC, when reviewing Tajikistan's initial report, expressed serious concern, among other things, over "the apparent lack of independence of the judiciary" and the extensive jurisdiction of military courts (UNHRC, 18 July 2005, Tajikistan).

There is little doubt that the "global campaign against terrorism" has reinforced the centrality of torture and other forms of ill-treatment in any consideration of the serious challenges confronting the administration of justice. As one analyst has pointed out "torture, in addition to being universally prohibited, undermines the goal of bringing terrorists to justice by tainting evidence and hindering effective international cooperation by virtue of the principle of *non-refoulement* (Flynn).

As the most recent global survey on the implementation of UNSCR 1373 indicates, this is another area that remains problematic:

> Some States have relied on special legal provisions or – as in a few cases – the imposition of states of emergency that have raised concerns of international mechanisms over possible infringement of the principles of necessity and proportionality and respect for non-derogable rights. Examples of special procedures include investigative or administrative detention regimes with limited judicial oversight, use of military tribunals, restrictions on access to counsel and evidence, and special powers granted to law enforcement authorities. (UNCTC 2009, p. 48)

These developments were clear indications of a UNSC milieu that could be characterized as being tone-deaf on human rights issues. The systematic neglect and concomitant marginalization of human rights issues persisted over a long period of time, despite repeated requests by human rights officials and experts in the United Nations system for quality control mechanisms and greater collaboration between the CTC and various human rights organs.

More specifically, the Office of the High Commissioner for Human Rights (OHCHR) submitted, very early on, a note to the chair of the CTC that included a set of principles that "could guide an analysis of counter-terrorism measures from a human rights perspective" (OHCHR, Note to the chair). The note reaffirmed the importance of the principles of legality, non-derogability, necessity and proportionality, nondiscrimination, due process, and non-refoulement.

Moreover, at a HRC meeting held with the legal expert of the CTC, HRC members expressed concern over the post-9/11 focus in states' legislation "on counter-terrorist measures while ignoring human rights" (UNHRC 2003, March 27). Some committee members pointed to instances of legislation, "which empowered the executive to accept as truth the designation made by foreign countries of organizations as terrorist organizations, without examining that designation on its merits," while one member warned "that some policies, supposedly aimed at combating terrorism, were simply policies of repression" (UNHRC 2003, March 27).

In response to these concerns and criticisms, the CTC eventually committed itself to ensuring a liaison between the Counter-Terrorism Committee Executive Directorate (CTED) and the OHCHR (UNSC 2004, August 12). Moreover, in 2005 the CTC agreed to the hiring by the CTED of its first human rights expert; however, the CTC limited the expert's portfolio to liaising activities with the UN human rights bodies and NGOs (Rosand et al. 2007, p. 16). In 2006, the CTC issued a policy guidance in which it reaffirmed the need for the CTED to liaise with the OHCHR, as appropriate, when analyzing states' implementation of Resolution 1373, as well as when preparing draft letters to states and organizing visits. In addition, the policy guidance stated that the CTC and the CTED, under the direction of the committee, "should incorporate human rights into their communication strategy" (UNSC 2006, May 25).

There are two areas where this incorporation can manifest itself in the working methods of the CTC and signal a more serious engagement with the human rights framework: the first relates to the issue of best practices in the area of counter-terrorism and human rights, and the second in the area of CTED on-site visits.

On best practices: In accordance with UNSCR 1377 (2001), 1456 (2003), and 1566 (2004), the CTC "has compiled a directory of recommended practices" to assist all states in their efforts to implement UNSCR 1373 (UNCTC Directory). The list of relevant best practices relates to specific provisions of the resolution. What is interesting about this directory is that there is scant reference to human rights instruments and hardly any reference to the relation of human rights standards to counter-terrorist practices. The most extensive reference in 1373 relates to the granting of refugee status (paragraph 3(f)), where the Convention relating to the Status of Refugees and the Convention Against Torture are included. However, the primary preoccupation with the Refugee Convention relates to the exclusion clauses (UNHCR, Background note). The only other relevant references are in the section on bilateral and multilateral cooperation instruments and agreements. Included in that section is a Council of Europe recommendation, issued by the Committee of Ministers, which emphasizes, in its preambular provisions, the need for compatibility of any international cooperation measures with the principles contained in the European Convention for the Protection of Human Rights and Fundamental Freedoms (Recommendation No. R (82) 1).

There is little doubt that more is needed in this area. There is already a factsheet that has been prepared by the OHCHR with the aim of strengthening "understanding of the complex and multifaceted relationship between human rights and terrorism" (OHCHR, Fact sheet #32). However, this is listed under a separate section entitled *Human Rights*. Moreover, the Human Rights Council has requested the Special Rapporteur on the promotion and protection of human rights and fundamental freedoms while countering terrorism, "to identify, exchange and promote best practices" on counter-terrorist measures that adhere to international human rights standards (Flynn). As the Senior Human Rights Officer of the CTC has noted, these and related resources "should be integrated into the Committee's work program and promoted more assertively by the Committee in its interactions with Member States" (Flynn).

On site visits: In March 2005, the CTC launched a program of state visits that always take place with the consent of the state concerned. In order to ensure "a more tailored approach" to the situation of the target country, the CTC created the following year a matrix, entitled Preliminary Implementation Assessment (PIA), which provides "a snapshot of the counterterrorism situation" in that country and includes information from the country itself, from relevant international organizations and other pertinent public sources; only the country concerned is privy to the information included in the PIA (CTED 2010).

Although the PIAs are expected to address all relevant provisions of UNSCR 1373, the aforementioned lack of proper integration of human rights into the Committee's work program, renders them (PIAs) questionable as a tool for promoting a more human rights-sensitive approach in the counter-terrorist effort. Yet, the PIAs could constitute a potentially critical entry point in this endeavor, because they frame the dialogue between the CTC and member states. In this context, it would also be important to ensure that the CTC's human rights expert is included in all on-site visits. Because the human rights expert is expected to prepare background notes for the CTED that address key human rights concerns relevant to the country's implementation of UNSCR 1373 and 1624,[11] this official's inclusion in the CTED delegation would ensure that all critical human rights issues receive due attention and inform the CTED's assessment of the overall situation in the country concerned.

Due Process in Listing and Delisting Practices

The listing and de-listing practices of the 1267 Sanctions Committee, which was established by the UNSC with the purpose of overseeing the implementation of sanctions imposed on individuals and entities belonging or related to the Taliban, Osama bin Laden and Al-Qaida, have raised critical questions concerning their adherence to international standards.[12]

The 1267 Committee was created in response to, among other things, the Taliban's continuing provision of "safe haven to [O]sama bin Laden;" in addition, the resolution cited the fact that the Taliban allowed bin Laden "and others associated with him to operate a network of terrorist training camps…and to use Afghanistan as a base from which to sponsor international terrorist operations." In a subsequent resolution, the UNSC requested the committee "to maintain an updated list, based on information provided by States and regional organizations, of the individuals and entities designated as being associated with [O]sama bin Laden, including those in the Al-Qaida organization" (UNSC 2000, December 19). Finally, in Resolution 1455, the UNSC emphasized the importance of the provision, by member states, of names and information to the committee, "so that the Committee can consider adding new names and details to its list" (UNSC 2003, January 17).

[11]Resolution 1624 calls upon states to, among other things, "prohibit by law incitement to commit a terrorist act or acts" and to "prevent such conduct." In addition, it reaffirms that all measures adopted in this context should be "in accordance with international law, in particular, international human rights law, refugee law and humanitarian law." The CTC "is mandated to include issues related to implementing the resolution in its dialogue with Member States" (United Nations Counter-Terrorism Committee Executive Directorate, CTED 2010).

[12]Part of this section follows Andreopoulos (2008, pp. 115–118).

According to the latest information provided by the Sanctions Committee, the list includes 137 individuals associated with the Taliban, and 257 individuals and 103 entities associated with Al-Qaida[13] (accessed June 20, 2010). The process by which individuals and institutions are listed and delisted has been challenged before regional and domestic fora.

One of the earliest cases involved three Swedish citizens of Somali origin – Abdirisak Aden, Abdi Abdulaziz Ali, and Yusuf Ahmed Ali – as well as the Al Barakaat International Foundation, a nonprofit association with which these men were affiliated. Their names and that of the association appeared on the Sanctions Committee list in November 2001 (Gutherie 2004, p. 511). U.S. intelligence provided the information that led to their listing, and this decision resulted in the freezing of their assets on the basis of a Commission of the European Communities regulation implementing UNSC sanctions.[14]

In response, the three individuals brought an action, before the European Court of First Instance (ECFI), against the commission and the Council of the European Union alleging that the UN-imposed assets freeze, implemented in the European Union via the aforementioned EC regulation, violated certain fundamental rights. Initially, the plaintiffs sought interim relief, which was denied.[15] At their request, the Swedish government initially petitioned the Sanctions Committee to have their names removed from the list, but with no success. A subsequent joint petition (with the U.S. administration) to the Sanctions Committee proved to be more successful, and led to the delisting of two of the three individuals in question (Gutherie 2004, p. 512). The third individual was eventually delisted on August 24, 2006.

The case of Yusuf Ahmed Ali and Al Barakaat was joined by another case brought by Yassin Abdullah Kadi, a resident of Saudi Arabia, before the ECFI; the court rendered its judgment on both cases on September 21, 2005 (ECFI 2005a, b). While the court rejected all of the applicants' arguments, it did note that the Charter of the United Nations "presupposes the existence of mandatory principles of international law, in particular, the protection of the fundamental rights of the human person.... Those principles are binding on the Members of the United Nations as

[13]The consolidated list was established and is maintained by the 1267 Committee with respect to al-Qaida, Osama bin Laden, and the Taliban and other individuals, groups, undertakings and entities associated with them. The list was last updated on June 4, 2010. Since the consolidated list's inception, 31 individuals and 33 entities have been removed from it. Retrieved from http://www.un.org/sc/committees/1267/consolist.shtml.

[14]The regulation in question is Commission Regulation (EC) No. 2199/2001 of November 12, 2001, amending for the fourth time, Council Regulation (EC) No 467/2001 prohibiting the export of certain goods and services to Afghanistan, strengthening the flight ban and extending the freeze of funds and other financial resources in respect of the Taliban of Afghanistan and repealing Regulation (EC) No, 337/2000; *Official Journal of the European Communities*, L295/16–18.

[15]Case T-306/01 *Abdirisak Aden, Abdulaziz Ali, Ahmed Yusuf and Al Barakaat International Foundation v Council of the European Union and Commission of the European Communities*. Proceedings for Interim Measures (2002/C 191/46), *Official Journal of the European Communities*, C191/26. The decision on interim measures can be found at: http://eur-lex.europa.eu/smartapi/cgi/sga_doc?smartapi!celexplus!prod!CELEXnumdoc&lg=en&numdoc=62001B0306.

well as on its bodies." It then went on to state: "The indirect judicial review carried out by the Court...may therefore, in some circumstances, extend to determining whether the superior rules of international law falling within the ambit of *jus cogens* have been observed...in particular, the mandatory provisions concerning the universal protection of human rights, from which neither the Member States nor the bodies of the United Nations may derogate because they constitute "intransgressible principles of international customary law."[16]

The plaintiffs appealed the ECFI decisions before the European Court of Justice (ECJ). In a decision issued on September 3, 2008, the ECJ set aside the judgments of the ECFI and ruled that the community judicature, contra the ECFI, does have jurisdiction to review measures adopted by the community giving effect to UNSC resolutions (ECJ 2008, September 3). Although the ECJ was careful to draw a distinction between the UNSC resolution and the regulation adopted by the Council of the EU, which implemented the said resolution, it found that the regulation in question infringed the affected parties' right to be heard before a court of law, the right of effective judicial review and the right to property (ECJ 2008, September 3).

The importance of this case cannot be overstated; its significance lies primarily in the fact that a court of ECJ's stature has ruled that the sanctions imposed, following a UNSC resolution, do violate certain fundamental human rights. Moreover, and despite the above-mentioned distinction drawn by the ECJ between the UNSC resolution and the EU regulation, the decision inescapably points to the conclusion that there is a limit to the powers of the UNSC.[17]

In a similar vein, the HRC, one of the major human rights treaty-based monitoring organs, has challenged the legality of a listing pursuant to UNSC 1267. The case involved two Belgian nationals, Nabil Sayadi and Patricia Vinck, whose names appeared on three lists (UNSC, European Union Council, and a Belgian ministerial order). As a result of these listings, and despite their clean records, all their financial assets were frozen; an act that prevented them "from working, travelling, moving funds and defraying family expenses" (ICCPR, United Nations 2008, December 29). Upon consideration of the communication submitted by Sayadi and Vinck under the Optional Protocol of the International Covenant of Civil and Political Rights (ICCPR), the HRC found that the facts before it disclosed a violation of Article 12 (liberty of movement) and Article 17 (freedom from unlawful attacks on one's honor and reputation) of the covenant.

It is instructive to note here that the 2004 UN report produced by the High-level Panel on Threats, Challenges, and Change is unusually candid about the critical issues raised by the modus operandi of the Sanctions Committee:

---

[16]Case T-306/01. The above passage is almost identical in both rulings.

[17]This, however, has not led to the closing of the case. The European Commission has enacted a new regulation (No. 1190/2008 of November 28, 2008), which provided for the continuation of the sanctions. Yassin Kadi and Al Barakaat International have filed challenges to their renewed listings in the ECFI (Analytical Support and Sanctions Implementation Monitoring Team 2009, October 2, p. 32).

> The way entities or individuals are added to the terrorist list maintained by the Council and the absence of review or appeal for those listed raise serious accountability issues and possibly violate fundamental human rights norms and conventions. The Al-Qaida and Taliban Sanctions Committee should institute a process for reviewing the cases of individuals and institutions claiming to have been wrongly placed or retained on its watch lists. (United Nations 2004, p. 50)

In a similar vein, the World Summit Outcome Document (2005) called upon the UNSC "to ensure that fair and clear procedures exist for placing individuals and entities on sanctions lists and for removing them, as well as for granting humanitarian exemptions" (UN General Assembly 2005, October 24, para. 109).

In response to these concerns, a series of studies have sought to address critical aspects relating to the fairness and transparency of listing and delisting procedures. Among the most widely discussed has been a study sponsored by the governments of Switzerland, Germany, and Sweden and conducted by the Watson Institute for International Studies at Brown University.

Among other things, the study noted that despite important improvements made over time, "criticisms persist about procedures related to the designation or listing of individuals, operations of committees, and the process for individuals and entities to be removed from the list." In addition, the study noted that "the lack of transparency of committee procedures and difficulties in obtaining information contribute to general perceptions of unfairness" (Watson Institute, p. 3). One of the key procedural recommendations of the study was the creation of a focal point within the Secretariat to handle all delisting requests, so that the petitioner would not have to do that through his or her state of citizenship or residence. With Resolution 1730, the UNSC adopted a modified version of this proposal and instructed the sanctions committees, including the 1267 Committee, to revise their guidelines accordingly (UNSC 2006, December 19).

More recently with Resolution 1904, the UNSC attempted to further enhance the transparency of the whole process. Among other things, the resolution directed the Sanctions Committee to make accessible on its website, once a name or names are added to the Consolidated List, "a narrative summary of reasons for listing for the corresponding entry or entries," and it established the Office of the Ombudsperson which will review requests for delisting submitted by individuals and entities. The main task of the office will be to "lay out for the Committee the principal arguments concerning the delisting request" (United Nations Security Council 2009, December 17). As a result of this development, the above-mentioned focal point will henceforth focus on delisting requests from other sanctions lists.

While this is a step in the right direction, other critical aspects of this problem, including the creation of independent review mechanisms, where individuals and entities may appeal decisions regarding their listing, are yet to be addressed. This, of course, is not a problem confined to the workings of the Sanctions Committee. The CTC's most recent global survey noted that "some states…lack effective procedures to allow persons affected by preventive measures to challenge such measures before independent bodies" (UNCTC 2009, p. 48).

Concluding Remarks

While the United Nations can play an important role in the development of counterterrorist strategies, its potential contribution has been undermined by policies and practices that have exhibited a serious human rights deficit. One of the strengths that an international organization such as the UN can bring to this effort is to develop and sustain state cooperation in accordance with certain agreed-upon standards. The promotion of human rights constitutes one of the main purposes of the organization. This has been reaffirmed in several recent resolutions such as 1624, which noted that all relevant measures taken by states must comply "with all of their obligations under international law, in particular international human rights law, refugee law, and humanitarian law" (UNSC 2005).

To be sure, interest-based considerations will remain paramount, especially in a body such as the UNSC. However, in recent years there has been a noticeable shift towards an effort at greater transparency and accountability. What led to this development? There are several contributing factors at work here: the work of the UN's human rights bodies (such as OHCHR and HRC); the advocacy of key human rights NGOs (such as Human Rights Watch); the applications filed by individuals and entities affected before regional judicial fora (such as the ECFI, the ECJ, and the European Court of Human Rights);[18] pertinent issues raised and debated in regional intergovernmental fora (such as the Council of Europe);[19] and legal challenges before domestic courts.[20] All these developments have increased the pressure on the UNSC to adjust its relevant policies and procedures.

This is a development consistent with what normative-oriented approaches would expect. More specifically, such approaches would focus on the relevance and resilience of fundamental norms (in this context, human rights ones) and the catalytic role of networks composed of actors interested in advancing and defending such norms (members of the Council of Europe, NGOs, UN bodies, and judicial fora). While a lot remains to be done in this issue area, one thing is clear: if the UN's counter-terrorist agenda is to advance, it needs to acquire a greater degree of legitimacy that only adherence to the said standards can provide.

---

[18]Youssef Mustafa Nada Ebada has brought a case before the European Court of Human Rights which is still pending (Analytical Support and Sanctions Implementation Monitoring Team 2009, October 2, p. 32).

[19]In Resolution 1597 adopted on January 23, 2008, the Parliamentary Assembly of the Council of Europe noted, among other things, that "the procedural and substantive standards currently applied by the UNSC and by the Council of the European Union, despite some recent improvements, in no way fulfill the minimum standards laid down above and violate the fundamental principles of human rights and the rule of law" (Council of Europe Parliamentary Assembly 2008).

[20]For a list of the legal challenges pending or recently concluded before domestic fora, see Analytical Support and Sanctions Implementation Monitoring Team, pp. 33–34.

References

Alvarez, J. (2003). Hegemonic international law revisited. *Am. J. Int. L. 97*(4), 873–888.

Analytical Support and Sanctions Implementation Monitoring Team (2009, October 2). Tenth report submitted pursuant to resolution 1822 (2008) concerning Al-Quaida and the Taliban and association individuals and entities, S/2009/502.

Andreopoulos, G. (2005). The impact of the war on terror on the accountability of armed groups. In: H.M. Hensel (Ed.), *The Law of Armed Conflict: Constraints on the Contemporary Use of Military Force* (pp. 175–177). Aldershot, Hants, UK: Ashgate.

Andreopoulos, G. (2008). The challenges and perils of normative overstretch. In: B. Cronin & I. Hurd (Eds.), *The UN Security Council and the Politics Of International Authority* (pp. 105–128). London: Routledge.

Council of Europe Committee of Ministers (n.d.). Recommendation No. R (82) 1 of the Committee of Ministers to member states concerning international cooperation in the prosecution and punishment of acts of terrorism. Retrieved from https://wcd.coe.int/com.instranet.InstraServlet?command=com.instranet.CmdBlobGet&InstranetImage=601006&SecMode=1&DocId=674292&Usage=2.

Council of Europe Parliamentary Assembly (2008). Resolution 1597, United Nations Security Council and European Union blacklists. Retrieved from http://assembly.coe.int/Main.asp?link=/Documents/AdoptedText/ta08/ERES1597.htm.

European Court of First Instance (ECFI). (2005a, September 21). Case T-315/01, Yassin Abdullah Kadi v. Council of the European Union and Commission of the European Communities. Retrieved from http://eur-lex.europa.eu/LexUriServ/LexUriServ.do?uri=CELEX:62001A0315:EN:PDF.

European Court of First Instance (ECFI). (2005b, September 21). Case T-306/01, Ahmed Ali Yusuf and Al Barakaat International Foundation v. Council of the European Union and Commission of the European Communities. Retrieved from http://eur-lex.europa.eu/LexUriServ/LexUriServ.do?uri=CELEX:62001A0306:EN:PDF.

European Court of Justice (ECJ). (2008, September 3). Judgment in Joined Cases C-402/05 P, and C-415/05 P, Yassin Abdullah Kadi and Al Barakaat International Foundation v. Council of the European Union and Commission of the European Communities. Retrieved from http://curia.europa.eu/jurisp/cgi-bin/form.pl?lang=en&Submit=Rechercher&alldocs=alldocs&docj=docj&docop=docop&docor=docor&docjo=docjo&numaff=C-402/05&datefs=&datefe=&nomusuel=&domaine=&mots=&resmax=100.

Flynn, E. (n.d.). Pushing the limits: Human Rights at the United Nations Counter-Terrorism Committee [Unpublished paper, on file with the author].

Gutherie, P. (2004). Security Council sanctions and the protection of individual rights. *New York University Annual Survey of American Law* (Vol. 60).

Human Rights Watch (2004, August 10). Hear no evil, see no evil: The UN Security Council's approach to human rights violations in the global counter-terrorism effort [briefing paper].

Keohane, R. (1997, Spring). International relations and international law: Two optics. *Harv. Int'l. L. J. 38*(2), 487–502.

Koskenniemi, M. (1995). The police in the temple – Order, justice and the UN: A dialectical view. *Eur. J. Int'l. L. 6*, 325–348.

Office of the High Commissioner for Human Rights (OHCHR). (n.d.). Note to the Chair of the Counter-Terrorism Committee: A human rights perspective on counter-terrorist measures. Retrieved from http://www.un.org/Docs/sc/committees/1373/ohchr1.htm.

Office of the High Commissioner for Human Rights (OHCHR). (n.d.). Human rights, terrorism and counter-terrorism. Fact sheet no. 32. Retrieved from http://www.ohchr.org/Documents/Publications/Factsheet32EN.pdf.

Philippine Action and Initiatives Against Domestic and International Terrorism (2001, December 27). S/2001/1290.

Rajagopal, B. (2003). *International Law from Below: Development, Social Movements and Third World Resistance*. Cambridge, UK: Cambridge University Press.

Republic of Tajikistan. (n.d.). Report submitted to the United Nations Counter-Terrorism Committee pursuant to paragraph 6 of Resolution 1373 (2001). Retrieved from http://daccess-dds-ny.un.org/doc/UNDOC/GEN/N04/669/99/PDF/N0466999.pdf?OpenElement.

Rosand, E., Millar, A., & Ipe, J. (2007). *The UN Security Council's Counterterrorism Program: What Lies Ahead?* International Peace Academy. New York.

Smith, M. (2007, December 13). *The Role of the United Nations in Counter-terrorism.* Keynote address at the Policing Across Borders Workshop, John Jay College of Criminal Justice, The City University of New York.

Talmon, S. (2005). Note and comment: The Security Council as world legislature. *Am. J. Int'l. L. 99*(1), 175–199.

United Nations (2003, January 12). *International covenant on civil and political rights (ICCPR).* Concluding observations of the Human Rights Committee: Philippines. CCPR/CO/79/PHL.

United Nations (2004). *Report of the High-Level Panel on Threats, Challenges and Change: A More Secure World: Our Shared Responsibility.* New York: United Nations Department of Public Information.

United Nations (2008, December 29). International covenant on civil and political rights (ICCPR). Communication No. 147i2/2006 Nabil Sayadi and Patricia Vinck v. Belgium, CCPR/C/94/D/1472/2006.

United Nations Counter-Terrorism Committee (accessed June 20, 2010). Directory of international best practices, codes and standards for the implementation of Security Council Resolution 1373 (2001). Retrieved from http://www.un.org/sc/ctc/practices.html.

United Nations Counter-Terrorism Committee (2009). Survey of the implementation of Security Council Resolution 1373 by member states. Retrieved from http://www.un.org/sc/ctc/pdf/GIS2009.pdf.

United Nations Counter-Terrorism Committee Executive Directorate (CTED) (2010). The role of the Counter-Terrorism Committee and its Executive Directorate in the international counter-terrorism effort. Retrieved from http://www.un.org/sc/ctc/pdf/presskit/FINAL_2010_Presskit_EN.pdf.

United Nations General Assembly (2005, October 24). 2005 World Summit Outcome, A/RES/60/1.

United Nations High Commissioner for Refugees (2003, September 4). Background note on the application of the exclusion clauses: Article 1F of the 1951 Convention relating to the Status of Refugees. Retrieved from http://www.un.org/sc/ctc/pdf/backgroundexclusion.pdf.

United Nations Human Rights Committee (2004, May 26). Consideration of reports submitted by states parties under Article 40 of the Covenant. Concluding observations of the HRC. Colombia. Retrieved from http://ods-dds-ny.un.org/doc/UNDOC/GEN/G04/419/122/PDF/G0441992.pdf?OpenElement.

United Nations High Commissioner for Refugees (2005, July18). Consideration of reports submitted by states parties under Article 40 of the Covenant. Concluding observations of the HRC. Tajikistan. Retrieved from http://www.unchr.ch./tbs/doc.nsf/(Symbol)/CCPT,CO.84TJK.En?OpenDocument.

United Nations Human Rights Committee (2003, March 27). HRC briefed on work of Counter-Terrorism Committee. Press release HR/CT/630.

United Nations Human Rights Committee (2005). International covenant on civil and political rights. General comment No. 29. States of emergency (Article 4). Retrieved from http://www.unhchr.ch/tbs/doc.nsf/898586b1dc7b4043c1256a450044f331/71eba4be3974b4f7c1256iae200517361/$FILE/G0144470.pdf.

United Nations Security Council (1999, October 15). Resolution 1267, S/RES/1267.

United Nations Security Council (2000, December 19). Resolution 1333, S/RES/1333.

United Nations Security Council (2001, September 28). Resolution 1373. Retrieved from http://www.un.org/sc/ctc/aboutus/html.

United Nations Security Council (2002, January 18). 4453rd meeting. S/PV.4453.

United Nations Security Council (2003, January 17). Resolution 1455, S/RES/1455.

United Nations Security Council (2004, August 12). Organizational plan for the Counter-Terrorism Committee Executive Directorate (enclosure). S/2004/642.

United Nations Security Council. (2005) Resolution 1624, S/RES/1624.
United Nations Security Council (2006, May 25). Security Council committee established pursuant to resolution 1373 (2001) concerning counter-terrorism. Policy Guidance PG2, S/AC.40/2006/PG2.
United Nations Security Council (2006, December 19). Resolution 1730, S/RES/1730.
United Nations Security Council (2009, December 17). Resolution 1904, S/RES/1904.
Watson Institute for International Studies at Brown University (n.d.). Strengthening Targeted Sanctions. Retrieved from http://watsoninstitute.org/pub/Strengthening_Targeted_Sanctions.pdf.

Can Domestically Seated War Crimes Tribunals Generate Positive Externalities? A Case Study of the Special Court for Sierra Leone

Christopher E.S. Warburton and Richard F. Culp

Introduction

With ratification of the treaty-based Rome Statute of the International Criminal Court (ICC) by a sixtieth country in 2002, the world community moved a step closer to institutionalizing the concept of universal jurisdiction[1] over genocide, war crimes, and other crimes against humanity. Among the supporting rationales for establishing the permanent ICC in The Hague, Netherlands, was the problem that ongoing security concerns in conflict regions of the world can forestall, perhaps indefinitely, the establishment of ad hoc tribunals in the countries where the crimes have occurred. In the past, domestic security concerns have served in part as a rationale for locating other international criminal tribunals outside the country where the atrocities were committed – e.g., the International Criminal Tribunal for the former Yugoslavia (ICTY) was located in the Hague and the International Criminal Tribunal for Rwanda (ICTR) in Arusha, Tanzania. Conversely, the assumed adequacy of domestic security played a role in the decision to locate the Special Panels for Serious Crimes (SPSC) in Dili, East Timor,[2] the Special Court for Sierra Leone in Freetown, and the Extraordinary Chambers in the Courts of

[1] "Universal" to the extent that countries are signatories of the treaty-based Rome Statute. As of July 2008, 108 countries had become States Parties to the Rome Statute of the International Criminal Court. The jurisdiction of the ICC is based on "complementarity", which allows national courts the first opportunity to investigate or prosecute.

[2] The SPSC experience in East Timor has not been very successful, due in part to difficulties in securing extradition agreements with Indonesia, where many of the indictees fled, and to continuing security threats to the stability of the East Timor government.

C.E.S. Warburton (✉)
Department of Economics, John Jay College of Criminal Justice and the Graduate Center, CUNY, New York, NY, USA
e-mail: cwarburton@jjay.cuny.edu

G. Anderopoulos et al. (eds.), *International Criminal Justice: Critical Perspectives and New Challenges*, DOI 10.1007/978-1-4419-1102-5_8,
© Springer Science+Business Media, LLC 2011

Cambodia (ECCC) in Phnom Penh. With the establishment of the ICC, there is now a permanent court in a single location with the ability to indict perpetrators of alleged war crimes emerging out of conflicts that have yet to be resolved. Indeed, the court has already indicted some of those alleged to have committed crimes against humanity during continuing conflicts in the Democratic Republic of the Congo, Uganda, the Central African Republic, and Darfur, Sudan.

The successful establishment of the ICC and its recent moves to address war crimes in ongoing conflicts present a strong case for discontinuing the practice of constituting ad hoc war crimes tribunals in countries that are recovering from civil conflict. However, locating a war crimes court outside of the country where the atrocities occurred has logistical and financial ramifications. Logistically, the distance from the scene of the crimes to the location of the trial poses many challenges in transporting, housing, and providing other support services to victims and witnesses. Similarly, the distance involved makes it difficult to actively engage the general public and the local news media of the victims' country in the day-to-day course of the trials. Although the ICC, the ICTY and the ICTR have taken measures to address this limitation, such measures can substantially increase the cost of conducting the trials.[3]

Moreover, locating a court in a distant location does little to help rebuild the justice system infrastructure and human resources of a country that has experienced prolonged conflict. In principle, spending a greater share of war crimes tribunal funds locally has the potential benefit of helping to rebuild and reform a post-conflict country's criminal justice system. Given that the absence of effective rule of law institutions is a common contributing factor in civil conflict,[4] domestically situated courts have the potential to kill two birds with one stone, holding accountable those responsible for atrocities and human rights abuses, while helping to develop local institutions that can serve to prevent such abuses in the future.

This chapter seeks to contribute to the debate over where best to locate war crimes trials by adding new data on the positive externalities that a domestically constituted tribunal can generate. Focusing on the criminal justice system of Sierra Leone, we show the deterioration of the security situation in the country over the course of the civil war, discuss the major internationally sponsored projects directed toward rebuilding it, and consider the various methods that have been used to place a value on justice-related activities. We then use the security budget of the Special Court over a 3-year period to estimate the shadow price of international investment in its operation. We argue that for poor countries in which the human and physical capital of justice system institutions has been destroyed as a result of civil war and war-related

[3]Notwithstanding efforts to control the myriad costs of housing a court in another country, the ICTY and the ICTR proved very expensive to operate – in 2000, the cost of operating the courts constituted a full 10% of the United Nations budget (Dougherty 2004).

[4]Kposowa (2006) makes the case that the underlying foundations of the Sierra Leone conflict were laid through general erosion in respect for the rule of law and a gradual breakdown in law and order for two decades before the conflict began in 1991.

atrocities, seating hybrid tribunals within the subject country generates positive externalities and helps subsidize the fiscal policy of post-conflict governments.

Problems with Seating and Operating Hybrid Tribunals

There are advantages and disadvantages, risks and opportunities, that occasion each option of where to locate a war crimes tribunal and the process of deciding is arguably more a matter of art than science. Principal concerns include whether the country has attained a sufficient level of peace and stability to withstand a war crimes trial and whether the country has sufficient infrastructure and human resources to conduct the court's business. In the case of both the International Criminal Tribunal for the former Yugoslavia (ICTY), which convened in the Hague, Netherlands, and the International Criminal Tribunal for Rwanda (ICTR), which meets in Arusha, Tanzania, the anticipated volume of potential defendants to be tried and the diminished post-conflict capacity of the local justice institutions to support the work of a domestic tribunal steered the decision away from holding the trials in-country (Beresford 2000–2001; Dougherty 2004).

As The Hague was home to the International Court of Justice and other international legal organizations, it was a logical site for locating a tribunal dealing with crimes against international law that occurred on European soil. In a similar way, Arusha was the eponymous location of the 1993 "Arusha Accords" between the Government of Rwanda and the Rwandan Patriotic Front (RPF) and the site of the Arusha International Conference Centre (AICC) where the tribunal could readily be housed. In each case, "administrative efficiency, including access to witnesses, and economy" (Beresford 2000–2001, p. 106) served as the guiding principle in locating the tribunals.

Both the ICTY and ICTR were established by UN Security Council resolutions and were "broadly mandated to try genocide, crimes against humanity and war crimes; premised on individual responsibility" (Dougherty 2004, p. 312). The scope of their mandates and the extent of atrocities in these conflicts led to the indictment of 120 persons by the ICTY and 90 persons by the ICTR. The judicial infrastructure to handle this volume of cases was simply nonexistent in either the former Yugoslavia or Rwanda. Indeed, it was unfortunately lacking in Tanzania as well, where a lack of rule of law infrastructure and a history of dysfunctional governance posed practical challenges to the efficient operation of the tribunal.

Early on, lawyers and judges were hampered by intermittent phone service, the absence of Internet access, and scant research support, so that the prosecution staff often could not communicate with investigators in the field. But even after the logistic headaches eased, the court was plagued by corruption, nepotism, and mismanagement. Squirreled away in east-central Africa in a jumping off spot for safaris and trips to nearby Mount Kilimanjaro, many staff members lazed about Arusha on cushy UN salaries. The court was so dysfunctional that a few of the early court reporters were found unable to type (Power 2002, p. 495).

The Special Court for Sierra Leone (SCSL), on the other hand, had a much narrower mandate than either the ICTY or the ICTR, handing down indictments to only a fraction of the number of defendants prosecuted by the other two courts. The SCSL was mandated to "prosecute persons who bear the greatest responsibility for serious violations of international humanitarian law and Sierra Leonean law committed in the territory of Sierra Leone since 30 November 1996"[5] (The Special Court for Sierra Leone 2002). Subject to the "greatest responsibility" and "after 1996" limitations, the SCSL indicted a total of just 13 persons. Other factors, including concerns over the availability of witnesses, the ease of citizen access to the trial proceedings, and the ability of local media to cover the trial were important points in the decision to hold the SCSL in Freetown (Elagab 2004). Ultimately, the decision on where to locate the tribunal is peculiar to the specific conflict involved.

Sierra Leone is a poor country with an average gross national per capita income[6] of U.S. $208 for the period 1964 (3 years after independence) to 2005 and $260 in 2007 (World Bank WDI 2009). In 1989, approximately a decade before the start of hostilities, about 57% of the population lived in extreme poverty, that is, on less than Le 2,111 (or slightly below US $1) per day. The most recent estimate puts 70% of the population below the extreme poverty line in 2004 (World Bank 2005) or at the national poverty line (World Bank 2008). The World Bank estimated the adult literacy rate to be 35% in 2006, and put life expectancy in the country at 41 years in 2005 and 43 years in 2007. The government's present value of debt as a percentage of gross national income was 40% in 2005. In 2007 the external debt stock as a percent of gross national income was 21.4%. Indebtedness is closely associated with public corruption and capital flight.

Transparency International rates the average perception of corruption between 2003 and 2008 to be exceedingly high (2.1) even after the cessation of hostilities.[7] Problems of resource constraint and corruption extended to the courts and the police, which were characterized by a lack of judges, magistrates, and prosecutors—a corrupt judiciary that was susceptible to manipulation and compromise of justice—inadequate law enforcement infrastructure; and a diminished and demoralized police force.[8]

[5]The "after November 1996" limitation was due to amnesty provisions of the Abidjan Peace Agreement of November 30, 1996.

[6]See World Development Indicator by the World Bank (2007).

[7]Transparency International (TI) is a global civil society organization which fights against corruption by bringing people together in a worldwide coalition to raise awareness of corruption and end the impact of corruption on humans around the world. The annual *Corruption Perceptions Index (CPI)* was first released in 1995 and it has gained extensive attention in business, political, and intellectual circles. The CPI ranks 180 countries by their perceived levels of corruption, as determined by expert assessments and opinion surveys. On a scale of 1–10, 1 is exceedingly corrupt, and 10 is superlatively clean (a rare and exceptional situation).

[8]For extended discussion of the problems, accomplishments, and challenges of the Court, see Human Rights Watch, Bringing Justice: the Special Court for Sierra Leone, September 7, 2004. Downloaded September 2008 from http://www.hrw.org/en/reports/2004/09/07/bringing-justice-special-court-sierra-leone-0: 1–55.

The civil war in Sierra Leone began in March 1991 with skirmishes between rebel fighters of the Revolutionary United Front (RUF) and the Army of the Government of Sierra Leone. The RUF sought the overthrow of then President Joseph Mohmoh's one-party government and a restoration of multiparty democratic rule. But the high-minded goals of the insurgency rapidly degenerated into an atrocity-ridden civil war that exacted a huge physical and psychological toll on the Sierra Leonean people and the infrastructure of the government (for a discussion of the broader effects of the war, see, e.g., Kaplan 1994 or Chege 2002). The war came to an official end following successful parliamentary elections in 2002.

In 2002, an agreement was reached between the government of Sierra Leone and the United Nations (UN) to establish a Special Court for Sierra Leone (SCSL). Established pursuant to Security Council Resolution 1315 of August 14, 2000, the SCSL was created to end impunity for perpetrators of crimes against humanity, war crimes, and other serious violations of international humanitarian law. The Security Council Resolution explicitly recognized the negative impact of the post-conflict security situation on the administration of justice in Sierra Leone and the importance of rule of law restoration to sustainable peace:

Recognizing that, in the particular circumstances of Sierra Leone, a credible system of justice and accountability for the very serious crimes committed there would end impunity *and would contribute to the process of national reconciliation and to the restoration and maintenance of peace* [emphasis added] (United Nations Security Council 2000).

As we shall see, not only was the hybrid tribunal able to function in a less-than-ideal security environment, but its existence and operations in Sierra Leone created positive externalities and subsidized the outlays of the Sierra Leone government, enabling it to rebuild human and physical capital and resuscitate the moribund Sierra Leone Police force, courts, and prison system.

There is no question that the capacity of the criminal justice system in Sierra Leone had been seriously diminished by the civil war and the ability of the country to host a war crimes tribunal was far from certain. All three major institutions of criminal justice – the police, the courts, and the prison system – were in disarray as the conflict in Sierra Leone came to an end.

The size of the Sierra Leone Police force declined steadily during the conflict as organized recruitment and training were functionally suspended nationwide: total personnel strength of the SLP dropped from over 10,000 before the civil war; to 9,300 in 1996; to 8,600 in 1998; to less than 6,600 in 2000 (Thompson 2000; Banya 1996; Commonwealth Police Development Task Force for Sierra Leone 1998; Meek 2003). According to some reports, as many as 900 police officers were killed during the war, with the January 1999 RUF attack on Freetown alone claiming the lives of more than 300 officers (Meek 2003).

As human resources declined, so too did policing infrastructure. The main police training facility at Hastings was severely damaged in two rebel attacks and training of new recruits was suspended indefinitely by the mid-1990s. Regional training centers in the provincial capitals of Bo, Kenema, and Makeni were abandoned as well (Meek 2003). By 1996, only 6 of the 23 largest police stations in the country had sufficient equipment to communicate with Police Headquarters in Freetown or with each other (Banya 1996). Routine maintenance of police stations in all of the SLP administrative divisions was seriously neglected during the war and several stations in areas contested by the rebels had been looted or burned to the ground (SLP officer interview, November 28–30, 2003). Where stations survived, routine supplies became nonexistent. By the mid-1990s new police uniforms were no longer being issued and officer dress lacked standardization. Police routinely had to purchase their own supplies, including uniforms, from street vendors. Few operable police vehicles survived the war and those that did were all at least 10 years old (SLP officer interview, November 28–30, 2003).

The court system in Sierra Leone suffered as well from the ravages of the civil war. Sierra Leone has a dual legal system, with common law and customary law systems operating concurrently. The common law is institutionalized into a four-level hierarchy of courts: a Supreme Court, the appeals court, high courts, and magistrate's courts. The magistrate courts serve as courts of original jurisdiction for criminal cases and for civil disputes involving Le 250,000 (approximately $106) or less. The high courts consider higher value civil disputes and more serious criminal cases.

In contrast to the common law courts, customary law prevails throughout the countryside, with local courts operating in each of the country's 149 chiefdoms. Jurisdiction of the local courts extends to most civil disputes and petty crimes with sanctions typically involving the payment of a fine or restitution. Before the conflict began, there were 26 full-time magistrate-staffed courts in each of 12 provincial districts; by 2000, there were only 15 magistrates, with the majority of them in Freetown. High courts had operated in the regional centers of Kenema, Bo, and Makeni before the war, but by 2000 they had not considered a single serious case for at least 6 years (Thompson 2002). As of 2004, only 150 lawyers remained in all of Sierra Leone (Kane et al. 2004), with 95% of them based in Freetown (James-Allen 2004). By way of comparison, in Rwanda in 1999 there were only 60 lawyers registered with the bar in the entire country (Salas 2002).

Like the Sierra Leone Police and the court system, the prison system went into a period of decline and neglect during the civil war. Prior to the war, there were 19 prison facilities in the country, but only 8 facilities survived the war intact (Kane et al. 2004). As in many African countries, prisons evolved in Sierra Leone as appendices to colonial military posts (Bernault 2003). Sierra Leone's largest prison, Central Prison on Pademba Road in Freetown, was originally built by British colonial authorities in 1816 and served as the colony's only prison for nearly 100 years. The current facility dates to 1914 and serves as the largest prison in the country. Though built for a population of 325, it regularly held as many as 1,000 inmates, many of whom were pretrial detainees who were routinely held for months or even years before being referred to a judge. Notwithstanding realistic concerns over whether Sierra Leone had the capacity to host a tribunal given the poor condition of its justice system, the prevailing view was that the democratically elected government, with the help of UN peacekeeping forces, was sufficiently stable to provide adequate court security and that the operation of the tribunal, along with other security sector development projects, could directly help in building the capacity of the domestic criminal justice system (Malan et al. 2003).

The overall security situation in Sierra Leone benefited greatly from the presence of international peacekeeping troops deployed under the UN Mission in Sierra Leone (UNAMSIL). The UNAMSIL commitment began in 1999 with the arrival 6,000 military personnel and incrementally increased to 17,000 troops by 2002. A major focus of United Nations operations involved the disarmament, demobilization, and reintegration (DDR) of combatants, including the organized collection of the surfeit of small arms and light weapons circulating in Sierra Leone as a result of the conflict. Another part of the UNAMSIL project involved a security sector reform (SSR) program that provided civilian police officers (CIVPOL) from UN member nations to help in monitoring Sierra Leone Police activities and assisting in the training of new recruits. At the height of CIVPOL involvement, a total of 87 officers were assigned to the program.

The UNAMSIL mission was gradually phased out and formally ended in December 2005. It was replaced by a much smaller UN Integrated Office in Sierra Leone (UNIOSL), which maintained a military deployment of about 1,000 and a reduced CIVPOL component of 20 police personnel. The trials began in the Special Court in 2003, at the height of UNAMSIL and CIVPOL involvement, and continued as the international peacekeepers were subsequently reduced.

Also, the government of the United Kingdom played a major role in helping to rebuild the security sector in Sierra Leone. In addition to providing about 10% of the total United Nations development assistance to Sierra Leone, the UK Department for International Development funded a number of security, governance, and humanitarian projects in Sierra Leone. In 2002, the UK Department for International Development (DFID) entered into a 10-year memorandum of understanding with the government of Sierra Leone by which DFID agreed to provide long-term support for a variety of criminal justice-related projects. Funds dedicated to these projects have helped in re-equipping and training the Sierra Leone Police and in rebuilding the court system through courthouse reconstruction and the training of judges, court clerks, and other judicial staff.

Notwithstanding the successes of UN peacekeeping and DFID security development projects, the decision to convene the Special Court in Freetown involved a leap of faith that overall security would be sufficient to provide a safe environment for the court. The government espoused the view that a hybrid tribunal could be capable of bringing perpetrators of war crimes to justice, while concurrently fixing a broken criminal justice system – a value-added dimension to transitional justice.

At the same time, in recognition that the security situation in the country was tenuous, the 2002 agreement between the government of Sierra Leone and the United Nations establishing the Special Court included a provision that the court "may be relocated outside Sierra Leone, if circumstances so require (Special Court 2000). Indeed, in 2006, when the Special Court sought to put former Liberian President Charles Taylor on trial, the court decided to transfer the Taylor case to the ICC in the Hague, citing concerns that "the presence of former President Taylor in the sub-region is an impediment to stability and a threat to the peace of Liberia and of Sierra Leone and to international peace and security in the region" (Amnesty International USA 2007).

The Challenge of Monetizing the Value of Justice and Security

Cost–benefit algorithms have been applied to the study of criminal justice as a way of quantifying the monetary impact of crime on its victims and measuring the relative efficiencies of different programs aimed at preventing and controlling its occurrence (Cohen 1998; Roman 2004). As crime and its consequences are obviously not market-traded commodities, CBA valuation methods involve the adoption of proxy measures that can be valued as a stand in for the nonmarket goods. The idea is that the benefit of a crime control measure is reflected in the value of crime averted. If a particular crime prevention measure costs x amount to implement and prevents y amount of crime, then the benefit-to-cost ratio is reflected in the equation y/x (y over x). The incremental benefit-to-cost ratio can be estimated in terms of marginal changes in cost and benefit.

The studies generally proceed from either an *ex ante* or an *ex post* perspective. *Ex ante* methods, such as contingent valuation or "willingness-to-pay," use survey methodology to ask respondents what they would be willing to pay in order to achieve a hypothetical social objective (e.g., less crime, a cleaner environment). Survey results are then generalized to the population as a whole to obtain an estimate of the societal cost of the phenomenon under study. Cook and Ludwig (2000), for example, used this methodology in estimating the annual cost of gun violence in the United States to be on the order of $100 billion. To our knowledge, there have been no published efforts to estimate willingness-to-pay to avoid being a victim of the extraordinary crimes prosecuted by a war crimes tribunal. The concept would be difficult if not impossible to operationalize in a developing country that lacks a Western-style, universal tax system or that has a police force with a history of corruption.

Nonetheless, a variant of willingness-to-pay for war crimes avoidance is suggested in the distribution of funds for Special Court for Sierra Leone activities vis-à-vis other important post-conflict development projects. While the monetary value of substantive transitional justice measures may be impossible to measure, the official mechanisms for distributing public goods have distinct costs and benefits, analysis of which may help us to better understand the value of distributive justice relative to other public goods.

For example, transitional justice in Sierra Leone is competing with many other needs, including resettlement and repatriation, health, food, education, and housing. Judging from how it chooses to allocate its aid to Sierra Leone, the international donor community places a high value on bringing war criminals to justice.

Table 1 shows the relative amounts of total international donations for the operation of the Special Court and for assistance to other sectors of the country.[9] For example, in 2004, international donors pledged a total of $13.35 million for

---

[9]The donor amounts are a part of the UN's consolidated appeal process and do not necessarily account for projects earmarked by donors for special projects delivered by NGOs. Unlike the ICTY and ICTR, financial contributions to the Special Court for Sierra Leone were voluntary and not assessed. The Secretary General suggested that contributions be assessed on members, but the Security Council opted for voluntary contributions. The viability of the Court at the inceptive stage of operation became severely threatened because of inadequate financial support.

Table 1 Comparison of donor support of special court with support of other sectors, 2004

	Amount (US$)
International donor commitments to the Special Court[a]	13,350,000
International donor commitments to other sectors[b]	
Agriculture	4,324,100
Coordination and support services	1,375,000
Economic recovery and infrastructure	15,080,000
Education	2,660,000
Family shelter and nonfood items	3,090,000
Food	200,000
Health	13,406,400
Multisector	9,497,100
Protection/human rights/rule of law	6,901,100
Water and sanitation	5,405,500
Total other sectors	61,939,200

[a]As the fiscal year for the Special Court is July through June, donor contributions for calendar year 2004 are calculated by averaging total contributions pledged for each of the two fiscal years July 2003–June 2004 and July 2004–June 2005. *Source*: Ayoola (2005) and Fernando (2006)
[b]Source: UN Office for the Coordination of Humanitarian Affairs (OCHA), Consolidated Appeals Process (CAP): Humanitarian Appeal 2004 for Sierra Leone, November 18, 2003

the operation of the court. This amount is comparable to the total amount pledged in support of economic recovery and infrastructure projects ($15 million) and health care (S13 million), while it is much more than the amount targeted at other important areas (e.g., $2.6 million for education, $3 million for family shelter, and $5.4 million for water and sanitation improvements). Monetizing the cost of running the court is certainly not the only way of valuing the justice that it dispenses, but it does provide a perspective on its value vis-à-vis other important development projects.

In contrast to the *ex ante* methods, *ex post* methods seek to retrospectively establish the costs of crime by examining both the tangible and intangible expenses associated with it. Tangible costs are easier to monetize, and can be drawn from such sources as the budgets of criminal justice agencies or jury awards that compensate victims for pain and suffering. Intangible costs (and benefits) are established through the concepts of opportunity cost and revealed preferences. For example, opportunity costs could include the lost work time a victim might experience. Revealed preferences include such things as preventive measures or avoidance behaviors that people undertake in order to avoid crime (Cohen 2005). But, like willingness-to-pay, the *ex post* method is perhaps more suitable to examining the costs of crime and justice in more developed societies. Further, some intangible costs – such as those involving crimes that betray the public trust or treason and, in the present case, crimes against humanity – are probably very high and very difficult to estimate (Cohen 2000, p. 287). The value of transitional justice which, according to the International Center for Transitional Justice, includes “achieving a holistic sense of justice for all citizens, establishing or renewing civic trust, or reconciling people and communities” (ICTJ 2008), is arguably beyond the realm of monetization.

We heed these cautions in limiting our analysis to the public benefit as reflected in the allocation of funds in the operation of the SCSL and the shadow price of social benefits that changes in allocation patterns might produce. The linear programming methodology is a useful estimating approach that combines the virtues of both the *ex ante* and *ex post* approaches to estimating opportunity cost and revealed preferences. It uses actual rather than contingent data for analysis of willingness to pay and the marginal costs and benefits that can be derived from both opportunity cost and revealed preference. Its flexibility and realism for comparative study minimize the challenges of internal and external threats that are frequently associated with surveys and inference.

Although linear programming is known to have existed before 1947 and was first proposed to deal with U.S. military planning activities in the 1940s, it gained widespread recognition and popularity after 1947 as a result of planning and optimization challenges in science, management, and economics. In academic circles, operations researchers, management scientists, mathematicians, and economists have written extensively on the subject (Dantzig 2002). Among the scholars studying its use and development, Leontief (1951) has largely been credited for the popularization of the linear programming algorithm in math and economics in the twentieth and twenty-first centuries. Dantzig notes that a major influence of the pre-1947 era was Leontief's work on the Input–Output Model of the Economy (1933). Leontief's matrix structure of the economy was simple, but found to be relevant to practical planning.

After World War II, economists and mathematicians became intrigued with the possibility that the fundamental problem of optimal allocation of scarce resources could be solved numerically. Although the world is nonlinear, systems of linear inequalities (rather than equalities) permit for the estimation of most nonlinear relations encountered in practical planning or challenges. Consequently, by the end of the twentieth century, planners became much more aware of the possibilities of optimizing objective functions while hedging against undesirable contingencies. This recognition evidently translates into the ability to state general objectives or problems and finding optimal policy solutions (the best policy solutions given identifiable constraints) to such objectives or problems. As such, linear programming in the post-1947 world is a revolutionary development that contemporaneously defines the ability to weigh incremental (marginal) benefits against marginal costs.

Linear programming is now routinely used by business enterprises for projecting optimal profitability when resource allocation decisions are subject to numerous constraints. Likewise, optimization modeling using linear programming has become a popular tool in policy analysis where a public goal (such as maximizing security) can be stated in the form of an objective function (Bardach 2004; Stokey and Zechhauser 1978).

Linear programming has also been used to some extent in development economics and conflict studies to estimate various economic and social welfare outcomes of alternative resource allocation scenarios. For example, Porter (1979) used linear programming to estimate the effect of international trade and capital sanctions on unemployment in South Africa during the apartheid era. More recently, Cisse et al. (2004) used linear programming to estimate the profitability of various Senegalese crops (groundnut, millet, sorghum, okra, and cowpea) optimized under the multiple constraints of food self-sufficiency, operating capital, and crop rotation. More germane to our present application, Misra and Kant (2005) used linear programming to project shadow prices of social and biological outputs of different village-level Joint Forest Management organizations in Gujarat, India.

Our use of the linear programming algorithm is consistent with the generic application of the method to optimization research, such as that of Jabeen et al. (2006), Reuss (1980), and Elobeid (1982). Jabeen et al. estimate the marginal value (benefit) of irrigation water through the linear programming technique to obtain the shadow price (sensitivity) of water to incremental changes in constraints. Of course, their objective is to maximize net returns from agricultural production, subject to production and resource constraints on water and land. Ours is to maximize welfare based on available financial resources.

Reuss draws attention to the use of the linear programming algorithm when empirical data are available because of its convenient format for stating problems of maximization or minimization and obtaining solutions through computer routines. An attractive property of linear programming that has general acclaim is the provision of shadow prices that give analysts information about constraints that most strongly affect the value of the optimal solution. This has been made evident in the papers of Elobeid (1982) and MacDonald (1995). We exploit this property to present the cost–benefit analysis of postponed and timely funding of the special court when actual data is available as opposed to extrapolations based on contingent valuation or willingness to pay.

Methodology

The Registrar of the SCSL produces an annual budget that details the court's expenses in two formats. The first format reports expenses as related to staffing levels in each of the court's four organs: the Chambers, the Office of the Prosecutor, the Registry, and the Defense Office. The second uses a program budget format, which divides all of the court's operational costs into units of activity, or "cost centers." Security is one such cost center. The security and witness and victim support services units of the Registry are among its most staff-intensive functions, with 35% of all Registry personnel working in these two areas (The Special Court for Sierra Leone 2009).

Under austerity measures undertaken by the Special Court, members of the Sierra Leone Police have been utilized in innovative ways to perform duties that would normally be performed by staff members. A number of Sierra Leone Police officers have been hired and trained to provide court security,[10] witness protection services, and prisoner transportation. Because of its prominence in the overall budget of the SCSL and use of Sierra Leone Police in its operations, we use the security budget of the Registry in our estimation procedures.

[10]Among all Registry areas in the annual budget, the "security" function has the single largest allocation of personnel assigned to it – 68 staff.

Based on the security budget of The Special Court for Sierra Leone, we use optimization by linear programming to determine the shadow price of security for the SCSL, or, more specifically, as a measure of the imputed worth of the court's security resources. Shadow price calculation thus provides an estimate of the amount the government of Sierra Leone can spend on other needed projects for every dollar of donor funds that are dedicated to the security function of the court. By extension, the shadow price estimates part of the opportunity cost of not having the Court seated in Sierra Leone. Further, the data provide a reasonable estimate of the cost of maintaining security for the Court, and, to some extent, policing for the general public in a state where police constables constitute a fraction of those living below the severe poverty line – barely above the extreme poverty line.[11] In sum, it provides an indication of what the government of Sierra Leone would have been willing to pay to establish minimum security if it had the ability to do so. Table 1 suggests that donors are very interested in a variety of development projects, but the viability of these projects is highly contingent on security and policing in what could otherwise be a dysfunctional state.

Three areas of security spending are of special interest to estimating the shadow prices: (1) contractual services; (2) general operating expenses; and (3) supplies and materials. Expenditures in these areas are associated with the Registrar (Table 2).[12]

Table 2 Security budget of the special court for Sierra Leone (US$): 2004–2007 (percentage of estimated outlay in parenthesis)

Year	Contractual services	General operating expenses	Supplies & materials	Total
2004–2005	215, 000 (92)	1,000 (4.3)	17, 500 (7.5)	233,500
2005–2006	260,300 (90)	6,000 (2.1)	23,100 (8.0)	289,400
2006–2007	250,400 (94)	2,000 (8.0)	14,200 (5.0)	266,600
	Average (92)	Average (1)	Average (7)	

Notes: Contractual services include: supplementary books; periodicals; subscriptions to electronic law libraries (e.g., LexisNexis and Westlaw); and security support by the Sierra Leone Police to the Special Court facilities, investigative units, detention facilities, residences of officials, witness protection, and meals for police officers. General operating expenses include: recurrent maintenance of miscellaneous and security equipments such as closed-circuit television (CCTV) system and X-ray machines. Supplies and materials cover seasonally sensitive gears for national and international duty officers, provision of ammunitions to enable officers to fire 50 rounds three times a year as continuation training, and replacement search mirrors, clothing, and uniforms, as well as replacement items for security staff at the detention centerSource: Special Court for Sierra Leone (percentages, supplied by authors). The fourth category, which is not included, deals with Acquisition and Equipments, such as handheld metal detectors for The Hague

[11]The World Bank classifies poverty into two categories: (1) extreme poverty (living on a dollar or less a day); and (2) severe poverty (living on two dollars a day). In 2001 and 2002, Sierra Leone Police officers were paid Le 42,000 approximately $21 a month. Inadequate income has been inextricably linked with corruption. Full time security officers of the Special Court for Sierra Leone were paid $200 a month, a very significant increase in income.

[12]Article 16 of the Statute of the Special Court for Sierra Leone gives the Registrar the overall responsibility for the administration and servicing of the Special Court. The other vital components of the Court include judges, chambers, office of the prosecutor, and the office of defense.

The shadow price performs a social value function and it takes the form:

$$S = \Delta\, Social Welfare\ \Delta\, / \Delta\, Spending \tag{1}$$

where S is the shadow price; Δ Social Welfare is the change in social welfare; and Δ Spending is the change in spending or financing. The shadow price measures the increase in social welfare as a result of a marginal (incremental) change in the availability and use of financial resources.[13]

We use the shadow price to estimate the amount by which the welfare improvement of the nation was subsidized for every US $100,000 that was spent by the Registrar on security on behalf of the SCSL[14]14 from 2004 to 2007. The SCSL as a social welfare maximizing agent of the government desired to optimally maximize the following objective function for the years 2004–2005 to 2006–2007:

$$Max: C \times 0.92 + G \times 0.01 + S \times 0.07 \tag{2}$$

where $C \times 0.92$, is the average percent of funds allocated to contractual services; $G \times 0.011$, is the average percent of funds allocated to general operating expenses; and $S \times 0.0682$, is the average percent of funds allocated to supplies and materials.

The Registrar of the SCSL is constrained by the expected annual funds from donor countries and policies of the Management Committee. It allocated its expected funds to reflect its priorities optimally subject to the following dual constraints:

$$\begin{aligned} 2004/5&: C \times 0.92 + G \times 0.004 + S \times 0.07 \le \$233,500, \\ 2005/6&: C \times 0.90 + G \times 0.002 + S \times 0.08 \le \$289,400, \end{aligned} \tag{3}$$

where $C, G, S \geq 0$ (the non-negativity condition for optimal solution).

We solve the optimization problem to derive the sensitivity effects (the shadow prices) for 2004–2005 and 2005–2006 and report the findings in Table 3.

Table 3 Sensitivity results of the linear programming model

Year	Shadow price	Right-side constraint	Allowable increase	Allowable decrease
2004–2005	0.635	233,500	16,831.03	175,620.00
2005–2006	0.373	289,400	54,233.33	609,76.09
2006–2007	0	266,600	0	13,191.89

[13]For further discussion and detailed analysis of cost-benefit analysis see Brent's *Applied Cost-Benefit Analysis.*

[14]This amount is also indicative of benefits that could have been achieved as a result of an aggressive pursuit of funds by the Management Committee, rather than the pursuit of severe cuts.

Findings

The sensitivity results indicate that based on the objective function of the security needs of the Court, for every US $100,000 increase in expenditure by the Registry, the improvement in national welfare could have been as much as US $64,000 in 2004–2005 and US $37,000 in 2005–2006 (see shadow prices in Table 3). These estimates are opportunity costs that could have been lost if the Court had been seated elsewhere. They do not presuppose the accrual of negative externalities by seating the court in The Hague or elsewhere. Rather, they suggest that external benefits emanating from infrastructural gains, as distinct from the evolution of judicial tradition and deterrence, are not maximized by the domestic country where atrocities took place when the tribunal is seated elsewhere. The quantitative or qualitative measure of prospective deterrence or enhancement of jurisprudence is beyond the scope of this discussion.

External financing realistically augments national government spending on security so that other areas of need, for example, health, education, and infrastructure, can be adequately funded when a tribunal is domestically seated. The findings suggest that although domestically seated war crimes tribunals are primarily viewed as a transitional justice mechanism, they also play a role in overall post-conflict development.

The empirical findings confirm the time value of money, meaning that funding hybrid tribunals expeditiously will generate the highest marginal impact on the welfare of troubled nations at the inceptive stage of tribunal operations. Table 3 shows that the maximum impact could have been obtained between 2004–2005 and 2005–2006. The optimal allocation of funds and shadow prices corroborate the argument that the early stages of operation usually require the largest amount of funding for immediate impact. Current allocations of the 2009–2010 budget (terminal budget) reflect such a view. Allocations for the SCSL in Freetown are reduced by about US $8 million (from approximately $18 in 1990 to $10 in 2010), while that of The Hague are also reduced by about US $8 million.[15]

The allowable increase/decrease in Table 3 denotes the range of optimal reallocation of money to the security sector that could be permitted to satisfy the results of the optimization problem. To obtain the maximum impact on welfare between 2004–2005 and 2005–2006 without altering the shadow prices, spending could have been increased by $175,620 in 2004–2005 or decreased by about $233,500. The allowable increase for the same result is comparatively larger, but the decrease is comparatively smaller.

This result confirms the idea that money has time value. This means that money has more value today relative to tomorrow. In developing models of transitional justice, architects should therefore pay very close attention to timely funding for optimal result. In this case the optimization objective shows that optimal results were obtained within the first 2 years of the tribunal given its objective and financial constraint.

[15]See the Sixth Annual Report of the President for the Special Court of Sierra Leone, obtainable from www.sc-sl.org.

Although we have not tested for longer-term effects, the seating of the SCSL in-country has the potential to contribute more broadly to the development of the Sierra Leonean domestic criminal justice system over time. Many of the personnel skills needed to operate a war crimes tribunal are identical to those of domestic courts that prosecute ordinary crimes, creating the opportunity for personnel and technology transfer to the domestic criminal justice system once the tribunal completes its work. The professional staff of an international tribunal (those holding jobs that require an academic background) constitute only about one-third of the total court personnel (CICC 2006). The other two-thirds work in support positions, where they perform functions that include personnel services, communications and information technology, language translation services, budgeting and finance, witness and victims support, procurement, and security – in other words, jobs that are fundamentally similar to those found in any well functioning court system.

The personnel of international tribunals are typically organized into four functional areas: Judicial Chambers, Office of the Prosecutor, the Defense Office, and the Office of the Registry. Their staffing structure is not unlike that of the proverbial iceberg, with only 10% of its mass visible above the water line; although the most conspicuous work of tribunals involves that of its trial chambers, only about 10% of all staff work in this area. Three-quarters of all staff work in the Registry, which provides behind-the-scenes administrative support for tribunal operations.

The SCSL was established as an independent special court and has greater flexibility in the hiring of Registry staff than the ICTY or the ICTR. Under these more internationalized institutions, staff hiring practice in the Registry is under the direct control of the UN Secretariat (Møse 2005), which selects personnel according to a formula that apportions representation relative to the total number of member states, a state's contribution to the budget, and its population size (CICC 2006). Although a breakdown of nationality of court staff is not readily available for the ICTR and ICTY, at the ICC, which uses a similar metric in selecting staff, 57.2% of personnel come from Western Europe and Others Group (WEOG) countries, 15.6% from the Group of Latin American and Caribbean Countries (GRULAC), 12.9% from Africa, 7.3% from Eastern Europe, and 7.1% from Asia (CICC 2006). The SCSL has greater latitude in this regard, with the net result that 53% of its full time personnel are citizens of Sierra Leone (King 2007).

Moreover, the staff comprising the SCSL have been actively involved in training staff from the domestic criminal justice system. During 2007–2008, for example, personnel from the SCSL provided training courses to nearly 600 domestic court staff on such topics as court records management, ethics of interpretation, and judicial management of juvenile cases. Similarly, SCSL staff worked with the Sierra Leone Prison Service to provide restraint training and detainee human rights training for prison guards (The Special Court for Sierra Leone 2009).

Other benefits of the domestically constituted court include infrastructural investments that will become the property of the host government once the court completes its work. In Sierra Leone, these investments include a newly built Special Court facility, the renovation of the Sierra Leone Prison Service's facility on Bonthe Island, and a new detention facility on the grounds of the SCSL. Possible uses of the court facility and grounds after the court completes its work include a regional judicial training facility, a memorial facility, or a court facility for the national judiciary (The Special Court for Sierra Leone 2009).

The Bonthe Island facility was loaned to the SCSL by the Sierra Leone Prison Service until a SCSL detention facility could be built. Funding for the SCSL was used to bring the Bonthe facility up to international prison standards, and it was subsequently returned to the Prison Service after the SCSL detention facility in Freetown had been completed. The new facility in Freetown, like the Bonthe Island renovation, was built to international standards for prison facilities and may serve as a Prison Service detention facility for women or juvenile offenders once the court completes its work. In the more internationalized ICTR, the UN Detention Unit in Tanzania, built in 1997 to hold Rwandan detainees, will be handed over to the government of the United Republic of Tanzania after the ICTR completes its work.

Conclusion

The seating of a hybrid tribunal in the location of hostilities has remarkable promise, not only in furthering transitional justice goals of holding perpetrators of extraordinary crimes accountable and thereby deterring their reoccurrence, but also in contributing to post-conflict development through the revitalization of physical and human capital. Although the cost of operation of hybrid courts can be relatively expensive, the efficient and optimal use of scarce resources and inflow of foreign capital have net positive externalities for poor countries that are recovering from devastating conflict experiences.

Apart from other positive externalities in such areas as education, economic recovery, and health, positive externalities from domestically seated hybrid tribunals inure to the benefit of policing, legal infrastructure, the correctional system, and general welfare. Shadow price estimates indicate that in the case of Sierra Leone, net welfare was improved as a result of incremental expenditures and funding of the hybrid tribunal. Although the creation of the International Criminal Court holds the promise of creating a single, centralized institution for prosecuting extraordinary crimes arising out of civil discord, the development-related positive externalities of domestically seated, ad hoc tribunals should be considered by policymakers, along with other factors, in deciding where to locate war crimes tribunals in the future.

A major difference between the international tribunals and the hybrid tribunals is in their funding mechanisms – the ICTY and ICTR are funded by UN assessments, whereas the ad hoc tribunals (East Timor, Sierra Leone, Cambodia, and Lebanon)[16]

[16]The Special Tribunal for Lebanon was established in 2007 with a mandate to prosecute persons responsible for the attack of 14 February 2005 resulting in the death of former Prime Minister Rafiq Hariri and in the death or injury of other persons. Fifty-one percent of the costs of the Special Tribunal are borne by voluntary contributions from supporting states, while the Government of the Lebanese Republic finances 49% of the costs.

are reliant on voluntary contributions from supporting states. Just as each of the hybrid war crimes tribunals has its own unique circumstances, funding streams, problems, and prospects, one should be cautious in generalizing too broadly on the basis of one court's experience. However, the cost of running these tribunals is dramatically lower than the fully internationalized war crimes tribunals (Cambodia, approx $5 million per year; East Timor, approx $5 million per year; SCSL, approx $16 million per year) compared to ICTY and ICTR annual budgets of $220 million and $180 million.

There are substantive policy implications for seating hybrid tribunals in the location of atrocities. When domestically seated hybrid tribunals are operated optimally and efficiently, justice can be meted out for less than extraordinarily huge amounts of money when the financial support is prompt and substantial. Between 2006 and 2007, the SCSL was constituted for about 10% of the estimated cost of the ICTR and about 9% of the estimated cost of the ICTY, in part due to its ability to rely upon the lower cost of local staff and resources in its operations (and partly because of the evident disparities in atrocities and method of funding).

The SCSL demonstrates that notwithstanding the problems with constituting hybrid tribunals, their expeditious financial support can generate positive externalities. Although the SCSL has espoused remarkable austerity and success, it has struggled to maintain bare minimum funding through the voluntary contributions mechanism. In light of the value-added dimension of in-country tribunals, policymakers have an additional rationale for pushing for assessed rather than voluntary contribution as a better proposition for making hybrid courts much more viable and effective in the future. In so doing, the international community can be summoned not only to create hybrid tribunals for the sake of pursuing transitional justice, but also for repairing broken infrastructure and improving national welfare, the lack of which is the very basis for political turmoil in troubled nations.

References

Amnesty International USA (2007). Special Court for Sierra Leone: Issues for consideration regarding the location of the trial of Charles Taylor. Retrieved from: http://www.amnestyusa.org/index.html.

Ayoola, E. (2005). *Second Annual Report of the President of the Special Court for Sierra Leone*. Freetown: Special Court for Sierra Leone.

Banya, S. (1996) *Report of the Dr. Banya Committee on the Republic of Sierra Leone Police Force*. Freetown: State House, Office of the President of the Republic of Sierra Leone.

Bardach, E. (2004). *A Practical Guide for Policy Analysis*, 2nd Ed. New York: CQ Press.

Beresford, S. (2000–2001). In pursuit of international justice: The first four-year term of the International Criminal Tribunal for Rwanda. *Tulsa J. Comp. Int'l L.* 8(1), 99–132.

Bernault, F.E. (2003). *A History of Prison and Confinement in Africa*. Portsmouth: Heinemann.

Brent, R.J. (1996). *Applied Cost–Benefit Analysis*. Cheltenham: Edward Elgar.

Cisse, A., Bravo-Ureta, B.E., Fuentes, P., &Thiam, A. (2004). An economic analysis of agricultural production in Senegal: A case study of the Thiѐns and Diourbel regions. *J. Devel. Soc.* 20(1/2), 3–19.

Chege, M. (2002). Sierra Leone: The state that came back from the dead. *Wash. Quart*. 25(3), 147–160.

Coalition for the International Criminal Court (2006). Scenarios on geographical representation within ICC staff. Retrieved from: http://www.iccnow.org.

Cohen, M.A. (2000). Measuring the costs and benefits of crime and justice. In: D. Duffee (Ed.), *Criminal Justice 2000: Vol. 4. Measurement and Analysis of Crime and Justice*. Washington, DC: National Institute of Justice, pp. 263–315.

Cohen, M.A. (2005). *The Costs of Crime and Justice*. New York: Routledge.

Commonwealth Police Development Task Force for Sierra Leone (1998) *Sierra Leone Police: Interim Report*. London: Marlborough House, Commonwealth Secretariat.

Cook, P.J., & Ludwig, J. (2000). *Gun Violence: The Real Costs*. New York: Oxford University Press.

Dantzig, G.B. (2002). Linear programming (50th anniversary issue). *Oper. Res.* 50(1), 42–47.

Dougherty, B.K. (2004). Right-sizing international criminal justice: The hybrid experiment at the Special Court for Sierra Leone. *Int'l Aff.* 80(2), 311–328.

Elagab, O.Y. (2004). The Special Court for Sierra Leone: Some constraints. *Int'l J. Hum. Rts.* 8(3), 249–273.

Elobeid, H.A. (1982). *Water Supply Controls and Economic Value of Irrigation Water in the Gezira Scheme, Sudan*. (Unpublished Master's thesis). Fort Collins: Colorado State University Department of Economics.

Fernando, R. (2006). *Third Annual Report of the President of the Special Court for Sierra Leone*. Freetown: Special Court for Sierra Leone.

Human Rights Watch (2004). Bringing justice: The Special Court for Sierra Leone: accomplishments, shortcomings, and needed support. *Human Rights Watch* 16(8A). Retrieved from http://www.hrw.org/reports/2004/sierraleone0904/.

International Center for Transitional Justice (2008). *ICTJ Mission and History*. Retrieved from http://www.ictj.org/en/about/mission/.

Jabeen, S., Ashfaq, M., & Baig, I.A. (2006). Linear program modeling for determining the value of irrigation water. *J. Agric. Soc. Sci.* 2(2), 101–105.

James-Allen, P. (2004). *Accessing Justice in Rural Sierra Leone: A Civil Society Response*. New York: Justice Initiatives, Open Society Institute.

Kane, M., Mackiggan, K., Mburu, C., Gassama, I., Morley, E., & Eldon, C. (2004). *Sierra Leone: Legal and Judicial Sector Assessment*. Washington, DC: The World Bank, Legal Vice-Presidency.

Kaplan, R.D. (1994). The coming anarchy. *Atlantic Monthly* 273(2), 44–77.

King, G.G. (2007). *Fourth Annual Report of the President of the Special Court for Sierra Leone*. Freetown: Special Court for Sierra Leone.

Kposowa, A. (2006). Erosion of the rule of law as a contributing factor in civil conflict: The case of Sierra Leone. *Police Pract. Res.* 7(1), 35–48.

Leontief, W. (1951). Input–output economics. *Sci. Am.* 185(4), 15–21.

MacDonald, Z. (1995). Teaching linear programming using Microsoft Excel Solver. *Comp. High. Educ. Econ. Rev.* 9(3), 7–10.

Malan, M., Meek, S., Thusi, T., Ginifer J., & Coker, P. (2003). *Sierra Leone: Building the Road to Recovery.* Pretoria. South Africa: Institute for Security Studies.

Meek, S. (2003). *Policing Sierra Leone*. In: M. Malan et al. (Eds.), *Sierra Leone: Building the Road to Recovery*. Pretoria, South Africa: Institute for Security Studies, pp. 105–116.

Misra, D., & Kant, S. (2005). Economic efficiency and shadow prices of social and biological outputs of village-level organizations of joint forest management in Gujarat, India. *J. Forest Econ.* 11(3), 141–160.

Møse, E. (2005). Main achievements of the ICTR. *J. Int'l Cri Just.* 3, 920–943.

Porter, R.C. (1979). International trade and investment sanctions. *J. Confl. Res.* 23(4), 579–612.

Power, S. (2002). *A Problem from Hell: America and the Age of Genocide*. New York: HarperCollins.

Reuss, J.O. (1980). *Matching Cropping System to Water Supply Using an Integrative Model* (Water Management Technical Report No. 62 Pakistan Project). Fort Collins: Colorado State University.

Roman, J. (2004). Can cost–benefit analysis answer criminal justice policy questions, and if so, how? *J. Contemp. Crim. Just.* 20(3), 257–275.

Salas, L. (2002). Reconstruction of public security and justice in post-conflict societies: The Rwandan experience. *Int. J. Compar. Appl. Crim. Just.* 26, 165–202.

Stokey, E., & Zechhauser, R. (1978). *A Primer for Policy Analysis*. New York: Norton.

The Special Court for Sierra Leone (2002). *Agreement Between the United Nations and the Government of Sierra Leone on the Establishment of a Special Court for Sierra Leone*. Retrieved from http://www.sc-sl.org/documents.html.

The Special Court for Sierra Leone (2009). *Sixth Annual Report of the President of the Special Court for Sierra Leone*. Freetown: The Special Court for Sierra Leone.

Thompson, B. (2000). *The criminal justice system of Sierra Leone*. In: O.N.I. Ebbe (Ed.), *Comparative and International Criminal Justice Systems: Policing, Judiciary, and Corrections*, 2nd Ed. Boston: Butterworth-Heinemann, pp. 91–112.

Transparency International (2007). *Corruption Perception Index*. Retrieved from http://www.transparency.org/.

United Nations (2004). *United NationsTransitional Appeal for Relief and Recovery, Sierra Leone 2004*. New York: United Nations.

United Nations Office for the Coordination of Humanitarian Affairs (OCHA) (2003). *Consolidated Appeals Process (CAP): Humanitarian Appeal 2004 for Sierra Leone*. New York: The United Nations.

United Nations Security Council (2000). Resolution 1315, adopted by the Security Council at its 4186th meeting, August 14, 2000.

World Bank (2005). World Development Indicator CD-ROM. Washington DC: The World Bank.

World Bank (2007). World Development Indicator CD-ROM. Washington DC: The World Bank.

World Bank. (2008). World Development Indicator CD-ROM. Washington DC: The World Bank.

World Bank. (2009). World Development Indicator CD-ROM. Washington DC: The World Bank.

Index

G. Anderopoulos et al. (eds.), *International Criminal Justice: Critical Perspectives and New Challenges*, DOI 10.1007/978-1-4419-1102-5,
© Springer Science+Business Media, LLC 2011

M

N

O

P

Q

R

FSC
www.fsc.org
MIX
Papier | Fördert
gute Waldnutzung
FSC® C083411

Kolibri 360 GmbH
Ferdinand-Jühlke-Straße 7
99095 Erfurt, Deutschland
produktsicherheit@kolibri360.de